THE LIVING WORD COMMENTARY

Editor
Everett Ferguson

The Revelation
to John
(The Apocalypse)

The Revelation to John (The Apocalypse)

J. W. Roberts

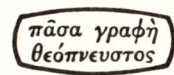

SWEET PUBLISHING COMPANY

Austin, Texas

Copyright © 1974 by Sweet Publishing Company
All rights reserved. No part of this book may be reproduced by any means without permission in writing from the publisher, except for brief quotations embodied in critical articles or reviews.

LIBRARY OF CONGRESS CATALOG CARD NUMBER: 73-20857

INTERNATIONAL STANDARD BOOK NUMBER: 8344-0074-X

PRINTED IN U.S.A.

Acknowledgment

This commentary is based on the text of the Revised Standard Version of the Bible, copyrighted 1946, 1952 and 1971 by the Division of Christian Education, National Council of the Churches of Christ in the U.S.A., and used by permission.

Writers in *The Living Word Commentary* series have been given freedom to develop their own understanding of the biblical text. As long as a fair statement is given to alternative interpretations, each writer has been permitted to state his own conclusions. Beyond the general editorial policies, the editors have sought no artificial uniformity, and differences are allowed free expression. A writer is responsible for his contribution alone, and the views expressed are not necessarily the views of the editors or publisher.

Contents

EDITOR'S NOTE	vi
I. INTRODUCTION	7
The Nature of Apocalyptic Writing	7
The Dating of Revelation	9
Systems of Interpreting Revelation	15
Lessons from Revelation	20
Outline of Revelation	21
Selected Bibliography	24
II. THE REVELATION TO JOHN (The Apocalypse)	27
The Prologue, 1:1-8	27
The Vision of the Son of Man, 1:9–3:22	32
The Son of Man, 1:9-20	32
The Seven Letters, 2:1–3:22	36
The Apocalyptic Vision, 4:1–16:21	52
The Divine Throne Room, 4:1–5:14	52
The Judgments of God, 6:1–11:19	63
The War of the Woman Against the Beast, 12:1–16:21	95
The Vision of Judgment, 17:1–21:8	134
The Judgment of the Great Harlot, 17:1–19:4	134
The Marriage Supper of the Lamb, 19:5-10	158
The Sequel to the Fall of Rome, 19:11–21:8	162
The Vision of the New Jerusalem, 21:9–22:5	184
The Epilogue, 22:6-21	195

Editor's Note

J. W. ROBERTS died during the time he was preparing this commentary. Chapters 17–22 were in final form (except for a few places). Most of the rest was in rough draft, although for some verses only a few notes had been made. Unfinished parts have been supplemented from mimeographed materials which he prepared and used in his classes and from tape-recorded lectures on Revelation. We can be certain that the present commentary represents in substance Prof. Roberts' approach, but we cannot be sure that we have his settled position on all details.

The editor has received invaluable assistance from Dr. Roberts' widow, Delno Roberts, in preparing the material for publication.

I

Introduction

THE NATURE OF APOCALYPTIC WRITING

Definition

THE BOOK OF REVELATION is an apocalypse, a work in which the message is couched in symbols and strange figures. The term apocalypse is Greek for "revelation," or more precisely, "an uncovering, a disclosure." It can refer to a divine revealing of hidden facts to a chosen person and in this sense corresponds to the Hebrew *galah*, "to reveal." This word is used of the revelation of God through the prophets (Deut. 29:29) and was closely associated with the revelation given to Daniel in Babylon (Dan. 2:22; 10:1) and to Isaiah (Isa. 22:14).

As a literary term apocalypse designates a type of treatise or book in which the theme is developed by use of symbols or visions such as sections of the book of Daniel and as the New Testament book of Revelation. "Apocalyptic" is an adjective defining the Jewish-Christian body of literature of this kind. The term was applied in the Old Testament and Jewish circles to certain books or sections of books which concern impending doom or deliverance, often connected with a judgment of God, either in some disaster or in connection with the end of the world and the future state.

Examples

There are several groups of apocalyptic writings belonging both to biblical (Old and New Testament) and non-

INTRODUCTION

biblical documents. Though Revelation is the only complete book of this type in the New Testament, it is not alone in utilizing the style. Individual sections of other books (such as Matt. 24; Mark 13; Luke 21; 1 Thess. 4:13ff.; and 2 Thess. 2) are written in the same imagery.

There had been for many years in the Judaism out of which Christianity sprang, a circle of pious people who lived in the expectation of the imminent ending of the age and the breaking in of the kingdom of God. The hopes of these people had long been expressed in this apocalyptic literature. Old Testament examples of this type of literature are Ezekiel 2:8ff.; 38, 39; Isaiah 24–27; 33–35; Joel 3:9-17; Zechariah 12–14; Daniel 2, 7, 8.

Non-canonical Jewish apocalypses stretch from 200 B.C. to A.D. 100 and later. Many of these can be read in R. H. Charles, *The Apocrypha and Pseudepigrapha of the Old Testament* (2 vols.). They include 1st Enoch, Testaments of the Twelve Patriarchs (esp. Levi, Judah, Zebulon, Dan); Psalms of Solomon; Assumption of Moses; Apocalypse of Baruch; 2nd Esdras; Apocalypse of Abraham; 2nd Enoch; and Sibylline Oracles.

Christians, too, wrote in this style in the early centuries with such works as Apocalypse of Peter; Vision of Isaiah; Shepherd of Hermas; 5th Ezra; 6th Ezra; Apocalypse of Paul. These may be read in such collections as *The Ante-Nicene Fathers* and E. Hennecke, *New Testament Apocrypha*.

Characteristics

Prophetic. Apocalyptic passages are included in Old Testament prophetic books. Apocalypses were predictive and served purposes of instruction and encouragement.

Reassuring. The literature dealt with the problem of evil in the world, especially that of the oppression of God's people by heathen rulers. The major theme was the surety of God's sovereignty over the world and his faithfulness to punish evil and reward the faithful. The form was often used in times of severe persecution (such as that of Antiochus Epiphanes, King of Syria, who suppressed Israel 175-163

B.C.). Thus it was a natural instrument of encouragement in the time of a severe persecution of Christians.

Poetic. The form of apocalypse is sometimes poetic. Much of the Hebrew Old Testament which uses it is in poetic form—parallelism. This can readily be seen by reading Ezekiel 38, 39 and Isaiah 24, 25 in the Revised Standard Version. Where the form of apocalyptic is not poetic, it still employs a symbolic imagery that is to be understood as such and not in a literal way. Poetic language is not to be interpreted in the same way as other forms of language.

THE DATING OF REVELATION

Two views have been generally accepted for the dating of the book of Revelation. The first is that the book was composed during the reign of the Emperor Domitian, who ruled A.D. 81 to 96. The second is that it was composed before the destruction of the city of Jerusalem (A.D. 70) and during the reign of Nero (A.D. 54 to 68). The earlier dating is generally connected with the interpretation that the visions of Revelation, in part at least, picture the persecution of the church by the Jews and foretell the destruction of Jerusalem and the consequent downfall of the Jewish state.

The early testimony is quite decisive for the Domitian or later date. In the last century some scholars, especially conservative ones, adopted the Neronic date. The modern opinion has definitely swung to the late date. This writer holds to the time of Domitian, and this study is written under this conviction. The following is a brief analysis of the two positions with the reasons for rejecting the early dating.

Arguments for the Traditional Dating

Both external and internal arguments favor the dating of the book in the reign of Domitian.

The external witnesses begin with Irenaeus (about 180), who affirmed the tradition of the early church, going back through Polycarp, for the residence of John in Asia Minor. Irenaeus in speaking of Revelation as the "apocalyptic vision" said that "that [vision] was seen not very long since,

INTRODUCTION

but almost in our day, toward the end of Domitian's reign" (*Against Heresies* V. 30). One may add to this testimony that of Clement of Alexandria (*Who Is the Rich Man* 42), Origen (*On Matthew* 16:6), Victorinus (*On the Apocalypse* 10:11), and Jerome (*Lives of Illustrious Men* 9). The only exceptions to this late dating are Epiphanius (he placed it too early, in Claudius' time), and Dorotheus, who misunderstood Irenaeus, supposing that he said that the exile of John to Patmos was in Trajan's reign.

The internal evidence is equally strong. The conditions of the churches in Asia Minor are not the same as those in the 50's and 60's as pictured in Acts of Apostles, the letters to Timothy and Titus, or 1 Peter. New opponents (Nicolaitans), new internal compromisers (Jezebel), new hazards (threat of death because of refusal to worship the Emperor) are present. References to growing cold and losing the first love and having a name but being dead indicate indifference due to the passing of time. There is no evidence for the requirement of emperor worship in Nero's time. The existence of the church at Laodicea amid wealth at the time of the writing is thought by some to be decisive against the early date, since Tacitus says that this city was destroyed by an earthquake in A.D. 60 and since his statement that the city was rebuilt by its own efforts without help would necessitate some time before a state of prosperity would again be realized.

Arguments for the Early Dating

The following are the main arguments for an early dating, together with some reaction to each.

Literary Style. The Greek of the book of Revelation differs markedly from that of the other books of John—the Gospel of John and the letters. Revelation is much poorer in style, especially in grammar. Since it is assumed that John was an Aramaic-speaking Jew, the conclusion seems correct that his Greek would improve with time and use. Hence he must have written Revelation early, when he spoke Greek poorly, and then at a time when his language had improved he wrote the other books. Dionysius of Alexandria (*Circa* A.D. 250) urged the differences in style as an argument that the

Date

author of the Apocalypse was different from the author of the Gospel.

There is some force to this observation. Although the differences have been exaggerated, Revelation is the poorer Greek when contrasted with the Gospel of John. It is not necessary, however, to resort to a theory of language improvement to explain the situation. The most common explanation is that New Testament writers often made use of scribes or literary assistants in writing. Paul wrote Romans by Tertius (Rom. 16:22); Peter used Silas (1 Pet. 5:12); while Paul mentions writing Galatians by his own hand (Gal. 6:11). It would be quite likely that if John had used help in composing his other books he would not have had such when in exile on Patmos. It has also been pointed out that in some sections of Revelation John writes quite good Greek. Most of the solecisms are in sections which seem consciously modeled on the language of the Old Testament. Hence the style may be intentional. Others have pointed out that Revelation was written when John was very old and in a state of excitement or agitation at the exile and the receiving of the visions. These factors could have influenced the style.

The Temple Still Standing. The commandment to rise and measure the temple (Rev. 11:1, 2) is often taken as referring to the Jewish temple in Jerusalem which was destroyed by the Romans in A.D. 70. Such identification would necessitate an early date for the origin of the book and would favor the age of Nero.

But the majority of commentators point out that the passage is obviously patterned after a similar incident in Ezekiel (chs. 40-48) and hence does not depend for its significance upon the Jewish temple as still standing in New Testament times. Furthermore, it is not the literal temple that is probably in view, but the temple viewed symbolically as the church (1 Cor. 3:16f.; 2 Cor. 6:16; Eph. 2:21; 2 Thess. 2:4). The temple which John was told to measure was not the one in Jerusalem but one in a vision which he had while on Patmos.

The Identification of the Woman Sitting on the Beast (Rev. 17:1—18:24). The woman of Revelation 17-18 is often identified with Jerusalem and is thought to represent the Jewish nation. Since the description is assumed to be a prediction of

INTRODUCTION

her fall, a date before the destruction of that city is presumed (A.D. 70). The principal reason for this identification is the assumption that the woman of chapter 17 is the same as that of chapter 12, pictured now as a fallen or apostate woman (church). The reasoning is that Rome, which most commentators think of as the more obvious or likely identification, has never stood in a spiritual relationship with God so as to fit the symbol of an apostate.

This view is extremely doubtful for several reasons. The book of Revelation itself gives no indication that the two women are two aspects of the same thing. On the contrary, all the symbols used to describe the woman indicate that the wanton and persecuting city of Rome is meant: the city sits on Rome's well-known seven hills (17:9); her universality is shown by the fact that she is mistress of "peoples and crowds and nations and tongues" (17:15), something which was not true of Jerusalem or the Jews in New Testament times. They were a subjugated people, while the woman, like Rome, "rules over the kings of the earth" (17:18). Nor do the descriptions of her persecution ("drunk with the blood of the saints," 17:6) really describe the Jews, who did offer local opposition to the church but were not in the position to offer a large-scale persecution of the church in the time of Nero. Finally, the universal commerce (Rev. 18:10-19) offers the most pointed identification of Rome rather than the capital of the remote Jewish province as the center of trade and commerce of the first-century world.

Some commentators contend that "harlot" and "fornication" used to describe the woman of chapters 17-18, when used figuratively, always imply spiritual unfaithfulness or apostasy and thus point to Jerusalem as the apostate church. This does not hold true, for there is Old Testament precedent for the use of such terms to depict the abominations of heathen cities (Tyre, Isa. 23:15-17; Nineveh, Nahum 3:4).

Evidence from the Syriac (Peshitta) Version. One argument which once had force but now is definitely known by biblical scholarship as false is based upon the title statement in the Peshitta Version of the New Testament that Nero banished John to Patmos. In the last century it was thought that the Peshitta was the early Syriac translation (made about

A.D. 125). Such an early testimony for the Neronian exile of John on Patmos was thought to be decisive.

Since the discovery of the Sinaitic Syriac it has been proved that the old Syriac Version of the second century is represented by the Sinaitic and Curetonian manuscripts but that the Peshitta is in reality a fifth-century revision of this version by Bishop Rabbula of Edessa (A.D. 411-435). An added and quite decisive fact against the contention is that the old Syriac Version did not even contain the book of Revelation. The Syrian churches did not accept the Revelation as canonical at this early date.

The Nero Redivivus Myth. Evidence that Revelation was written during Nero's reign is to be found, according to some, in the reference to the myth that Nero would return to life and reestablish himself at Rome. It is generally agreed that the reference to the death wound of the beast which was healed (see comments on Rev. 13:3) refers to this legend; hence, it is argued that this prediction would place the writing of the Revelation in Nero's time.

Actually the facts should be taken in just the opposite order. There is no proof that this legend, current after the death of Nero, was current during his life and during the time when he was persecuting the churches. Hence the theory actually supports the later date.

A date for the composition of Revelation in the reign of Domitian fits the facts well. Domitian was the second emperor to persecute the Christians, so his persecution was actually a revival of Nero's policy. In this respect (if this is the correct interpretation of the death wound), Domitian was "Nero come to Life." The argument is actually a stronger one for the later date.

Historical Setting

The case for the traditional dating of Revelation rests solidly upon the early evidence from Western Asia Minor, which was the place of John's residence in his later life. Objections raised against dating the writing of the book in Domitian's time show no reason for setting aside this early testimony. The interpretation of Revelation ought to proceed on the assumption of the late dating. Circumstances leading

INTRODUCTION

up to the writing of Revelation do, however, go back to Nero's time.

The great fire of Rome in A.D. 64, which many suspected to have been set by the Emperor Nero, became the occasion for a new appraisal of the status of Christianity. Hitherto the Christians had apparently been taken as a sect of the Jews. In the investigations which grew out of Nero's choice of Christians as the scapegoat for the fire, the Romans came to look upon them as proponents of a new religion, one without legal status.

In its rapid growth the church encountered many difficulties. Its converts from Judaism, proselytes, and Greek God-fearers aroused the opposition of the Jews. In time, the Greek neighbors of the Christians came to regard them as antisocial. To their inherited suspicions of weird practice (from their Jewish past), others were added. Tacitus says that the Romans were ready to accept the charges against Christians because they were already "detested for their outrageous practices."

Roman religion was largely national and closely connected with the state. As far as the individual was concerned, it was mostly a matter of public ceremony. Joining in this public ceremony was a patriotic duty, and official recognition of noncompliance could only be considered treason, a crime against the state worthy of death. In practice this did not mean that all except the official religion was put down. The empire was of such a mixture, especially in the provinces, that foreign and especially eastern religions were tolerated. The basis of toleration was that they operate unobtrusively without causing a disturbance of the peace or interfering with the official cult. Violations were generally a matter for the local police and magistrates. Though Christians found themselves in a difficult position, the situation was not impossible.

As the decades passed, the dark cloud on the horizon was the rise and spread of the cult of emperor worship. In the provincial sponsorship of this cult and the demand that all people conform at least in token participation in homage to the divinity of the emperor, that cloud began to overshadow the church in a fearful manner. What Augustus had permitted in Asia in the form of religious honors to himself a mad

Interpretation

Caligula demanded for a short period, and toward the end of the century the Flavian emperor Domitian openly claimed.

SYSTEMS OF INTERPRETING REVELATION

The book of Revelation offers a series of visions of strange things or events that are symbolic of something about to happen to the churches and the world (Rev. 1:1). Since the language and pictures are symbolic and representative, rather than real or actual, how are they to be taken?

In the history of Christian interpretation several different schools or systems of interpretation have evolved. They comprehend the different ways in which the book can logically be approached, and they are customarily named from the point of view in time of the readers of the book. Each method of interpreting Revelation has been represented by devout and learned students of the book. Except for the fact that one of them (the left-wing preterist) has been associated with the liberal or modernist school which denies the inspiration and historical value of the book, and another (the futurist) with the extreme wing of Protestant thought known as premillennialism, or dispensationalism, they are all equally adaptable by believers and unbelievers.

The Preterist School

Preterists (meaning "the past") claim that, with the exception of the specific happenings of the second coming, everything *has been fulfilled* in the time of John and in the years immediately following. There are two schools of those who think the Revelation concerns events which are, from our point of view, past. They have been referred to as the left-wing and right-wing preterists.

Left Wing. This school includes many of the most learned but at the same time the most radical scholars of recent decades. This group thinks the author of Revelation shared the ideas of most Jewish apocalyptists, who thought that the messianic age would be preceded by severe upheavals of the earth and visitations of God upon the unrighteous. Though allowing for the use of apocalyptic and symbolic visions and language, they think that John was actually predicting a series of events in his immediate future which would include the rise of an antichrist and the destruction of the city of Rome and its empire. In this they think John was wrong, as Rome did not fall in the immediate future. They further think that John closely identified the end of the world with the impending destruction of Rome.

Right Wing. The preterists who believe in the inspiration and accuracy of the book see Revelation 6:1—16:21 as referring to the history of the church during the age of the martyrs or the age of the persecution of the church, ending with the defeat of the persecuting forces at the downfall of their power. This means that this section is believed to predict the history of the church roughly from John's time until the conversion of Constantine and the Edict of Toleration (A.D. 311). The three and one-half years of the rule of the beast and the harlot represent this "little season" of the dominance of the Roman Empire. The binding of Satan is interpreted as the downfall of the persecuting power in which the cause of the saints (6:9ff.) is "resurrected" (the first resurrection), and the one thousand years is the longer period of the triumph of the biblical faith. Rather than being a series of literal events (as the futurists and to some extent the left-wing preterists hold), the visions *symbolize* historical happenings. Such events are not meant as consecutive but as repeatable happenings. This interpretation normally takes an a-millennial view of chapter 20. The right-wing preterist interpretation is the standpoint adopted in this commentary.

The Futurist School

This method of interpreting Revelation believes that nothing in the book beyond the fourth chapter has yet been fulfilled or will be fulfilled until just before the coming of the Lord. Futurists usually hold that chapters 14-19 describe events which will take place in a three and one-half year period immediately preceding the second coming of Christ. They often connect this with the seventieth week of Daniel 9:24ff., which is cut off in the middle and thereby separated by many centuries from the previous weeks.

Interpretation

An extreme literalism usually characterizes the futurist treatment. While admitting that some things are obviously symbolic and cannot be taken literally, this school still insists that the normal assumption should be that the figures represent literal events. For example, the earthquakes and the stars falling of the sixth seal are taken as literal events. The temple measured in chapter 11 is a literal one, which must be rebuilt by the Jews before the end of time. The witnesses of this chapter are Moses and Elijah returned to earth.

A personal antichrist is a central part of the futurist interpretation. The first beast of Revelation 13 refers to the great symbol of personal unrighteousness (Dan. 7:25; 8:25; 11:26), which is the same as Paul's man of lawlessness (2 Thess. 2) and which is understood to be a personal worldly ruler of great wickedness who will arise at the period of the end. The second beast is his helper. Actually, the term "antichrist" occurs in the New Testament only in the letters of John (1 John 2:18, 22; 4:3; 2 John 7), where it does not describe one particular person but identifies any one denying that Jesus has come in the flesh (1 John 2:18, 22).

Instead of seeing the book as consisting of a series of cycles or recapitulations, or seeing it as divided into two major parts between chapters 11 and 12, the futurists see the book as one continuous series of events. Belief in a literal millennium—a thousand years of rest, happiness, and prosperity during a future earthly reign of Christ between his second advent and the resurrection—is held by most futurists. This materialistic and literalistic speculation has plagued the Christian movement since early times. Since so much published comment on Revelation is of this nature, it is wise for the student to know the background of this concept.

Millennialists are of two varieties. First, there is what might be called the historic classical premillennialism, or chiliasm, which merely thinks that Christ will come back to earth and reign at the end of the age. Then dispensationalism (Darbyism) adds to this the complete rearrangement of biblical interpretation, including the kingdom postponement, two resurrections, rapture, reestablishment of Judaism, rebuilding of the temple during the millennium, etc.

INTRODUCTION

The roots of classical millennialism lay in the speculations of Jewish apocalyptic literature about a thousand-year period of prosperity at the end of the age. This idea was applied to the interpretation of Revelation 20 by early Christian writers like Papias, Justin Martyr, Irenaeus, Tertullian, and Hippolytus. These writers freely admitted that others thought that their idea was wrong. Then the views were refuted by such able writers as Origen, Dionysius, and Gaius. The great theologian Augustine (d. 430) so argued for a non-literal interpretation that the literal concept was killed until it was resurrected by John Albrecht Bengel (d. 1752). The opposite literal view that the millennium is a period of peace and prosperity before the coming of Jesus (postmillennialism) was developed by Daniel Whitby (d. 1726). Dispensationalism developed from the speculations of John Nelson Darby in the nineteenth century. Non-millennialist interpreters who are still futurists are rare, but Abraham Kuyper and Theodor Zahn are examples of futurist a-millennialist interpreters.

Objections to the Futurist School. The literal interpretation of such obvious figurative and pictorial language is the most serious objection to the futurist view. In ordinary prose the literal sense is to be expected unless something in the context makes it impossible. In such material as the apocalypse, the opposite method ought to be expected.

The interpretation of the visions as one continuous series is objected to on obvious grounds. Not only does the book seem to divide itself into two main sections in the visions, but chapter 12 obviously cuts the visions in two, by returning to the birth of Jesus (the woman and the man-child). This must be denied by the futurists. The futurist interpretation also divorces the book from its first-century setting. What possible encouragement to a suffering church would there be in a book which must be interpreted as referring to events centuries in the future?

The Continuous Historical or Chronological School

Those who hold this view see the Revelation as a symbolic picture of the events of the church from Pentecost until the end of time. They are anxious, therefore, to know where our era is pictured and think to see specified in the book actual battles (Battle of Tours), movements (rise of Mohammedanism, the Protestant Reformation), individuals (Napoleon, the Pope, Hitler), or events (Constantine's Edict of Toleration).

It has been asserted that these identifications are so vivid and detailed that all one needs to convince any infidel of the truth of Christianity is a copy of the book of Revelation and Gibbon's *Decline and Fall of the Roman Empire*. On the other hand, nearly every interpreter has made different interpretations of details. As history has stretched out, new identifications have been required to include great events of more recent times.

Objections to the Continuous Historical Interpretation. This interpretation divorces Revelation from the history of the early church and people to whom it was written. Yet it was to show them "what must shortly come to pass."

The continuous historical interpretation attaches too much importance to the Roman Catholic Church. It sees the Reformation largely as the only great event since the time of Constantine, and it limits the history of the Christian movement to the West. What about the movements of the East and of Africa?

This view also leads to false calculations of time. It is based on the assumption that the time periods of Revelation are to be taken as the "one day = one year" theory (Num. 14:34; Ezek. 4:4-6; Dan. 9:25). For this there is no proof. Yet this has been responsible for most timetables for the Lord's coming. This system usually leads to the belief that the interpreter's own time is near the end.

Finally, this interpretation is not based upon anything in Revelation itself. Conversely, the book implies the connection of the church in John's day with the events themselves, not just the first one.

The Philosophy of History School

The fourth method of interpreting the book of Revelation, commonly called the philosophy of history school, thinks that Revelation does not refer to specific events at all but to the great principles of God's dealing with the church in

INTRODUCTION

history. This school admits that the Revelation was set in the events of first-century persecution, but it sees the solution worked out as that which will be typical of any such confrontation of truth and error in any age. The book is thus ideal and completely symbolic. Its truth may be seen by the church to "fit" its situation whenever it is confronted by persecution or opposition.

The criticism offered by many to this viewpoint in its extreme form is that it divorces the book too much from the events of the age in which it was written. It makes the visions mere idealization, rather than thinking that they referred to historical events and receive a second or double fulfillment in later, possibly similar situations.

It should be noted that many interpreters are not pure representatives of the above four schools but have absorbed elements from other viewpoints into the principal scheme to which they adhere. Some follow a given scheme unconsciously, without realizing its assumptions.

LESSONS FROM REVELATION

There are powerful lessons to be learned from the Revelation of Jesus given to John. Regardless of which of the systems of interpretation is adopted, these lessons still stand out. They are a part of the total picture and do not depend on the meaning of the symbols in chapters 6-20. The churches of today face many problems and situations in which these lessons are needed. The following are some of these lessons:

Jesus' presence is still guaranteed to the churches. He walks in the midst of the candlesticks, the churches. Just as he promises to be with the church always through the Spirit whom he would send to abide forever, so he knows the churches and hears their pleas. He acknowledges the cries of martyrs for vengeance; prayers rise to him from the hearts of his worshipers.

The Almighty Father, creator of the universe, and Jesus Christ the Redeemer enthroned in heaven are the proper objects of worship and adoration of saints, the created things, and heavenly creatures. Throughout the book, but especially in chapters 4 and 5, the worthiness of God and the Lamb to be

Outline

praised and worshiped is emphasized. Warnings are given against ascribing worship or ultimate loyalty to anything else, whether a false religion or an angel or other servant of God.

The patience of the saints is of the utmost importance. Patience here is loyalty in worship and life and endurance in the face of persecution even unto death. Even the Lord of life suffered and died. He does not take his followers out of the world. Instead he upholds them in suffering, that they may be kept from the evil one. Even their death is precious in his sight.

The defeat of evil and the devil and all his agents is certain. God uses the natural forces of the world (like the four horsemen) to accomplish his purposes. Evil has its own seeds of destruction in it. Satan himself has already been overthrown and defeated. No matter how powerful an earthly force may be which sets itself against God's cause, its defeat and final overthrow are certain.

The final triumph of the church is certain and glorious. The cause of truth may seem weak, but even the earth helps her from her enemies. Her leader is the Word of God out of whose mouth the sharp two-edged sword proceeds. The church militant will become the church triumphant. The Lord will come to claim his bride. She must be ready, adorned with righteousness, and faithful, to be received.

The second coming of the Lord will bring about the end of the world as we know it. "The heaven and the first earth are passed away." And, "Behold, He comes with the clouds, and every eye shall see him." The church must learn to pray, "Even so come Lord Jesus."

Final reward and retribution will be given by the great Judge at the day of all days. The principle of divine justice is "each shall be judged out of the books according to his works." Either the second death or the heavenly Jerusalem will be the abode of all throughout all eternity. All the dead, "the great and the small," will meet that final appointment.

OUTLINE OF REVELATION

The following is an outline or analysis of the book of Revelation from the preterist or contemporary historical interpretation.

INTRODUCTION

The book is divided into four unequal parts by the expression "in the Spirit," which signifies the beginning of an ecstatic vision. These are (1) The Vision of the Son of Man (1:10ff.), (2) The Apocalyptic Vision (4:2ff.), (3) The Destruction of Rome (17:3ff.), (4) The New Jerusalem (21:10ff.). To these are to be added the Title and Address, which make up the Prologue (1:1-8), and the Epilogue (22:6-21).

I. THE PROLOGUE, 1:1-8
   A. The Title, 1:1-3
   B. The Address, 1:4-8

II. THE VISION OF THE SON OF MAN AND THE SEVEN LETTERS, 1:9–3:22
   A. The Vision of the Son of Man, 1:9-20
      1. The Introduction of John, 1:9-11
      2. The Vision of the Son of Man, 1:12-20
   B. The Seven Letters, 2:1–3:22
      1. To Ephesus, 2:1-7
      2. To Smyrna, 2:8-11
      3. To Pergamum, 2:12-17
      4. To Thyatira, 2:18-29
      5. To Sardis, 3:1-6
      6. To Philadelphia, 3:7-13
      7. To Laodicea, 3:14-22

III. THE APOCALYPTIC VISION, 4:1–16:21
   A. The Divine Throne Room, 4:1–5:14
      1. The Creator of All Things, 4:1-11
      2. The Scroll and the Redeemer, 5:1-14
   B. The Pageant of Divine Judgments, 6:1–16:21
      1. The First Section. Theme: The Judgments of God upon the World of Wickedness, 6:1–11:19
         a. The Preparation for the Judgments, 6:1–8:1
            (1) The First Four Seals, 6:1-8—The Four Horsemen: The Agents of the Judgment
            (2) The Fifth Seal, 6:9-11—The Souls under the Altar: The Occasion for the Judgment
            (3) The Sixth Seal, 6:12-17—The Cosmic Earthquake: Terror at the Impending Upheaval of the Temporal Power
            (4) A Parenthesis: The Sealing of the Saints, 7:1-17—The Martyrs Exempt from the Terror of the Judgment
         b. The Judgments Delivered—The Seven Trumpets, 8:1–11:19
            (1) The Seven Angels with Trumpets, 8:1-5

Outline

- (2) The First Four Trumpets: Natural Disasters, 8:6-12
- (3) The Demonic Judgments, 8:13–11:19—The Three Woes
  - (a) The First Two Woes, 8:13–9:21
  - (b) Two Intervening Visions, 10:1-11—The Vision of the Little Book; and 11:1-14—The Measuring of the Temple/Two Witnesses
  - (c) The Seventh Trumpet: The Third Woe, 11:15-19
- 2. The Second Section. The War of the Woman and Her Seed Versus the Beast and His Allies, 12:1–16:21
  - a. The Protagonists of the War, 12:1–14:20
    - (1) The Woman and her Child, 12:1-6
    - (2) The War in Heaven, 12:7-12
    - (3) The War on Earth, 12:13-17
    - (4) The Two Great Beasts, 13:1-18
    - (5) The Forces of the Lamb, 14:1-20
  - b. The War with the Beast, 15:1–16:21
    - (1) The Song of Moses and the Lamb, 15:1-8
    - (2) The Plagues upon the Great City, 16:1-21

IV. THE VISION OF JUDGMENT OF THE GREAT HARLOT, 17:1–21:8
  A. The Fall of Rome, 17:1–19:4
    1. The Identity of the Woman and the Beast, 17:1-18
       a. John Carried into the Wilderness, 17:1-6
       b. The Secret Revealed by the Angel, 17:7-18
    2. The Dirge over the Fallen City, 18:1–19:4
       a. The Fall of the City Announced, 18:1-8
       b. The Lament for the City, 18:9-20
       c. Stone Cast into the Sea, 18:21-24
       d. Praise for God's Judgments, 19:1-4
  B. The Marriage Supper of the Lamb, 19:5-10
  C. The Sequel to the Fall of Rome, 19:11–21:8
    1. The War between Christ and the Beast, 19:11-21
    2. The Thousand-Year Reign, 20:1-6
    3. Satan Loosed, 20:7-10
    4. The End of the Conflict: The Final Judgment, 20:11-15
    5. The New Heaven and New Earth, 21:1-8

V. THE VISION OF THE NEW JERUSALEM, 21:9–22:5
  A. John Invited to View the Holy City, 21:9, 10
  B. The City's Outward Appearance, 21:11-23
  C. The Inhabitants of the City, 21:24-27
  D. The Provisions of the City, 22:1-5

VI. THE EPILOGUE, 22:6-21

INTRODUCTION
SELECTED BIBLIOGRAPHY
General Introduction

CAIRD, G. B. "On Deciphering the Book of Revelation," *Expository Times* (1962-63), 13-15, 51-53, 81-84, 103-105.

DANNER, DAN. "A History of Interpretation of Revelation 20:1-10 in the Restoration Movement," *Restoration Quarterly,* 7 (1963), 27-35.

FEUILLET, ANDRÉ. *The Apocalypse,* trans. by T. E. Crane. Staten Island: Alba House, 1964.

HOPKINS, MARTIN. "The Historical Perspective of Apocalypse 1-11," *The Catholic Biblical Quarterly,* 27 (1965), 42-47.

ISBELL, ALLEN. "The Dating of Revelation," *Restoration Quarterly,* 9 (1966), 107-117.

MINEAR, PAUL S. "Ontology and Ecclesiology in the Apocalypse," *New Testament Studies,* 12 (1966), 89-105.

RISSI, M. "The Kerygma of the Revelation to John," *Interpretation,* 22 (1968), 3-17.

ROBERTS, J. W. "The Interpretation of the Apocalypse: The State of the Question," *Restoration Quarterly,* 8 (1965), 154-162.

_____. "The Meaning of the Eschatology in the Book of Revelation," *Restoration Quarterly,* 15 (1972), 95-110.

ROWLEY, H. H. *The Relevance of Apocalyptic.* London and Redhill: Lutterworth Press, 1944.

RUSSELL, D. S. *The Method and Message of Jewish Apocalyptic.* Philadelphia: Westminster, 1964.

Commentaries

Since commentaries differ, depending on the system of interpretation followed, it seems best to list them accordingly. Those on the Greek text are marked with an asterisk.

Preterist

Right Wing

*BECKWITH, ISBON T. *The Apocalypse of St. John.* London: Macmillan, 1919.

Bibliography

CAIRD, G. B. *The Revelation of St. John the Divine.* Harper's New Testament Commentaries. New York: Harper and Row, 1966.

*DUESTERCLIEK, F. *Critical and Exegetical Handbook to the Revelation of St. John.* Funk and Wagnalls, 1887.

PIETERS, ALBERTUS. *Studies in the Revelation of St. John the Divine.* Grand Rapids: Eerdmans, 1942.

SCOTT, C. ANDERSON. *Revelation.* New Century Bible.

*SWETE, H. B. *The Apocalypse of St. John.* Macmillan, 1906.

Left Wing

*CHARLES, R. H. *The Book of Revelation.* International Critical Commentary. Scribner's, 1920.

*MOFFATT, JAMES. *Revelation.* Expositor's Greek Testament.

RIDDLE, M. *Revelation.* Moffatt Commentaries, 1940.

SCOTT, E. F. *The Book of Revelation.* London, 1939.

Futurist

KUYPER, ABRAHAM. *The Revelation of St. John.* Grand Rapids: Eerdmans, 1935.

LADD, GEORGE ELDON. *A Commentary on the Revelation of John.* Grand Rapids: Eerdmans, 1972. (N.B.—Ladd's view is futurist, combined with preterist. He is a premillennialist but not a dispensationalist.)

TENNY, M. C. *Interpreting Revelation.* Grand Rapids: Eerdmans, 1957.

Dispensationalist

ERDMAN, W. J. *Notes on Revelation.* New York: Revell, 1930.

FROST, HENRY W. *The Second Coming of Christ.* Grand Rapids: Eerdmans, 1934.

SCOFIELD, C. I. *The Holy Bible: Scofield Reference Edition.* New York: Oxford, 1917. New Edition, 1967.

Anti-Dispensationalist

MASSELINK, WM. *Why the Thousand Years?* Grand Rapids: Eerdmans, 1930.

INTRODUCTION

Historical

BARNES, ALBERT. *Notes on the New Testament.* New York: Harper's, 1852. Also Postmillennial.

CARROLL, B. H. *The Book of Revelation.* New York: Revell Co., 1913. Postmillennial.

ELLIOTT, E. B. *Horae Apocalypticae.* London: Seeley, 1844. 4 Vols. Premillennial but not dispensational.

> *Recapitulationist View* (Cyclist). Takes the view that it is historical but not continuous. Seven stages or pictures each covering the entire period of the Christian dispensation.

BOWMAN, JOHN WICK. *The Drama of the Book of Revelation.* Westminster Press, 1955.

_____. "Revelation," *Interpreter's Dictionary of The Bible,* Vol. IV. George Buttrick (ed.). New York: Abingdon, 1963.

HENDRIKSEN, W. *More Than Conquerors.* Grand Rapids: Baker, 1940.

Philosophy of History

*ALFORD, HENRY. *The Greek Testament.* New York: Harper, 1862.

BENSON, E. W. *The Apocalypse, an Introductory Study of the Revelation of St. John the Divine.* London: Macmillan, 1900.

*LENSKI, R. C. H. *The Interpretation of St. John's Revelation.* Columbus, Ohio: Wartburg Press, 1943.

MILLIGAN, WM. *The Book of Revelation.* Expositor's Bible. New York, 1893.

MORRIS, LEON. *The Revelation of St. John.* Tyndale Bible Commentaries. Grand Rapids: Eerdmans, 1969. (Philosophy of history combined with preterist. Refuses to align himself with any of the usual schools.)

II

The Revelation to John (The Apocalypse)

THE PROLOGUE, 1:1-8

The Title, 1:1-3

IN THE TITLE John sets forth the subject of his book. It is a revelation of things about to happen. The origin and authority or sanction behind the Revelation are affirmed: It comes from God through his ordained messengers, who include Christ, his angel, and John himself, a prophet commissioned by God to receive the Revelation in visions.

[1, 2] As noted in the introduction, the **revelation** (Greek *apocalypse*) identifies this book with the type of Jewish literature called apocalyptic, to which Daniel and many other books belong. The experiences of Daniel and his companions were used to console Jewish sufferers in the trials to come under the Syrian king Antiochus Epiphanes (204-165 B.C.—see Dan. 8, esp. vss. 21ff.). The book of Daniel in turn was imitated by a whole list of later Jewish books of the same type (e.g., Enoch, 2 Esdras). While the similarity with these books helps in understanding the imagery of Revelation, John's book is also different. John insists that he stands in the line of Old Testament prophets and that his book is one of prophecy (vs. 3). But John's Revelation is also that given by Jesus Christ.

Jesus gives the revelation **to show his servants** what must happen soon. By **servant** is usually meant someone entrusted with special work or responsibility: the Old Testament

REV. 1:1-3 *The Reader*

¹**The revelation of Jesus Christ, which God gave him to show to his servants what must soon take place; and he made it known by sending his angel to his servant John,** ²**who bore witness to the word of God and to the testimony of Jesus Christ even to all that he saw.** ³**Blessed is he who reads aloud the words of the prophecy, and blessed are those who hear, and who keep what is written therein; for the time is near.**

---

prophets (10:7; 11:18), Moses (15:3), the apostles (Acts 4:29), Paul (Rom. 1:1), an evangelist such as Epaphras (Col. 4:12) or Timothy (2 Tim. 2:24). In a sense, all believers are servants, and this is probably meant here, since all are to hear and read this book. The revelation concerns **what must soon take place.** This phrase is identical with the Septuagint rendering of Daniel 2:28, 45, except that the revelation to Nebuchadnezzar was to be fulfilled "in the last days" or "after this." By saying that events are to happen quickly John means that God will take an immediate hand in the events happening among the churches. He does not mean that everything envisioned will happen immediately, nor does he mean the second coming is about to happen (see comments on vs. 9). In 6:11 the martyr spirits are told that the period of martyrdom must be extended. The future end-time was still further beyond (also see 10:6, 7; 22:10).

[3] It was common in ancient times for the scribe or author of a work to pronounce a blessing concerning the treatise. John pronounces a blessing upon the one who reads the Revelation aloud in the public assembly (the Greek word means this), as well as the congregation who hears, and then upon those who keep or pay attention to what is written therein. Time and again, the book will emphasize that God gives the revelation for the instruction of his saints, hence the frequent "let him who has ears to hear, hear" and the "this is the mind of wisdom" (2:7, etc.; 17:9).

The Address, 1:4-8

The address contains the central theological affirmations of the book. They are set forth primarily in a series of divine names and epithets expressive of the attributes of the

Seven Churches REV. 1:4

⁴John to the seven churches that are in Asia:
Grace to you and peace from him who is and who was and who is to come, and from the seven spirits who are before his throne,

---

Godhead and chosen with special reference to the problem of the book—the Christians' reaction to the stark reality of the powerful, persecuting world power Rome.

[4] Though the letter is the Revelation of Jesus Christ, John is the one to whom it was made known and the one commissioned to write to the churches. So Revelation comes in the general style of epistles of the times: **John to the seven churches of Asia.** By **Asia** here is meant the Roman province combining the former geographical areas of Mysia, Lydia, and Caria. Since there are known to be more than **the seven churches** at the time in the province—Colossae (Col. 1:2), Troas (Acts 20:5), Hierapolis (Col. 4:13), and probably Magnesia and Tralles, John must be using the number seven in its symbolic sense of completeness. The Revelation is addressed to these seven churches as a cross section of the church and thus to the church as a whole. In further epistolary style, the salutation **Grace to you** is given, and the document is identified as coming from the three persons of the Deity. As is frequent in Greek salutations, the descriptive words of those who authorize the letter say a great deal. God the Father is described in terms of his everlasting being; he is the one **who is** (the Greek form of the I Am of Ex. 3:14; cf. Jer. 1:6; 14:13), the one **who was** (here John invents some grammar, as he uses the Greek article with the imperfect of the verb *to be*; the imperfect had no participle), and the one **who is to come.** God is the God of the past, present, and future. So the book which is to concern itself with the church's crisis in history is addressed by the God of history who has manifested, continues to manifest, and will yet manifest himself in history. Likewise, the greeting from the **seven spirits** before the throne is meant to convey the perfection of the Holy Spirit (see 3:1; 4:5; 5:6). This is indicated by the obvious coordination in the context with the Father and Son and by the dependence of the language on Zechariah 4:10. It has been suggested that John follows the language of

REV. 1:4, 5 *Jesus Christ*

⁵ **and from Jesus Christ the faithful witness, the firstborn of the dead, and the ruler of kings on earth.**
To him who loves us and has freed us from our sins by his blood

---

later Judaism, according to which the chiefs of the angelic band of spirits are seven in number.

[5] Greetings to the churches come also from the Lord, whose revelation this is, and his descriptive titles are given in view of the situation which calls forth the visions. **The faithful witness** looks back to the "testimony" which Jesus gives (vs. 2) and also recalls the death of Jesus Christ on the cross as a witness to the world. Those called upon to be faithful unto death (2:10) could remember that he, too, was a faithful witness. For the Old Testament background from which the term is quoted, see Isaiah 55:4 (and cf. Prov. 14:5; John 3:11, 32f.; 8:14f.). To those about to die Jesus addresses himself as one who also has died but is the conqueror of death. As Paul had said (Col. 1:18), he is **the firstborn of the dead.** Others had been raised from death through God's power, but Jesus was the first to be raised to die no more. Early Christians saw great significance in Jesus' resurrection as the conquering of death (Heb. 2:9ff.; 1 Cor. 15:20; Rom. 8:11). As the resurrected Lord, Jesus is also **ruler of the kings of the earth**; he has been given dominion over all (see 5:12; Eph. 1:20f.; 1 Cor. 15:25ff.). John paraphrases and alludes to Psalm 89:27f. (cf. vs. 48). Even the rulers before whom Christians must stand and be judged for their faith in Jesus owe allegiance to the risen Lord. A part of the purpose of Revelation is to show the ultimate triumph of the rightful ruler of the universe.

Next, in a manner quite common to the documents of the early church, is a doxology—a spontaneous hymn of praise. The description of the person and work of Jesus is continued by ascribing to him **glory and dominion for ever and ever** on the grounds that he **loves us and has freed us from our sins by his blood.** John uses the present tense of the participle to express Jesus' love. This is his continuing characteristic; not only on the cross did he love, but he continues to do so in his presence with the church. But above all, on the cross, where he loosed us **from our sins by his blood,** his love was shown.

Coming Again REV. 1:5-7

⁶**and made us a kingdom, priests to his God and Father, to him be glory and dominion for ever and ever. Amen.** ⁷**Behold, he is coming with the clouds, and every eye will see him, every one who pierced him; and all tribes of the earth will wail on account of him. Even so. Amen.**

There is a variation in the manuscripts between "freed" (from *luō*) and "washed" (from *louō*). Both ideas, however, fit the context well. The phrase is a graphic expression of the significance of the death of Jesus.

[6] Finally, John applies to the saints the prerogatives of Israel. They became (as God had promised Israel at the making of the covenant, Ex. 19:9) **a kingdom, priests to his God and Father.** The exact grammar of the phrase is difficult, but whether the original promise is rendered "a royal priesthood" or by *hendiadys* **"a kingdom** (kings) **and priests,"** the ideas are similar. Compare 1 Peter 2:9, 10, where the same Christian application is made of these covenant promises, as well as the repetition in Revelation 5:10.

[7] Appended to the doxology is a promise of the **coming** of Christ, a promise emphasized at the end of the book by the Lord himself (22:7, 12, 20). The Greek of **he is coming with the clouds, every eye** especially they **who pierced him will see him**, and **all the tribes of the earth will wail on account of him** is a combined quotation from Daniel 7:13 and Zechariah 12:10—13:1. The combining of the descriptions occurs also in Jesus' sermon on Olivet (Matt. 24:30). The words give assurance to a generation whose hope of the parousia had seemed unrealized that the promise still stands, and they also describe the grief the world will voice as it sees doom being realized.

It would be impossible to deny that the promise has primary reference to the second coming. But all Jesus' actions in history are to be seen against that coming. Jesus' coming to the churches may be in other ways, too. He may come to sup with the faithful (3:20) or to remove the candlestick of a church whose love has grown cold (2:5). Jesus' repeated promises to come in judgment upon the enemies of the church surely anticipate the second advent but are not limited to it.

REV. 1:8-10　　　　　　　　　　　　*Alpha and Omega*

⁸ "I am the Alpha and the Omega," says the Lord God, who is and who was and who is to come, the Almighty.

⁹ I John, your brother, who share with you in Jesus the tribulation and the kingdom and the patient endurance, was on the island called Patmos on account of the word of God and the testimony of Jesus. ¹⁰ I was in the Spirit on the Lord's day, and I heard behind me a loud voice like a trumpet

---

[8] The climax of the opening of the book is reached by the direct words ascribed to God, the Almighty: **I am the Alpha and the Omega,** the beginning and ending letters of the Greek alphabet, which are later repeated with the interpretation that their use signifies the "beginning and the end" (21:6). The letters, joined with the previous identifications of **God** as the one **who is, and who was and who is to come,** emphasize the eternal nature of God. The Old Testament has "first and last" in Isaiah 41:4 (Greek); 44:6 (Hebrew). But to this eternalness there is added the characteristic of power: God is **the Almighty.** The Greek *pantokrator* is one of the several ways the Greek translates the phrase "Yahweh of Sabaoth," the powerful, avenging, conquering Lord of the "hosts." Nine times it is used to describe God's omnipotence: 4:8; 11:17; 15:3; 16:7; 14; 16:6, 15; 21:22. These are especially passages where God's triumph is achieved by the blood of Christ and of the martyrs.

THE VISION OF THE SON OF MAN, 1:9—3:22

Having completed the varied introductions to the book, the writer turns to the initial vision of the series which are to make up his book. He records Christ's appearance to him at his place of exile on a Sunday. Jesus Christ appeared to him with instructions to send a record of his visions to the seven churches of the province of Asia (1:9-20) and to include a message to each church (2:1—3:22). The carrying out of these instructions forms the base of this section of the Revelation.

The Son of Man, 1:9-20

[9, 10] In the manner of older apocalyptic (Dan. 8:1;

10:2; Enoch 12:3) the writer identifies himself: **I John, your brother,** ... Whoever "John" was, the churches knew him. Patmos was an island off the coast of Asia Minor. The evidence suggests (Tacitus *Annals* 3.68; 4.30; 15.71; Juvenal *Satires* i. 73; vi. 563) that the island group to which it belonged was often used as a place of exile for imperial prisoners. John was there on **account of the word** (message of preaching) of God. His work as an evangelist of Jesus Christ had led him to be arrested and exiled.

The vision took place on a **Lord's day**, or the first day of the week, when saints in the churches would be meeting to celebrate the resurrection of their Lord. John was **in the spirit**; that is, he was caught up in ecstasy (for so the expression is to be interpreted, 4:2).

With these identifications of John the writer, the stage is set. But perhaps more significant is John's identifying himself as a **brother** and one who **in Christ** (that is, as a Christian) shares with his readers the **tribulation** and **the kingdom** and the **patient endurance**. These descriptions go to the heart of the problem facing Christians in a time of coming peril. The readers would know that John had been arrested for the faith; his persecution foreshadowed their own affliction which was coming to try the whole world (3:10). That he had been true to his faith and had not denied his Lord in the hearing in which he was sentenced would also be known; this is an example for their own call to patient endurance (see 14:12).

But the **kingdom** or sovereign reign of God which he shared with them was not something objective and empirical like persecution and endurance. The reality of the kingdom is apprehended with the eye of faith, a vision that may grow dim at the taunts of the crowd or the court in the time of trial. Second Peter (3:4) bears out what was being hurled at Christians: questions like "Where is the promise of his coming?" Beside the stern, brute facts of the kingdom of Caesar, the eternal kingdom might seem to lack reality. Only those who knew, with John, that in Christ they shared the ultimate reality (God's kingdom on earth) could face what was coming upon the churches.

REV. 1:11-14 *Seven Lampstands*

¹¹ saying, "Write what you see in a book and send it to the seven churches, to Ephesus and to Smyrna and to Pergamum and to Thyatira and to Sardis and to Philadelphia and to Laodicea."

¹² Then I turned to see the voice that was speaking to me, and on turning I saw seven golden lampstands, ¹³ and in the midst of the lampstands one like a son of man, clothed with a long robe and with a golden girdle round his breast; ¹⁴ his head and his hair were white as white wool, white as snow; his eyes were like a flame of fire,

---

[11, 12] The voice which John heard behind him instructed him to write what he saw **in a book** and **send it to the seven churches**. When John turned, he saw **seven golden lampstands**. Zechariah 4, a passage which furnishes background for much of the book, uses the candelabrum in the temple to suggest the idea of Israel as the light. This concept is heightened in other places by the idea of the church as the light of the world (Matt. 5:14; Phil. 2:15). The imagery is twofold: The churches on earth are the lights; the stars (vs. 16) are their heavenly counterpart. This is in accord with the well-known Jewish idea of the stars representing angels as the ministering spirits entrusted with the fortunes of earthly institutions and individuals.

[13, 14] Jesus is described in great detail **walking in the midst of the seven lampstands**. This certainly calls attention to the presence of the exalted Christ among the earthly congregations of his people. The resurrected Lord had promised that he would be with his disciples always even to the end of the age (Matt. 28:20). Though absent, Jesus knows and cares what happens in the churches (2:2, 9, 13, 19, etc.). Even the stars (angels), who represent the churches, are held in his right hand (vs. 16).

John describes the present Lord of the churches as **one like a son of man.** Whether this is merely the Hebrew way of expressing the likeness of a human being, or whether John is using the well-known title of Jesus from the Gospels, which was adopted by Jesus as a special title of self-designation, is much argued. John's going on to describe him in terms reminiscent of Daniel 7:13ff., especially in that **his hair was**

Son of Man REV. 1:13-20

¹⁵ his feet were like burnished bronze, refined as in a furnace, and his voice was like the sound of many waters; ¹⁶ in his right hand he held seven stars, from his mouth issued a sharp two-edged sword, and his face was like the sun shining in full strength. ¹⁷ When I saw him, I fell at his feet as though dead. But he laid his right hand upon me, saying, "Fear not, I am the first and the last, ¹⁸ and the living one; I died, and behold I am alive for evermore, and I have the keys of Death and Hades. ¹⁹ Now write what you see, what is and what is to take place hereafter. ²⁰ As for the mystery of the seven stars which you saw in my right hand, and the seven golden lampstands, the seven stars are the angels of the seven churches and the seven lampstands are the seven churches.

---

white as wool, and his later use of the title in 14:14 seem to argue the latter. His description of the **son of man** bears resemblance to that of the angelic being who was Daniel's guide (Dan. 10:5ff.), and whom Daniel described as like a son of man (10:16), and the Ancient of Days (7:9). The **long robe** is that of the high priest (Ex. 28:4; 39:29), a visible emblem of Jesus' atoning office. The **girdle** is not of one who runs and toils, but is around his heart as one who has entered the repose of sovereignty.

[15, 16] The description continues to draw on Old Testament language, especially at this point Ezekiel: **burnished bronze** (Ezek. 1:7) and **sound of many waters** (Ezek. 1:24; 43:2). Jesus holds the fortunes of the churches (**stars**) **in his right hand**, and **his face was shining**, reminiscent to John of Jesus on the Mount of Transfiguration (Matt. 17:2), in a brightness exceeding that of Moses (Ex. 34:29).

[17, 18] Jesus is the **first and last** (Isa. 44:6). The consolation is already offered that he has conquered death and is alive. Thus he controls access to and can give release from **Death. Hades** is Greek for the grave, the underworld, the realm of the dead, and is equivalent here to **Death** (Acts 2:24, 27, 28).

[19, 20] The churches might seem isolated from each other and helpless as they faced the coming trial to their faith.

But such is not the case. Each is a part of the mystic number seven. Each is held by the unseen presence of the risen son of man. As a seven-branched candelabrum or lampstand (the menorah) had become the standing symbol of the Jewish community in the ancient world, so each church, as the new Israel, is represented by a **lampstand**. The angels of the churches have been variously interpreted, principally as human representatives of the church or as guardian angels standing for the church itself. That the lampstands are on earth and the **angels (stars)** are in Christ's **hand** favors the latter. In this view, the angels are the heavenly counterpart of the earthly reality of the church.

The vision of the son of man is set here at the beginning partly because it gives the explanation of John's call to write. Furthermore, it is characteristic of John's method to set Christ in the forefront as the key to what **is to take place** in history.

The Seven Letters, 2:1—3:22

The seven letters, together with the vision of chapter 1, are a kind of cover letter and introduction to John's apocalyptic visions, which begin in chapter 4. From the divine promises made in the letters (especially to "those who conquer") the readers are prepared to learn of the nature of their ordeal, to be disclosed in the apocalypse proper (chs. 6-20). The letters force the recipients to look at themselves before they are introduced to the apocalyptic horrors. Note the theme of repentance (2:5, 16, 19; 3:3, 19). The persecuted church is not one that can afford to feel superior. Christ wants to come back into the church (3:20). When this point is appreciated, it serves to moderate the vindictiveness that is naturally expressed by a persecuted church (6:10).

Sir William Ramsay (*Letters to the Seven Churches*) has shown that the letters indicate an intimate knowledge not only of the churches and their history but of the history, topography, economics, and religious life of the cities where the churches were located. They reflect the actual life situations of the respective churches in the first century. As already suggested, seven churches were selected to give a cross section of the universal church.

Seven Letters REV. 2:1, 2

¹ "To the angel of the church in Ephesus write: 'The words of him who holds the seven stars in his right hand, who walks among the seven golden lampstands.

² "'I know your works, your toil and your patient endurance, and how you cannot bear evil men but have tested those who call themselves apostles but are not, and found them to be false;

The letters have a common fourfold plan. Each begins with a description of the Christ, the Lord of the churches. These descriptions emphasize qualities drawn mostly from the vision of chapter 1 and seem selected in relation to the condition of each congregation addressed. Next, the good qualities of the churches' records are noted and praised (except in the case of Laodicea, where nothing praiseworthy is found). Then comes blame for the failings and deficiencies of the local groups (Smyrna and Philadelphia have only praise). In these praise and censure sections the local situations over against paganism, Judaism, and the internal struggle of the churches are revealed. At the conclusion there are beatitudes or promises of blessings—some general, and to each church a promise to "him who conquers." The letters constitute what may be called an "inspection" of the churches to establish whether they are prepared for their ordeal, the coming persecution.

Letter to Ephesus, 2:1-7. [1, 2] The letter is addressed **to the angel**, by which John means the heavenly representative of the church (1:20). The beginning of the letter stresses the benevolent care of the Lord **who holds the seven stars** (the angels, 1:13, 20) **in his right hand** and also his intimate knowledge as the **one who walks among the seven lampstands** (the churches themselves, 1:20). The first part of the scrutiny is complimentary to Ephesus. The Lord **knows** (is acquainted with and approves) the church's **works, toil, and patient endurance.** Through the years the members had dedicated themselves to good works (Eph. 2:10). The phrase **I know . . .** is repeated of Sardis (3:1), of Philadelphia (3:8), and of Laodicea, but not always in a complimentary sense. **Toil** (cf. 14:13) and **patient endurance** signify that the persecution to

REV. 2:1-4 *False Apostles*

³I know you are enduring patiently and bearing up for my name's sake, and you have not grown weary. ⁴But I have this against you, that you have abandoned the love you had at first.

---

be visited anew on all has been visited on Ephesus through the years (cf. Paul's trouble in the city and notice the implications of Eph. 6:10-20). Another compliment to the Ephesian church is: **they cannot bear evil men** some of whom **call themselves apostles but are not.** The term apostle is used in several senses in the New Testament: to describe Christ the messenger of the Father (John 20:21; Heb. 3:1); to designate the twelve apostles of Christ selected by him to be sent as his representatives (Mark 3:14); to include similarly chosen and qualified men such as Paul, James the Just (Gal. 1:19), Barnabas (Acts 14:14), Andronicus and Junias (Rom. 16:7); and finally, to indicate local messengers or "apostles of the churches" (2 Cor. 8:19, 23) such as Epaphroditus (Phil. 2:25). One phenomenon of the early church was the pretense of a group of false apostles, evidently claiming the credentials of the wider group of the apostles of Christ (2 Cor. 3:1ff.; 12:11 ff.). John was to tell the churches of Asia Minor (1 John 4:1 ff.) to test such men by their message. Here Ephesus has **tested** them and found that they are **false**.

[3] The Spirit repeats the complimentary feature, **enduring patiently**, expanding it to their **bearing up** for the sake of Christ's "name" and **not** growing **weary**. All this reflects their faithfulness in persecution and their activity for Christ's sake.

[4] But after the compliment comes the censure. The Lord has against them that they **have abandoned** their former **love** (contrast 1 Thess. 1:3). The Greek refers to the love characteristic of former times, like "first" or "former" pledge (1 Tim. 5:12). Such love might refer to God or, ethically, to fellowmen. The noun in the Christian context usually has the ethical sense—the distinctive quality of positive regard even for one's enemies. The praise given for patient endurance and labor seems to be against the idea that they no longer loved the Lord as in former days. The loyal spirit of defense of the truth had bred an attitude of intolerance and

Love Needed REV. 2:4-7

⁵Remember then from what you have fallen, repent and do the works you did at first. If not, I will come to you and remove your lampstand from its place, unless you repent. ⁶Yet this you have, you hate the works of the Nicolaitans, which I also hate. ⁷He who has an ear, let him hear what the Spirit says to the churches. To him who conquers I will grant to eat of the tree of life, which is in the paradise of God.'

---

spite toward those in error. Paul reminded Timothy in charging those who taught a different doctrine that "the end of the charge is love out of a pure heart" (1 Tim. 1:5). Patience and meekness must be shown those who oppose themselves (2 Tim. 2:25). This in their zeal Ephesus had forgotten.

[5, 6] In view of their leaving their former love, the Ephesians are admonished to **remember from what you have fallen**, which was their place of favor with God, and to repent or turn again in moral earnestness to **do the works you did at first**. It may seem strange that a church so loyal and steadfast should have been considered fallen because it was lacking in this one respect: the spirit in which they did their works. But it should be remembered that the essence of the gospel is God's love for erring humanity. Any attempt to make the gospel effective which distorts this central fact is a distortion of the gospel itself.

Unless such repentance is forthcoming, Christ warns: **"I will come to you and remove your lampstand"**; that is, the impending crisis of judgment will come upon them and in their deficiency they will cease to be regarded by Christ as a true church of his. This interpretation implies what has already been claimed: that the coming of Christ here (and elsewhere in the book) does not represent an imminent coming of Christ to end the world in what is called his parousia. Rather, the term is used in the Jewish secondary sense in which every visitation of God is seen as his coming. On **Nicolaitans**, see 2:15.

[7] The one **who conquers** is particularly the martyr, the one who is faithful in persecution. Such a person is especially in need of the promise that he will enjoy **the paradise of God** (Gen. 2:9).

REV. 2:8, 9 *Persecution by Jews*

⁸ "And to the angel of the church in Smyrna write: 'The words of the first and the last, who died and came to life.
⁹ "'I know your tribulation and your poverty (but you are rich) and the slander of those who say that they are Jews and are not, but are a synagogue of Satan.

Letter to Smyrna, 2:8-11. [8] The message of this letter is one of encouragement in the face of coming persecutions. The Smyrneans are reminded that Christ himself, the eternal one, shared a martyr's death but lived again. **The first and last** is repeated from 1:17. **Died and came to life** picks up 1:18.

[9] Christ encourages the angel of the church at Smyrna by saying that he knows their **tribulation and poverty**. Though lacking in earthly possessions, they are rich (cf. James 2:5 and contrast Rev. 3:17). What the church has already suffered is not said, but it seems to have been motivated by the calumny of the Jews (cf. Acts 13:50; 1Thess. 2:14ff.; Rev. 3:9). Since the destruction of Jerusalem (A.D. 70) the antagonism between Jews and Christians had grown, until it resulted in a curse against the Christians being included in the synagogue prayers. Much later, when Polycarp was martyred at Smyrna, Jews took a leading part (*Martyrdom of Polycarp* 12f.; 17f.). The attack upon Christians, resulting from the rejection of Jesus as Messiah, meant that the Jews had forfeited their privileges and had become a **synagogue of Satan**.

This striking phrase reflects both the attraction and the tension between Judaism and the early church (cf. again 3:9). Although *sunagogē* is used once in the New Testament for a Christian assembly (James 2:2), it rapidly gave way to the more popular term *ekklesia*. Both Jews and Christians maintained that they were a "synagogue (assembly) of the Lord" (see Num. 16:3). In John's gospel, however, Jesus denies that those who oppose the Christ are the true children of Abraham or of God (John 8:31-47). By their slander of the new Israel of God (Gal. 6:16), hostile Jews showed themselves to be the assembly of the Slanderer (Grk. *sātānas*).

Second Death REV. 2:10-12

¹⁰Do not fear what you are about to suffer. Behold, the devil is about to throw some of you into prison, that you may be tested, and for ten days you will have tribulation. Be faithful unto death, and I will give you the crown of life. ¹¹He who has an ear, let him hear what the Spirit says to the churches. He who conquers shall not be hurt by the second death.'

¹² "And to the angel of the church in Pergamum write: 'The words of him who has the sharp two-edged sword.

---

[10] John forecast that soon members of the Smyrna church would endure a short trial (**ten days**; cf. Dan. 1:12, 14). **Prison** in the ancient world was a place for those awaiting trial. They must be ready for the extreme penalty if it should come to that, as it had at Pergamum (2:13). Many Christians would be tempted to put a pinch of incense on Caesar's altar or call Caesar "Lord" in order to escape death, but this is to be recognized as a pitfall of Satan with terrible consequences to the compromisers (14:9-11). Satan's design to tempt would be God's test. God would turn the martyrdom into his own purpose and bestow a **crown of life. Crown** in the Old Testament refers to honor and dignity (Pss. 8:5; 103:4); in the New Testament it is used of the eschatological victory over evil (1 Cor. 9:25; 2 Tim. 4:8; James 1:12).

[11] **He who conquers** (as Jesus conquered by his own death) will **not be hurt by the second death,** the gehenna of fire which will destroy both soul and body. The Spirit's message to the churches does not offer immunity from death but from hell and the annihilation of the soul. **Second death** has been documented as a description for hell in the Jewish targums. The first death would be natural death, to which all are subject; the **second** is eternal **death,** to which the condemned are given over at the judgment (20:6, 14; 21:8). Here the reward (of 2:7) is stated more specifically, for it is contrasted with the martyr's death (vs. 10).

Letter to Pergamum, 2:12-17. [12] The Roman proconsul ruled by **the sword.** When Christ addresses the church in the provincial capital, it is fitting that he has the **sharp two-edged sword** (cf. 1:16) to counterbalance the **sword** of the proconsul.

REV. 2:13, 14 *Antipas the Martyr*

[13] "'I know where you dwell, where Satan's throne is; you hold fast my name and you did not deny my faith even in the days of Antipas my witness, my faithful one, who was killed among you, where Satan dwells. [14] But I have a few things against you: you have some there who hold the teaching of Balaam, who taught Balak to put a stumbling block before the sons of Israel, that they might eat food sacrificed to idols and practice immorality.

---

[13] At least three explanations have been offered on Pergamum as **where Satan's throne is:** the great altar of Zeus (now reconstructed in Berlin) which crowned the city's acropolis; the sanctuary of Asclepius, whose emblem (a serpent entwined around a staff) would immediately remind Jews and Christians alike of Satan; and the imperial cult. The last is most likely correct in view of the theme of the whole book and the later identification in the book of imperial power with the ancient beast who gives his power to the dragon-serpent (chs. 12, 13).

Despite the situation of the church in the seat of Rome's power, they had **held fast the** Lord's **name** and **did not deny** his **faith**. Pliny's letter to Trajan (X. 96) and the *Martyrdom of Polycarp* indicate that, when arrested as a Christian, one was asked to deny his connection with Christ and was offered an avenue of escape in doing so. That local persecutions had occurred before the time of this letter is shown by the fact that Antipas, one of their number, had been killed, either by the officials or by mob violence. This in turn exposed other Christians to danger. Still no Christian had denied Christ. Antipas had been faithful in giving his witness when brought to trial. The expression **even in the days of Antipas** implies that the time of his death was not the only occasion when the church there had been in danger. Pergamum, with pride in its priority in honoring the divinity of the emperors, would most likely be in the forefront of opposition to Christianity.

[14] Although the Christians of Pergamum had held their loyalty to Christ, there were some efforts to compromise. The story of Balaam is told in Numbers 22-25 (cf. 2 Peter 2:15; Jude 11). As a result of his suggestion, the women of Moab were brought among the Israelites (see Num. 25:1f.) to

Religious Compromise

15 So you also have some who hold the teaching of the Nicolaitans.

---

entice them to **eat food sacrificed to idols and to practice immorality** (Greek, "fornication"), and twenty-three thousand were slain in one day (1 Cor. 10:8, 9). The Old Testament subsequently used Balaam as a warning to God's people (Micah 6:5) and later Jewish writers adopted him as a symbol of covetousness and sponsor of religious syncretism (Philo, *Life of Moses* I. 53-55; 264ff.; Josephus, *Antiquities* IV. vi. 126ff; *Pirke Aboth* 5:19). So John here uses Balaam for such a symbol, without naming the actual people who claimed that compromise was permissible. John may use "fornication" in a metaphorical sense for idolatry (spiritual adultery). On the other hand, there were those at Corinth who argued fornication was permissible (1 Cor. 6:12ff.), and actual fornication was involved in the story of Balaam, even as it was common in various temple cults of the Near East.

There were plausible arguments to support an accommodation to the claims of the state and to local religious practices. Both Peter and Paul (1 Peter 2:13ff.; Rom. 13:1ff.) had taught that the Roman state was divinely ordained and deserving of support. The divinity of the emperor was generally not taken seriously and was considered by most a pious fiction which served state policy well. Only a token of submission to demonstrate loyalty was demanded. Moreover, Paul had taught that an idol was nothing and that meat sacrificed to idols might be eaten (1 Cor. 8) except in actual worship (1 Cor. 10:19ff.). What harm, then, these Christians at Pergamum perhaps asked, is there in engaging in the practices to the extent of demonstrating loyalty to the emperor and thus giving Caesar his due (Matt. 22:21)?

John's answer is indicated by his reference to the false prophet and by his demand to repent (vs. 16). For John's abhorrence of compromise, see also 9:20f.; 14:9-11; 21:8.

[15] John seems to impute this laxity of teaching also to the sect of the **Nicolaitans** (already mentioned in 2:6). We know little for sure about them. John's word **so** may indicate that this was the actual identification of those to whom he had attached the symbolic name Balaam.

REV. 2:16-19 *Burnished Bronze*

¹⁶ Repent then. If not, I will come to you soon and war against them with the sword of my mouth. ¹⁷ He who has an ear, let him hear what the Spirit says to the churches. To him who conquers I will give some of the hidden manna, and I will give him a white stone, with a new name written on the stone which no one knows except him who receives it.'

¹⁸ "And to the angel of the church in Thyatira write: 'The words of the Son of God, who has eyes like a flame of fire, and whose feet are like burnished bronze.

¹⁹ "'I know your works, your love and faith and service and patient endurance, and that your latter works exceed the first.

---

[16] The demand is that these compromisers **repent**. If they do not, Jesus threatens to come, not his advent at the end of time, but a visitation in some historical event of judgment (cf. 2:5, 22) or disaster (8:7ff.).

[17] Once again the promise is made **to him who conquers**, i.e., the martyr who overcomes by his faithful testimony. Jewish writers refer to the legend that the pot of manna in the ark of the covenant (Ex. 16:32ff.; Heb. 9:4) had been hidden by the prophet Jeremiah when the temple was destroyed and would reappear in the messianic age (2 Maccabees 2:4-8; 2 Baruch 29:8; Hagigah 12b). Thus a hidden and heavenly food is promised to those who did not eat at the pagan banquets. The white stone has been taken to be an amulet, but it possibly was a ticket to a banquet and so continues an allusion to the messianic banquet (19:5ff.).

Letter to Thyatira, 2:18-29. [18] Christ is identified in the same terms as in 1:14, 15. The word translated **burnished bronze** occurs only in the book of Revelation and may have some reference to the guilds of bronze workers in the city, which are known from inscriptions. Another suggestion is that the descriptive eyes and feet consciously refer to claims and attributes of the Thyatirian sun-god. This would strike significantly with "worshipers of God."

[19] Unlike Ephesus, the church at Thyatira had experienced constant growth in the Christian graces (cf. 1 Thess.

Jezebel REV. 2:20-23

[20] But I have this against you, that you tolerate the woman Jezebel, who calls herself a prophetess and is teaching and beguiling my servants to practice immorality and to eat food sacrificed to idols. [21] I gave her time to repent, but she refuses to repent of her immorality. [22] Behold, I will throw her on a sickbed, and those who commit adultery with her I will throw into great tribulation, unless they repent of her doings; [23] and I will strike her children dead. And all the churches shall know that I am he who searches mind and heart, and I will give to each of you as your works deserve.

1:3). The opening compliment, however, is followed by a serious indictment.

[20] The teaching of **Jezebel** coincides with that accepted at Pergamum (2:14, where see notes). The woman who is given the name of the Old Testament queen (1 Kings 16:21) claimed to be **a prophetess** and was evidently accepted and respected in the church. One reason, perhaps, was a promotion of the works of love and service for which the church is commended in verse 19. Allusion is made to the apostolic letter of Acts 15:28, 29 (see also verse 24, below) in the practices encouraged by the prophetess. She may not have been a personal participant in fornication but an advocate of compromise with pagan cults (as at Pergamum) in which this was a feature.

[21, 22] The command to **repent** and the stern warnings give some indication of the serious threat this modern Jezebel's teaching posed for the church. As the ancient Jezebel had led Israel into idolatry in her promotion of the worship of Baal, so her namesake was erasing a necessary line of separation between Christianity and paganism.

[23] The seriousness of the situation is further emphasized by the threat against the offspring of this woman. This would guarantee cutting off the line of its most likely continuation. **He who searches mind and heart** is an Old Testament description of God (Jer. 11:20; 17:10). God's requital of man according to his deeds was declared in the Old Testament (e.g., Ps. 62:12, Prov. 24:12) and finds frequent affirmation in the New Testament (Matt. 16:27; 2 Cor. 5:10; 11:15).

REV. 2:24–3:1 *Morning Star*

²⁴But to the rest of you in Thyatira, who do not hold this teaching, who have not learned what some call the deep things of Satan, to you I say, I do not lay upon you any other burden; ²⁵ only hold fast what you have, until I come. ²⁶He who conquers and who keeps my works until the end, I will give him power over the nations, ²⁷ and he shall rule them with a rod of iron, as when earthen pots are broken in pieces, even as I myself have received power from my Father; ²⁸ and I will give him the morning star. ²⁹He who has an ear, let him hear what the Spirit says to the churches.'

¹ "And to the angel of the church in Sardis write: 'The words of him who has the seven spirits of God and the seven stars.

"'I know your works; you have the name of being alive, and you are dead.

---

[24] The **deep things of Satan** may be an ironic reversal of a claim by the followers of Jezebel to know divine mysteries, or alternatively it may be a repetition of the claim by the prophetess' followers that one must experience all aspects of pagan society, either to know what was evil in it or to bring Christian teaching to bear on it. In the crisis before the church no other **burden** or requirement was necessary than the separation from the pagan world (see on vs. 20).

[25-29] It was necessary to hold fast to the Christian profession until Christ came in visitation through the trials soon to confront the churches. The one who conquers is promised rule and power in the same terms as that exercised by his Lord (Ps. 2:8f. and cf. the use made of the Psalm in Rev. 12:5; 19:15). The **morning star** is Christ himself in 22:16.

Letter to Sardis, 3:1-6. [1] This letter has similarities to that to Ephesus, already evident in the description of the sender (cf. 1:16 and 2:2). Having the **seven spirits** (see 1:4 and 4:5), Christ is shown as controlling the divine action in the churches. And the church needs the life-giving Spirit of God. Christ knows their works (2:2); and, although they seem to be **alive,** they **are dead.**

White Garments — REV. 3:2-6

² Awake, and strengthen what remains and is on the point of death, for I have not found your works perfect in the sight of my God. ³ Remember then what you received and heard; keep that, and repent. If you will not awake, I will come like a thief, and you will not know at what hour I will come upon you. ⁴ Yet you have still a few names in Sardis, people who have not soiled their garments; and they shall walk with me in white, for they are worthy. ⁵ He who conquers shall be clad thus in white garments, and I will not blot his name out of the book of life; I will confess his name before my Father and before his angels. ⁶ He who has an ear, let him hear what the Spirit says to the churches.'

[2, 3] The exhortations of verses 2 and 3 reflect the history of Sardis, a city normally impregnable that had twice fallen to invaders because of lack of watchfulness. The church was going the same way the city had gone; hence, the need to be alert (**awake**) and to persevere. Christ knows their works (2:2); they seem to be alive but **are dead.** The phrase **like a thief** was current among the early Christians (1 Thess. 5:2; Matt. 24:43; 2 Peter 3:10; Rev. 16:15); it is used here of Christ's coming in judgment on the church at Sardis. The repeated **awake** and reference to a **thief** show that the problem at Sardis was a loss of eschatological fervor.

[4-6] Only a **few who have not soiled their garments** indicates that many had come to live lives indistinguishable from their pagan neighbors. The unbecoming soiled **garments** contrast with the promised white. All the faithful will wear **white** (a symbol of purity and victory), especially the conqueror. When he shall confess Christ before the authorities, he shall have his name acknowledged by Christ **before the Father** (Matt. 10:32). Greek and Roman cities kept an official register of citizens. Christ has already had to **blot out** the names of most of the Sardis Christians from the heavenly city register. But some names at Sardis remained in God's register as worthy, until the time of the companionship and the walk with Christ. The idea of one's name being written in **the book of life** is a common biblical image (Ex. 32:32; Isa. 4:3; Ps. 69:28; Phil. 4:3; Heb. 12:23) frequently employed in Revelation (13:8; 17:8; 20:12, 15; 21:27).

REV. 3:7-9 *Open Door*

⁷ "And to the angel of the church in Philadelphia write: 'The words of the holy one, the true one, who has the key of David, who opens and no one shall shut, who shuts and no one opens.

⁸ "'I know your works. Behold, I have set before you an open door, which no one is able to shut; I know that you have but little power, and yet you have kept my word and have not denied my name. ⁹ Behold, I will make those of the synagogue of Satan who say that they are Jews and are not, but lie—behold, I will make them come and bow down before your feet, and learn that I have loved you.

The Letter to Philadelphia, 3:7-13. [7, 8] Like Smyrna, the church at Philadelphia had trouble with her neighbors in the Jewish synagogue; yet this constituted her great opportunity. Most of the letter concerns this relation of Jews and Christians. This probably accounts for the fact that the descriptions of Christ center on him as the Messiah. He is **the holy one** and **the true one.** In this context these terms referring to Jesus describe his holiness and truthfulness in relation to the Father and the Spirit (Mark 1:24; Luke 1:35; 4:34; John 6:69; 1 John 2:20; Acts 3:14; 4:27, 30). In Revelation they are also applied to God. Besides thus ascribing deity to Jesus, their connection with his messiahship is shown in: he has **the key of David,** he **opens and no one shall shut,** he **shuts and no one opens,** figures borrowed from Isaiah 22:22, where David entrusted the **key** to the house of David to Eliakim his steward. That symbol of royal power and access is now entrusted to the Christ. The shutting is used in reference to an **open door,** which the Lord says **I have set before you.** The **open door** is a symbol of a promising new missionary work, like the one Paul faced at Troas (2 Cor. 2:12) or at Ephesus (1 Cor. 16:9). That opportunity evidently has to do with the Jews, and success may be anticipated, because the **door** is one **which no one is able to shut.**

[9] The opportunity is now explained; Jesus will make **those of the synagogue of Satan . . . come and bow down before your feet.** In the increasing antagonism between church and

Dwellers on the Earth REV. 3:9, 10

¹⁰Because you have kept my word of patient endurance, I will keep you from the hour of trial which is coming on the whole world, to try those who dwell upon the earth.

---

synagogue following the destruction of Jerusalem in A.D. 70 (mentioned earlier in connection with Smyrna), bitterness was engendered. In aligning themselves with the enemies of the church the Jews ceased to be a true Israelite group and became **a synagogue of Satan** (2:9). That **they are to come and bow** before the church may well mean that this particular group will be converted, though some commentators insist that only a grudging admission on their part of the church's rightful position as God's people is intended. The open door seems to prove that conversion is meant. Many Old Testament references (Isa. 45:14; 49:23; 60:3, 14; Ps. 86:9) predicted that the Gentiles would acknowledge the God of Israel, coming and bowing down before his people. John is here drawing upon these promises, but he turns them around to predict these Jews as acknowledging that Christ has **loved** the church by giving himself for it.

[10] The church at Philadelphia is commended for having kept the Lord's **word of patient endurance,** and though they have only a **little power,** Christ promises to keep them from **the hour of trial** that is **coming on the whole world to try those who dwell upon the earth.** Who are the dwellers upon the earth? The term **the whole world,** which may mean the whole inhabited earth (Ps. 24:1; Luke 4:5), is more generally a technical term for the Roman Empire. John's own usage of the term **those who dwell upon the earth** shows that he means the enemies of the Christian community. This term occurs seven times elsewhere in Revelation. In 6:10 it designates the persecutors against whom the souls under the altar cry; in 8:13 they are the recipients of the triple woe; in 11:10 they rejoice over the death of the two witnesses; in 13:8, 14 they worship the beast from the sea (idolatry is hardly to be expected of the Jews); in 17:8 they marvel at the beast. Clearly they are the Roman followers of the beast opposed to the Christians.

¹¹I am coming soon; hold fast what you have, so that no one may seize your crown. ¹²He who conquers, I will make him a pillar in the temple of my God; never shall he go out of it, and I will write on him the name of my God, and the name of the city of my God, the New Jerusalem which comes down from my God out of heaven, and my own new name. ¹³He who has an ear, let him hear what the Spirit says to the churches.'

¹⁴ "And to the angel of the church in Laodicea write: 'The words of the Amen, the faithful and true witness, the beginning of God's creation.

¹⁵ "'I know your works: you are neither cold nor hot. Would that you were cold or hot! ¹⁶So, because you are lukewarm, and neither cold nor hot, I will spew you out of my mouth.

[11-13] Elsewhere in Revelation **the temple** is heaven (7:15; 11:19; 14:15, 17; 15:5, 6, 8; 16:1, 17) but here the **temple** seems to be the church as the spiritualized equivalent of the Old Testament temple (1 Cor. 3:16; Eph. 2:20; 1 Peter 2:5). The **name of God** was put on every Israelite in the priestly blessing (Num. 6:27). The conqueror bears not only the name of God and Christ but also **the name of the city of God. City** is one of John's important words. He often contrasts the earthly city with the heavenly one. Here the reference is to the **New Jerusalem, which comes down from heaven** (cf. 21:2, 10). The Gospel of John uses the idea of coming down from heaven in reference to the incarnation of Jesus (John 3:13; 6:33, 38—as the bread of heaven Jesus comes down and gives life). Here the emphasis is on the origin of the city in God.

Letter to Laodicea, 3:14-22. [14] The author is everything the lukewarm Laodiceans were not: loyal to the promises of God (cf. 2 Cor. 1:20), **faithful, and true** (cf. 19:11). These qualities led Antipas to martyrdom (2:13), but such was not to be expected among the self-satisfied Laodiceans. Yet all of the material prosperity at Laodicea came through Christ, **the beginning** (or source, cf. Col. 1:15) **of God's creation.**

[15, 16] The Laodicean church, in contrast to its Lord and to his desires for it, was neither one thing nor another; it

I Stand and Knock REV. 3:17-22

[17] For you say, I am rich, I have prospered, and I need nothing; not knowing that you are wretched, pitiable, poor, blind, and naked. [18] Therefore I counsel you to buy from me gold refined by fire, that you may be rich, and white garments to clothe you and to keep the shame of your nakedness from being seen, and salve to anoint your eyes, that you may see. [19] Those whom I love, I reprove and chasten; so be zealous and repent. [20] Behold, I stand at the door and knock; if any one hears my voice and opens the door, I will come in to him and eat with him, and he with me. [21] He who conquers, I will grant him to sit with me on my throne, as I myself conquered and sat down with my Father on his throne. [22] He who has an ear, let him hear what the Spirit says to the churches.'"

---

was **neither cold nor hot.** Its tepid spirit of accommodation would be violently ejected by Christ.

[17, 18] The author's knowledge of local conditions is never more in evidence than in the description of the church at Laodicea. The references to wealth (**rich**), **garments,** and **salve** apply to the church what is known of the circumstances of the city. What the church did not know was its spiritual condition, exactly the opposite of its material resources: **poor, blind,** and **naked.** But if the author's counsel were accepted and he were recognized as the source of aid (a great storehouse, abounding in garments and ointments, with the best gold to buy more), such a wretched, pitiable condition could be alleviated.

[19, 20] One of the most powerful and moving pictures of Christ is sketched in these verses. The loving father will **reprove and chasten** (Prov. 3:12; Heb. 12:6). He who knows the works of the church (vs. 15) issues the call to **repent** (2:5). His insistent **knock** (cf. Luke 12:36), if refused, issues in judgment (James 5:9). But if the **door** is **opened,** there is a sharing in the messianic banquet (Luke 22:30; 24:30; Rev. 19:9).

[21, 22] Christ offers to the one **who conquers** a share in his own rule. The victor only follows in the steps of Jesus. The identification of Christ and his people is such that they are several times spoken of as sharing rule from his **throne**

REV. 3:21–4:1 *The Second Vision*

¹**After this I looked, and lo, in heaven an open door! And the first voice, which I had heard speaking to me like a trumpet, said, "Come up hither, and I will show you what must take place after this."**

(2 Tim. 2:12; Rev. 20:4, 6). Sharing his suffering is the path to a share in his glory (Rom. 8:17; 1 Peter 4:13). As an esteemed Bible teacher used to say, "Cross-bearing precedes crown-wearing." And nowhere in all of scripture does Christ express more graphically then here that he has been full circle and made victory possible for his followers.

THE APOCALYPTIC VISION, 4:1—16:21

The Divine Throne Room, 4:1—5:14

The first vision (1:9–3:22), including the seven letters, has prepared the churches for the tribulations that they are about to undergo (3:10) and serves as a cover letter for the heavenly visions which are now to begin (4:1ff.) and to continue through 22:5. Chapters 4 and 5 introduce these visions. The vision of God as Creator on his throne and Christ as the Lion/Lamb worthy to open the book to reveal the secret of God's plan in the persecution furnishes the foundation of assurance that in all the experiences of the churches God is in control. He has, in fact, through his Son already won the decisive victory upon the cross which proves the key to understanding what is about to happen. This is the backdrop against which the coming events are to take place. The same truths concerning God as the eternal, all-powerful being and the Son as the faithful witness, etc., have been set forth by the epithets in the address (1:4-8).

The Creator of All Things, 4:1-11.[1] The new aspect of the visions is introduced by **After this,** referring to the previous vision, which had introduced the risen Christ (1:12ff.; cf. 7:1, 9; 15:5; 18:1). There are two other indications, structurally, that John is coming to the second and principal part of his visions. First, he says that **the first voice which I had**

Heaven Opened REV. 4:2

² **At once I was in the Spirit, and lo, a throne stood in heaven, with one seated on the throne!**

---

heard speaking to me like a trumpet (referring to the first vision in 1:10) spoke again.

[2] Also, as in 1:10, John says that **At once** he was **in the Spirit,** a statement that introduces each of the four main groupings of visions (1:10; 4:2; 17:3; 21:10).

The first vision was given to John as Christ appeared personally to him on Patmos. Now, however, John sees **in heaven an open door!** That door stood **open** for John to enter and see. He was to be shown **what must next take place** (cf. 1:1 and 22:6). The idea of an opening into heaven through which a prophet or seer is transported to heaven for a revelation is familiar from the Old Testament (Ezek. 1:1; 1 Kings 22:19). Paul also had a vision in which he was caught up "to the third heaven" (he did not know whether he was in the body or out of it) and heard things he could not utter (2 Cor. 12:1f.). Jewish apocalyptic writers adopted this as a device to indicate the beginning of their visions (Enoch 14:13; Test. of Levi 5). From an Old Testament point of view, the fact that the prophet is privy to the councils of the Father in heaven is the surest mark of a prophet. Jeremiah assured his readers that the true prophet has "stood in the council of the Lord to perceive and to hear his word" (Jer. 23:18; cf. Amos 3:7). This is one of John's claims that his is a book of prophecy (1:3; 10:11; 22:7, 10, 14).

The one seated is identified in verse 8 as "the Lord God Almighty." Frequently in the Old Testament heaven is God's **throne** (Isa. 66:1) or (as here) he is enthroned in heaven (Ps. 11:4). John makes various uses of the **heaven** into which he is now invited to look. It is not always merely heaven; at times it is a temple with an altar and sacrifice (a frequent Old Testament figure also); then like a synagogue where a scroll is read (5:1), or a court where the prosecuting attorney loses his case and is banished from the court (12:10); and above all (since one of John's principal figures of the course of cosmic events is a battlefield), it is the headquarters for God's forces in the great struggle with Satan and his forces.

REV. 4:3, 4 — Twenty-four Elders

³ **And he who sat there appeared like jasper and carnelian, and round the throne was a rainbow that looked like an emerald.** ⁴**Round the throne were twenty-four thrones, and seated on the thrones were twenty-four elders, clad in white garments, with golden crowns upon their heads.**

---

[3] Unlike the vision of Ezekiel (1:26), in John's vision there is no description of the form of God. All details by which God is described in human terms are avoided (contrast 1:13-16). What is emphasized is his striking majesty and brilliance, described under the likeness of precious stones **jasper and carnelian. Around the throne** there **was a rainbow** that had the appearance of **emerald** or green color. Most commentators see in this a symbol of the mercy of God coupled with his faithfulness to the covenant made with Noah.

[4] **Around the throne** of God sat **twenty-four elders** on as many thrones. These may best be interpreted as angels, especially as they may be the heavenly counterpart of the council of spiritual Israel. In the vision of the future splendor of the saints in heaven in Isaiah 24:23 it is said that God will be glorified "before his elders" or "ancient ones." Here undoubtedly reference is to the heavenly council of God, which the Bible speaks of often and in various ways.

The most common idea among commentators is that the **elders** represent the twenty-four courses of priesthood of the Old Testament (1 Chron. 24:1-6). This may be so, but the **elders** of Revelation do not function as priests. Another idea put forward is that they represent the twelve patriarchs of Israel and the twelve apostles of the Lord, whose names are inscribed upon the gates and walls of the New Jerusalem (21:12ff.). One really needs no theory of their presence. They are heavenly creatures and are revealed as a part of the heavenly scene. Probably one should be content with this. They are not chief actors in the drama which is to be unfolded in the visions, though they do occasionally take a lead in the action (5:5ff.; 7:11, 13; 11:16; 14:3; 19:4). Mostly they are the leaders of the heavenly chorus ascribing worship to God in his majesty.

Sea of Glass REV. 4:5-7

⁵**From the throne issue flashes of lightning, and voices and peals of thunder, and before the throne burn seven torches of fire, which are the seven spirits of God;** ⁶**and before the throne there is as it were a sea of glass, like crystal.**

And round the throne, on each side of the throne, are four living creatures, full of eyes in front and behind:

---

[5] The sights and sounds which accompany the vision enhance the impression of God's majesty. These are the **flashes of lightning** and **the voices** or sounds **and peals of thunder**, which probably are intended to be reminiscent of God's revelation at Sinai (Ex. 19:16). Then John saw **seven torches** (the word is different from the lamps in chapter 1) burning **before the throne**. John himself needs no explanation of their symbolism. He recognized them as **the seven spirits** before God (1:4; 3:1). They probably represent the Holy Spirit.

[6a] In his description of the heavenly scene John further says that before the throne of God there was **as it were a sea of glass, like crystal.** Something likened to a sea is described as **like crystal.** This is probably an allusion to the Old Testament imagery of the sea. This heavenly crystal sea occurs in Ezekiel's vision of Jehovah's throne (Ezek. 1:22, 26; cf. Ex. 24:10). See further on 15:2, 3, where those who have been victorious over the beast are seen standing "beside the sea of glass." This sea is, therefore, (typically) the heavenly counterpart of the Red Sea, identified in the Old Testament with the forces of evil over which God's people had achieved a great victory in their defeat of Pharaoh (cf. Ezek. 29:3). The victory over Egypt at the Sea (Ps. 74:13f.) was but a repetition of the original victory over the forces of evil at creation, when God brought order out of chaos (represented by the sea and sea monsters—Job 9:13; 38:8-11; Pss. 89:10; 104:5-9; Prov. 8:27-39). This imagery was used for anticipated acts of God's salvation (Isa. 11:11, 15, 16; 27:1; 51:9-11; Ezek. 29:3-5) and is extensively employed in Revelation (e.g., 13:1; 21:1).

[6b, 7] As John continues his description, he says that he saw **around** and **on each side of the throne four living creatures full of eyes in front and behind.** Furthermore, the creatures

⁷the first living creature like a lion, the second living creature like an ox, the third living creature with the face of a man, and the fourth living creature like a flying eagle. ⁸And the four living creatures, each of them with six wings, are full of eyes all round and within, and day and night they never cease to sing,
 "Holy, holy, holy, is the Lord God Almighty,
 who was and is and is to come!"
⁹And whenever the living creatures give glory and honor and thanks to him who is seated on the throne, who lives for ever and ever, ¹⁰the twenty-four elders fall down before him who is seated on the throne and worship him who lives for ever and ever; they cast their crowns before the throne, singing,

---

were **likened** to **a lion, an ox,** and **a flying eagle,** and one had **the face of a man.** These **creatures** are enigmatic, as John never explains their presence or identity. However, in two Old Testament visions similar to John's they are explained: In Ezekiel 1:5ff., "four living creatures" are seen just as here, and the descriptions also include the features of a lion, an ox, a man, and an eagle. Isaiah's creatures (Isa. 6) are not numbered but bear striking resemblances to John's.

[8] In both Old Testament visions the creatures had six wings, and they sang **"Holy, holy, holy, is the Lord God Almighty."** What is helpful is that in the two Old Testament passages the creatures are identified. In Isaiah 6:2 they are "seraphim" and in Ezekiel they are several times called cherubim (10:1ff., esp. vs. 15). In Revelation we are probably to understand John's four creatures as heavenly seraphim or cherubim.

[9, 10] Whatever symbolic meaning, if any, the **living creatures** have in this vision, it is clear that their function, along with the elders, is to lead the hosts of heaven in the worship of God, **who is seated on the throne and who lives for ever.** John sees that when they **give glory and honor** to God, **the twenty-four elders** follow them in doing the same; they fall down before him and cast their crowns in adoration to God for his eternal nature: He lives **for ever and ever. Throne** is a central theological description of God in the Revelation, the word occurring over forty times.

God the Creator REV 4:11–5:1

¹¹"Worthy art thou, our Lord and God,
to receive glory and honor and power,
for thou didst create all things,
and by thy will they existed and were created."
¹And I saw in the right hand of him who was seated on the throne a scroll written within and on the back, sealed with seven seals;

---

[11] The worshiping creatures of heaven recognize that it is fitting and right for God's creatures to ascribe unto him **glory and honor and power.** In view of the larger context of the drama of Revelation, we need not doubt that the praises given here to God are chosen in this instance in the light of the central problems. Here the Revelation is laying the foundation for the central doctrine of the book, which is also central to the entire Christian faith; that is, the eternal God, enthroned in heaven, is the central power of the universe. This is true because as Almighty God he is the creator of the universe. The hint to be understood here, and to be worked out later, is that if there is evil in the world, it must some way be fitted theologically into the understanding of the sovereignty of the God who made all things and who has not abdicated his throne.

The Scroll and the Redeemer, 5:1-14. [1] The heavenly scene, which began with the invitation of John to "come up here," continues as John sees **a scroll in the right hand of the one seated on the throne.** The word for scroll here means a papyrus roll made of pasting sheets of papyrus side-to-side and then rolling the whole from one end. Such books ordinarily were written only on one side, except in case of overflow. Hence fullness of message is indicated by its being **written within and on the back.** The scroll was **sealed.** Seals were made up by melting wax on the edge of the rolled-up scroll. Before the wax hardened, usually a ring or seal bearing the mark of the sender was pressed into it. Often messages were sealed more than once, but **seven** seals would mean that it was to be overly secure.

The description of this scroll resembles that given by Ezekiel in 2:9f., which contained "words of lamentation and mourning and woe." The scroll signifies the message which

REV. 5:1-3 *Worthy to Open the Scroll*

²and I saw a strong angel proclaiming with a loud voice, "Who is worthy to open the scroll and break its seals?" ³And no one in heaven or on earth or under the earth was able to open the scroll or to look into it,

---

had been promised to John. Twice he had been told that "what must shortly come to pass" would be revealed to him (1:1; 4:1).

[2] John wept when he thought no one was **worthy to open** the book, evidently in disappointment because the promised revelation was so close and yet was not to be revealed. There has been much difference of opinion as to what it means **to open the scroll.** We have already indicated our belief that John's message pertained to the immediate problem of the persecution of the church under Domitian, which posed the problem of how such suffering was possible in a world ruled by Almighty God. Seen from this viewpoint, and anticipating the fact that the scroll could be opened by Jesus because he had been crucified and raised (5:9), the purpose of the scroll is seemingly to show how the current problems of the church fit in with the redemptive purpose of God and what the outcome of that persecution will be. The book shows God's judgment on the world, but also his redemptive purposes.

After seeing the book, John hears **a strong angel:** The term occurs again (as "mighty angel") in the visions of 10:1 and 18:21. The angel's question has to do with the moral right (**worthy,** not "able") of **the angel** to open the book. Jesus is later said to be **worthy** to do this by virtue of his death and resurrection (vss. 5, 9). Hence the revelation contained in the scroll concerns events or truths dependent upon the death of the Lord.

[3] John does not indicate how the search to find someone worthy **to open the scroll** was carried out or how long it took. Perhaps it is merely implied that after the announcement went forth for someone to open it, no one from any of the regions **in heaven** or **on earth** or **under the earth** could come forward claiming to be worthy to open it. The reason is clear from what we have seen above. To open the scroll is to take the commission to bring its contents to pass.

Lion of Judah REV. 5:4-6

⁴and I wept much that no one was found worthy to open the scroll or to look into it. ⁵Then one of the elders said to me, "Weep not; lo, the Lion of the tribe of Judah, the Root of David, has conquered, so that he can open the scroll and its seven seals."

⁶And between the throne and the four living creatures and among the elders, I saw a Lamb standing, as though it had been slain, with seven horns and with seven eyes, which are the seven spirits of God sent out into all the earth;

---

[4] When John realized that no one was able to open the scroll, he **wept.** His disappointment that the divine mysteries would remain undisclosed expresses the yearning to catch a glimpse of God's plan.

[5] The one who is able to **open the scroll and its seven seals** is identified as the **Lion of the tribe of Judah** and **the Root of David.** These descriptions from the Old Testament identify the Jewish Messiah. Beginning with the promise in Genesis 49:9f. that the sceptre would not depart from Judah and that the obedience of the nations would be his, the Old Testament looked for a ruler after the prototype of David (Isa. 11:1-10; Ps. 89:20; and from the New Testament cf. Rom. 15:12; Heb. 7:14). The fierce kingly attributes of the anointed one to be raised up were emphasized (Ps. 2; 110). This expectation was current in Judaism before Jesus was born. The Psalms of Solomon (ch. 17) reveal a Jewish expectation that God would soon raise up a Messiah, a military commander who would expel the Romans and establish the rule of God on earth. The elders' words are intended to assure that such expectations have been fulfilled. But the Jewish expectation was not the fulfillment that the church had been led to accept. The kingly concept had to be transformed.

[6] When John turned to look, he saw among the elders and living creatures, not a **Lion,** but a **Lamb standing, as though it had been slain.** There was another expectation among the prophets, set forth particularly by Isaiah (40-66) of a servant of God, who seems at first to be Israel itself (Isa. 41:8ff.), then the faithful remnant of Israel (probably to be explained by the Hebrew concept of corporate representation), and finally of an individual servant who would suffer

REV. 5:6-8 — The Lamb

⁷and he went and took the scroll from the right hand of him who was seated on the throne. ⁸And when he had taken the scroll, the four living creatures and the twenty-four elders fell down before the Lamb, each holding a harp, and with golden bowls full of incense, which are the prayers of the saints;

---

vicariously for God's people; he would be led as a lamb to the slaughter (Isa. 53:7). According to some interpretations God had himself combined the ideas of Davidic kingship and the Suffering Servant at the baptism of Jesus: the reference "Thou art my Son" being drawn from Psalm 2, which emphasizes kingship, and "my beloved in whom my soul delights" being the opening of the poem about the servant of the Lord (Isa. 42:1f.). The Christian faith therefore saw Jesus as fulfilling the Davidic expectations of kingship, not through military might, but only through the path of suffering and crucifixion. The messianic Son of David is redefined in terms of the Suffering Servant. For New Testament references see such passages as John 1:29; Acts 8:32ff.; 1Peter 2:21ff. The unwillingness of the Jews to accept this reinterpretation led to the cross as a stumbling block (1 Cor. 1:23) and to the preaching of the necessity of the Christ to suffer (Luke 24:46; Acts 17:3). Such is the background of John's vision.

In addition to the Lion/Lamb description, the vision emphasized that Christ was seen **with seven horns** (symbol of strength, Deut. 33:17; 1 Kings 22:11) **and with seven eyes,** in turn interpreted as the seven spirits of God sent out into all the world and symbol of national or kingly might (Zech. 1:18-20; Dan. 7:7ff.) In the Revelation generally, horns symbolize the might of the persecuting power (12:3; 13:1; 17:3ff.). Though he is a Lamb sacrificed, Jesus is seen in his heavenly position exercising power over all flesh (Matt. 28:18; John 17:1; Eph. 1:21). The Lamb's all-seeing vision is emphasized by his having **seven eyes**. The Old Testament counterpart of this is Zechariah's vision of the seven lamps which are said to be the seven eyes of the Lord, "which range through the whole earth" (Zech. 4:2, 10). These are now further explained as **the seven spirits sent out into all the earth** (note 1:4; 3:1; 4:5, indicating the Spirit's worldwide mission).

[7, 8] The action which is to carry forward the drama

A New Song REV. 5:7-9

⁹ **and they sang a new song, saying,**
  "Worthy art thou to take the scroll and to open
  its seals,
  for thou wast slain and by thy blood didst
  ransom men for God
  from every tribe and tongue and people and
  nation,

---

begins when the Lamb **took the scroll from the right hand** of God, at which point the living creatures and the elders fell down before the Lamb. In their hands these heavenly inhabitants held a harp (symbol of praise) and **golden bowls full of incense**. The incense is a symbol of **the prayers of the saints** (cf. Ps. 141:2; Rev. 8:3). The prayers of the saints on earth are mighty before God (James 5:16). These heavenly inhabitants thus represent the saints on earth who have prayed for the coming of the events now to be worked out and who add their praise and prayer for the accomplishment of God's purpose.

[9] After offering the praise and prayers of the saints to God, the living creatures and the elders begin their own song of praise. It is called **a new song**, a term frequently used in the Old Testament (Pss. 33:3; 40:3; 96:1; 98:1-9; 149:1; Isa. 42:10) for any new or recently composed hymn, but especially for a composition in honor of a special occasion. In most of the passages the occasion is the celebration of God's coming in judgment and worldwide victory.

The **new song,** repeating the former declaration of the worthiness of the Lamb to open the scroll, now states the reason for that worthiness. As he had formerly been seen as a Lamb slaughtered, so now his position as one who can open the seals and bring about the anticipated events is directly connected with his sacrifice on the cross: **for thou wast slain and by thy blood didst ransom men.** Christians firmly believed that the sacrificial death of Jesus, in which he vicariously gave his lifeblood for the sins of men, served as the ransom price for men from the slavery of sin (1 Peter 1:18ff.; Acts 20:28; 1 Cor. 6:20). The former slaves to sin were thus purchased (see the metaphor used in 1 Cor. 6:20; 7:23; Gal. 4:5; Rev. 14:3; 2 Peter 2:1).

> [10] **and hast made them a kingdom and priests to our God, and they shall reign on earth."**

This ransoming was for God, in that they are now destined for his service.

[10] Here, as in 1:5, 6, Christians are accorded the role of a "royal priesthood" which was promised to Israel at the giving of the Law (Ex. 19:6; cf. 1 Peter 2:9). Isaiah had foreseen that the Lord's anointed would cheer the hearts of the mourners and make them to be called "priests of the Lord . . . ministers of our God" (Isa. 61:3, 6).

There is a textual variation at this point of the song. Some manuscripts read the future (adopted by the RSV, on somewhat better textual evidence) **and they shall reign on the earth.** The context, however, seems to demand the present tense. Already John has emphasized (1:5f.; and the present passage) that the ransomed are now kings and priests. If John did write the future, then he must refer to the future immediately subsequent to the appointment of each as king and priest. The reference is not to a futurist reign with Christ on earth (the promise of 20:6 is the special privilege of the martyrs and is not said to be on earth) nor to the heavenly eternal reign of the New Jerusalem (22:5). John is speaking of the prerogative of service as kings and priests for all those purchased by the blood of Christ.

The universality of the privilege of priestly service has already been potentially realized in the cross of Christ. **Every tribe and tongue and people and nation** have been purchased to God for priestly service. The message of the book is that this goal will be achieved through the cross of Christ, combined with the service of his earthly representatives (martyrs) purchased for God's service. This provides the key to the theology of suffering in the book. As Christ exercises God's rule in virtue of his conquering through the cross, so he consecrates the redeemed as a "royal house of priests" who in the same way—through their sacrifice—**shall reign on the earth** with him. The scroll will reveal how this is to be.

Honor and Glory REV. 5:11-14

[11] Then I looked, and I heard around the throne and the living creatures and the elders the voice of many angels, numbering myriads of myriads and thousands of thousands, [12] saying with a loud voice, "Worthy is the Lamb who was slain, to receive power and wealth and wisdom and might and honor and glory and blessing!" [13] And I heard every creature in heaven and on earth and under the earth and in the sea, and all therein, saying, "To him who sits upon the throne and to the Lamb be blessing and honor and glory and might for ever and ever!" [14] And the four living creatures said, "Amen!" and the elders fell down and worshiped.

[11, 12] In addition to the chorus of the four **living creatures and** the **elders**, John **heard the voice of many angels, numbering** into the **myriads and thousands**, who joined the praise of the Lamb who was slain. Again, because of his death he is described as being worthy **to receive power, wealth, wisdom, might, honor, glory, and blessing.** Undoubtedly "to receive" does not mean to be given what he did not possess; rather, as in the praise of God in 4:9, 11, the idea is to be given recognition and praise for those characteristics which belong to him by reason of his being and work. The Bible emphasizes that angels, though not immediate actors in the drama of man's redemption, were concerned and interested spectators (Eph. 3:10; 1 Peter 1:12). They know and acknowledge with praise the wonder and efficacy of his death.

[13, 14] To the heavenly chorus are added the voices of **every creature in heaven and on earth and under the earth and in the sea**, this time ascribing **blessing and honor and glory and might for ever** to both the Father as the one who sits upon the throne and to the Lamb. They find their worship seconded by the **"Amen"** of the living creatures and the prostration of **the elders**. Significantly, the same praise is given to both the Father and the Lamb.

The Judgments of God, 6:1—11:19

The principal apocalyptic section of Revelation is made up of the visions of 6:1-16:21, with chapters 4 and 5 serving as an introduction to the visions. Though still in the style of

¹Now I saw when the Lamb opened one of the seven seals, and I heard one of the four living creatures say, as with a voice of thunder, "Come!" ²And I saw, and behold, a white horse, and its rider had a bow; and a crown was given to him, and he went out conquering and to conquer.

---

an apocalypse, the destruction of the city (17:1–21:8) is set off as a separate vision by the phrase "in the Spirit" (17:3).

The material in 6:1–16:21 is divided into two parts: 6:1–11:19 and 12:1–16:21. The latter part is a doublet, or repetition of the former. The evidence for this is in the vision of the "little scroll" of chapter 10. There it is said that in the days of the sounding of the seventh angel, "Then will be finished the mystery of God" (10:7). In the same vision John is told that the "little scroll," which he had been commanded to eat, meant that he "must prophesy *again* about many peoples and nations and tongues and kings" (10:11). The first part is a general treatment of God's judgments on the world of wickedness (6:1–11:19); whereas the second part is a more detailed picture, particularly of the church's struggle with the beast (12:1–16:21).

The First Four Seals: The Four Horsemen, 6:1-8. The opening of the seven seals of the book which John had seen in the right hand of God marks the beginning of the promised revelation of "what must soon take place." A sealed scroll could not be unrolled until all seals were broken; hence the question of the relation of the first six seals and the seventh (which brings the seven trumpets of judgment) is raised. The scenes revealed with the breaking of the seals may be merely preliminary to the contents of the scroll, which are made known only after the seventh seal is broken. Nevertheless, the revelation is never said to depend upon reading the scroll. It is plausible, therefore, that what accompanies the opening of the seals is intended to represent a proportionate part of the scroll's content.

[1, 2] The first four seals are a unit. Each seal is introduced by a call of one of **the four living creatures**, and each reveals a **horse** and its **rider**. The four horsemen here obviously parallel visions given to Zechariah (1:8-11 and 6:1-9), who twice saw four colored horses, one group with riders,

Four horsemen REV. 6:1-6

³ When he opened the second seal, I heard the second living creature say, "Come!" ⁴ And out came another horse, bright red; its rider was permitted to take peace from the earth, so that men should slay one another; and he was given a great sword.

⁵ When he opened the third seal, I heard the third living creature say, "Come!" And I saw, and behold, a black horse, and its rider had a balance in his hand; ⁶ and I heard what seemed to be a voice in the midst of the four living creatures saying, "A quart of wheat for a denarius,ª and three quarts of barley for a denarius; but do not harm oil and wine!"

ª The denarius was worth a day's wage for a laborer.

---

another pulling chariots which were sent out to patrol the earth. Zechariah's horses, related to the four winds (cf. Rev. 7:1ff.) seem to be symbolic, as in other places (Jer. 49:36; Dan. 7:7; 8:8), of agents of judgment.

The rider of the **white horse** here resembles that of 19:11ff., which is definitely to be identified with Christ; and many commentators have so interpreted this rider. The resemblance, however, is certainly coincidental, and in the Greek the two riders wear different kinds of crowns. The evident unity of the four horses and four winds indicates that they together symbolize the forces of punishment—conquering military power, civil strife, famine or scarcity, and death.

The bow of the rider on the **white horse** symbolizes his warlike role, and his **going forth conquering and to conquer**, together with the color **white**, depicts his victory. No woe accompanies the first horse; none is needed, as conquest itself is destructive and carries its own woe. No definite historical conquest (Parthians from the East, etc.) need be supposed. The use of **was given** (also 6:4; cf. 13:5, 7, 14, 15) indicates that divine permission was granted to evil powers to carry out their work. The emphasis is that God is in control; the evil forces cannot act on their own.

[3, 4] The **red horse** follows the second command to **come**. His color symbolizes slaughter. He is given power **to take peace from the earth so that men should slay one another.** Thus his weapon is **a great sword**.

[5, 6] At the third living creature's **"Come,"** a **black horse**

REV. 6:5-10 *Death*

⁷When he opened the fourth seal, I heard the voice of the fourth living creature say, "Come!" ⁸And I saw, and behold, a pale horse, and its rider's name was Death, and Hades followed him; and they were given power over a fourth of the earth, to kill with sword and with famine and with pestilence and by wild beasts of the earth.

⁹When he opened the fifth seal, I saw under the altar the souls of those who had been slain for the word of God and for the witness they had borne;

---

appears. His **rider** represents famine; he has a **balance in his hand** for measuring. The voice describing the scene indicates the extreme scarcity of the staple foods: **a quart of wheat** costs **a denarius** (see Matt. 20:2), and **three quarts of barley** (a less desirable product) costs the same. The price would ordinarily be much less. The injunction **Do not harm oil and wine** (not necessarily luxuries, but ordinary products of the area, Deut. 11:14; Hos. 2:8; Joel 2:19) is probably to indicate that the judgments symbolized are not total. Famines do not usually destroy all (cf. 7:8; 9:5, where limits are similarly fixed).

[7, 8] With the opening of the **fourth seal** a **pale horse** appears, whose **rider's name was Death, and Hades followed** with **him**. This **rider** and his accompanist (on their combination, cf. 1:18) symbolize destruction by various other means besides in battle (numbers one and two) and that indirectly on men by injury to vegetable life (number three). The four means of death—**sword** (that is, murder, etc.), **famine, pestilence** (literally "death" but used in Greek to render the Hebrew word for pestilence, cf. Jer. 14:12), and **wild beasts**—are frequently grouped together as the ordinary means of death in unstable society (Lev. 26:22ff.; Ezek. 14:21; Jer. 15:2f.). Again the forces of judgment symbolized are limited: they may exercise authority only **over a fourth of the earth**.

The Fifth Seal: Martyrs' Cry for Judgment, 6:9-11. [9, 10] After the revelation of the natural agents of God's judgment under the symbol of the four horsemen, the vision then depicts **the souls** of the martyrs **underneath the altar**. This is

Plea for Vengeance REV. 6:9-11

[10] they cried out with a loud voice, "O Sovereign Lord, holy and true, how long before thou wilt judge and avenge our blood on those who dwell upon the earth?" [11] Then they were each given a white robe and told to rest a little longer, until the number of their fellow servants and their brethren should be complete, who were to be killed as they themselves had been.

---

intended evidently to set the stage for the judgments (avenging the martyred saints) and also explaining the delay in that judgment, that is, to fill up the number of the martyrs. The **altar** must refer to the heavenly altar (8:3, 5; 14:18) in the analogy of heaven as the temple of God (11:19; 14:15; 15:5; cf. Ps. 18:6; Hab. 2:20; Micah 1:2). The reference is to the altar of burnt offering (not of incense), because the blood of the slain Christians is thought of as being poured out as an offering (see Phil. 2:17; 2 Tim. 4:6), like the offering of the animal sacrifice.

It is often said that this plea for vengeance falls below the prayer of Stephen "Lord, do not hold this sin against them" and is unworthy of the teaching of Jesus. But this ignores the circumstances. The **marytrs** have been condemned and sentenced as worthy of death in a Roman court. Unless that verdict is reversed by God's judgment on the unjust judges and courts, the whole Christian cause stands condemned. This natural human cry expresses the conviction that the just will be vindicated. The cry for just judgment is like that of the whole church (22:17) for the speedy coming of the kingdom (so often in the Old Testament, Ps. 79:5-10, as well as in the New, Luke 18:7; Heb. 12:24).

O Lord, holy and true is an appeal to the absolute holiness of God (which cannot tolerate the inequity perpetrated) and to the one who is true to that holiness. **Those who dwell on earth** refers to the world in its hostility to God (see 3:10).

[11] No definite answer is given. God's concern is broader than that of the questioners (cf. 2 Esdras 4:33ff.). Instead, the martyrs were each given a **white robe** (cf. 3:4f.), symbol of purity, garments of heavenly ones (7:9, 13; Dan. 7:9; Matt. 28:3). They are not taken

REV. 6:11-17 *Cosmic Upheavals*

¹²When he opened the sixth seal, I looked, and behold, there was a great earthquake; and the sun became black as sackcloth, the full moon became like blood, ¹³and the stars of the sky fell to the earth as the fig tree sheds its winter fruit when shaken by a gale; ¹⁴the sky vanished like a scroll that is rolled up, and every mountain and island was removed from its place. ¹⁵Then the kings of the earth and the great men and the generals and the rich and the strong, and every one, slave and free, hid in the caves and among the rocks of the mountains, ¹⁶calling to the mountains and rocks, "Fall on us and hide us from the face of him who is seated on the throne, and from the wrath of the Lamb; ¹⁷for the great day of their wrath has come, and who can stand before it?"

---

to heaven but are only shown to share heaven's glory. They should **rest** (cessation from toil, labor, or affliction), here, relief from their distressful yearning and crying for coming judgment. With assurance of the full glory later, they are to await consummation in patience and peace until the number of their fellow sufferers should be complete. The period of waiting is (like the devil's time of persecution in ch. 12) a little time. On the role of the martyrs, see comments on l2:11-13.

The Sixth Seal: Cosmic Upheavals, 6:12-17. [12-17] With the opening of the **sixth seal** a series of cosmic disturbances are accompanied by the terror of men as they see what is happening. The upheavals are to be interpreted as representative of the social and civil disturbances.

Commentaries usually see in these events the description of the breakup of the natural world at the second coming of Christ and the end of the world. These disturbances are not occurring under the seventh seal, which symbolizes the end (10:7), but under the sixth. It is true that the four horsemen representing the judgments of God have been revealed, but the judgments have not yet fallen upon men. The identity of these horsemen with the four winds seems assured, and they are allowed to hurt the earth only after the saints are sealed. (7:1; 8:6ff.); thus the sequence is wrong for this to be the end of time. The calamities are not the end; for, after they occur,

Judgment on Persecutors REV. 6:12–7:1

men still are alive and asking for the mountains to fall upon them.

The most decisive feature is the fact that the paragraph describing these events is a carefully composed mosaic of phrases and terms drawn from the language of the Old Testament. In their original use these passages do not concern the end of time but clearly represent the destruction and judgment of God on the nations and cities involved in Israel's history. The Jews had a kind of double eschatology which saw all such visitations as a day of the Lord, typical of the End, which would come at the close of history.

One source of these terms is Joel 2:28ff., where **the sun became black** and **the moon became like blood** before the great and notable day of the Lord comes (cf. Jer. 4:23, 28, in its woe to Jerusalem). Peter gave this passage a figurative meaning and considered it fulfilled on Pentecost (Acts 2). Other sources are Isaiah 2:12-22; 24:2-4, 21-23; 34:4; Hosea 10:1-8; Malachi 3:2; Zephaniah 1:14.

One can hardly escape the conclusion, therefore, that the **sixth seal** anticipates, in Old Testament symbols, the fear of wicked men when the time comes that God visits the power which was persecuting his people. Undoubtedly the church stood in awe at the power and might of Rome. But Israel's ancient enemies had been mighty also. God foretold their destruction and passing from the earth. So also at the beginning of the drama of Revelation, the mighty society and civil structures which oppose the people of God are set for destruction (cf. 18:19).

A Parenthesis: The Sealing of the Saints, 7:1-17. The opening of the seventh seal, expected immediately, is delayed by two episodes (vss. 1-8 and 9-17). Something of the same occurs in chapters 10 and 11 between the blowing of the sixth and seventh trumpets. The purpose of the intervening visions here is to show the preparedness of the church for the coming ordeal of judgment in contrast to the terror of men, which has already been seen under the sixth seal. God's servants are sealed for protection, which answers the question of 6:17, "Who can stand?"

REV. 7:1-3 *Four Winds*

¹ **After this I saw four angels standing at the four corners of the earth, holding back the four winds of the earth, that no wind might blow on earth or sea or against any tree.** ² **Then I saw another angel ascend from the rising of the sun with the seal of the living God, and he called with a loud voice to the four angels who had been given power to harm earth and sea,** ³ **saying, "Do not harm the earth or the sea or the trees, till we have sealed the servants of our God upon their foreheads."**

[1, 2] After the picture of terror associated with the cosmic upheavals of the sixth seal, John saw **four angels standing at the four corners of the earth**. The idea of the earth having four quarters or angles from which four winds blow is a convention frequently mentioned in the Old Testament (Isa. 11:12; Ezek. 7:2; four winds—Zech. 2:6; Dan. 7:2; 8:8; 11:4). This convention says nothing about the Hebrew worldview; they also knew the other points of the compass and could speak of twelve winds as well as four (Enoch 76:7).

Angels managing the **winds** is in keeping with other physical phenomena, as the angel of the fire (14:18) and of waters (16:5). That these winds are simply another symbol for the four horsemen of the first four seals seems to be one of the most definite identifications of the Apocalypse. In Zechariah's vision, on which the Apocalypse continuously draws, the four horsemen are explicitly said to be **the four winds** of the heaven (Zech. 6:5). Furthermore, the idea of the winds as God's avenging spirits or of the Lord coming in vengeance, riding upon the clouds or winds, is so commonplace in the Old Testament that it is difficult to mistake (Isa. 19:1; 66:15; Pss. 18:10; 104:3f; Jer. 4:11-13; 23:19). This is another reason for rejecting the idea of these visions as representing chronological historical events. It is significant that the four angels are seen **holding back the winds**. They **have power to harm the earth**, but they are thus far being restrained.

[3] The **earth, sea, and trees** are mentioned in prospect of injury from the powerful winds, probably because when the judgments are at last unloosed, the first will be against the natural elements rather than men (8:7-13). Prohibiting or restraining the injury represents the postponement of the judgments until the churches have been fully prepared for it.

144,000 REV. 7:3-8

⁴And I heard the number of the sealed, a hundred and forty-four thousand sealed, out of every tribe of the sons of Israel, ⁵twelve thousand sealed out of the tribe of Judah, twelve thousand of the tribe of Reuben, twelve thousand of the tribe of Gad, ⁶twelve thousand of the tribe of Asher, twelve thousand of the tribe of Naphtali, twelve thousand of the tribe of Manasseh, ⁷twelve thousand of the tribe of Simeon, twelve thousand of the tribe of Levi, twelve thousand of the tribe of Issachar, ⁸twelve thousand of the tribe of Zebulun, twelve thousand of the tribe of Joseph, twelve thousand sealed out of the tribe of Benjamin.

The **servants** have been **sealed**—have had a mark of identity—**upon the forehead** (see Ezek. 9:4, 6 for marking on the foreheads of the innocents to be saved). In the counterpart here, the martyred saints are protected, destined by God for another fate. The martyr does not fear the disasters which afflict the world of nature and social structures of men, because it is his part to fill up what is lacking in the suffering of Christ (Col. 1:24). He has a different destiny from that of God's enemies. Death by disasters visited on the natural world holds no terror for those marked for martyrdom (cf. 2 Tim. 4:18).

[4-8] The number of the sealed is **a hundred and forty-four thousand out of every tribe** of the sons **of Israel**. The servants of God who were to be sealed are therefore in some way representative of Israel. Some would take this literally and explain these as the martyrs of the Jewish church and take the later group (vss. 9-12) who come from all nations and tongues as the Gentile church. But the facts hardly justify this. The listing of the tribes does not follow any natural listing of the sons of Israel or the tribes of the physical Israel (Levi and Joseph are never in Old Testament listings). In New Testament times the twelve tribes of national Israel no longer existed except in some fanciful ideal of Jewish restoration gained from taking Old Testament predictions literally.

The hundred and forty-four thousand must represent the whole church of the New Testament as spiritualized Israel. There is much evidence for such a view. The book of James addresses itself to the "twelve tribes of the dispersion" (James 1:1); and 1 Peter is directed, similarly, to "the exiles

REV. 7:4-9 *Spiritual Israel*

⁹After this I looked, and behold, a great multitude which no man could number, from every nation, from all tribes and peoples and tongues, standing before the throne and before the Lamb, clothed in white robes, with palm branches, in their hands,

---

of the dispersion" (1 Peter 1:1). Those to be in the kingdom, according to the Lord (Luke 22:30), were called the "twelve tribes of Israel" (cf. Matt. 19:28). With this might be compared also the statements of Paul in Galatians 6:16 ("the Israel of God") and Philippians 3:3 ("we are the true circumcision"). It is no coincidence that the New Jerusalem has the names of the twelve tribes of the sons of Israel on the gates, while the foundations represent the twelve apostles of the Lamb (Rev. 21:12-14). Finally, **the hundred and forty-four thousand** here strikingly resemble the army of the same number on Mt. Zion with the Lamb (14:1ff.), who represent the "redeemed from the earth" and those who have **the names of the Lord and the Father on their foreheads**. Those sealed here are the martyrs of the whole church, who are not to be killed by the plagues accompanying the trumpet blasts, but who are reserved to be killed as God's witnesses by the beast which rises out of the sea (11:7).

[9] A second great group is seen by John: **a great multitude which no man could number**. This universal host—**from every nation, from all tribes and peoples and tongues**—was already in the heaven of John's vision, **standing before the throne of God and before the Lamb** arrayed in white as a symbol of their righteousness. The symbols of victory, the palm branches, are in their hands.

Though the first group was sealed, this group is not so described. The reason is that these have already passed through the great ordeal, whereas the first group still faced it (vs. 14). The first group are the servant-martyrs still on earth and subject to the wrath of the coming judgments (from which they are sealed) and facing martyrdom. It is the Church Militant (as it is often described from Rev. 19:11ff.). The other company is the heavenly chorus of the martyrs daily being received into the presence of God, where they need no sealing but receive the comforting of the Father: the

The Martyrs REV. 7:9-17

¹⁰ and crying out with a loud voice, "Salvation belongs to our God who sits upon the throne, and to the Lamb!" ¹¹ And all the angels stood round the throne and round the elders and the four living creatures, and they fell on their faces before the throne and worshiped God, ¹²saying, "Amen! Blessing and glory and wisdom and thanksgiving and honor and power and might be to our God for ever and ever! Amen."

¹³ Then one of the elders addressed me, saying, "Who are these, clothed in white robes, and whence have they come?" ¹⁴ I said to him, "Sir, you know." And he said to me, "These are they who have come out of the great tribulation; they have washed their robes and made them white in the blood of the Lamb.

Church Triumphant, as it is commonly called. The first group represents the one generation of Christians who in John's day faced the great tribulation; the second represents the church of all generations who conquer through the blood of the Lamb.

[10] Salvation here has the Old Testament sense of victory. **Salvation** belongs to **God** and **the Lamb** (12:10; 19:1) who bestow it on these who have white robes and palm branches, namely these who remain faithful and so are victorious.

[11, 12] As the redeemed throng ascribe their victory to God and to the Lamb, **all the angels, the elders,** and **the living creatures** prostrate themselves in **worship** before **God** and add their praise to the chorus. Because of his great wisdom and love in making possible this victory scene, he is shown to deserve the adulation which the redeemed have given him. The heavenly **"Amen"** (so be it) makes that praise their own. But they enlarge the hymn. For his mighty works of love, God deserves to be given **blessing, glory, wisdom, thanksgiving, honor, power, and might**, not only at this point in the vision but **for ever and ever.**

[13-17] The picture anticipates the new exodus of the martyrs. (Compare the new exodus and Song of Moses and the Lamb in 15:2-4). They pass through the great tribulation, sustained by the blood of the Lamb, into the bliss of heavenly joy and praise.

> ¹⁵ Therefore are they before the throne of God,
>   and serve him day and night within his temple;
>   and he who sits upon the throne will shelter
>   them with his presence.
> ¹⁶ They shall hunger no more, neither thirst
>   any more;
>   the sun shall not strike them, nor any
>   scorching heat.
> For the Lamb in the midst of the throne will
>   be their shepherd,
>   and he will guide them to springs of living water;
> ¹⁷ and God will wipe away every tear from their eyes."
> ¹ When the Lamb opened the seventh seal, there was silence in heaven for about half an hour. ² Then I saw the seven angels who stand before God, and seven trumpets were given to them. ³ And another angel came and stood at the altar with a golden censer; and he was given much incense to mingle with the prayers of all the saints upon the golden altar before the throne; ⁴ and the smoke of the incense rose with the prayers of the saints from the hand of the angel before God. ⁵ Then the angel took the censer and filled it with fire from the altar and threw it on the earth; and there were peals of thunder, voices, flashes of lightning, and an earthquake.

Seven Angels with Trumpets, 8:1-5. The **seven trumpets** announce the judgments of God, which come in symbolic form, on the earth. The climax is the **earthquake** (symbol of the change in the world structure) following on the seventh trumpet (11:19). **The seven angels** herald both natural disorders (the first four trumpets) and demonic disasters (the three woes). Their purpose is to work repentance (9:20). Before the final trumpet, there are two visions (cf. the interruption between the sixth and seventh seals in chapter 7) which give John's actual program.

[1-5] As in Joel's plague of locusts (Joel 2), the judgment—called there "the day of the Lord"—is introduced by the blowing of **trumpets**, here **seven** in number. Before the blowing of the trumpets **another angel mingled incense with the prayers of the saints** (cf. 5:8). The scene

Natural Disasters REV. 8:1-7

⁶Now the seven angels who had the seven trumpets made ready to blow them.

⁷The first angel blew his trumpet, and there followed hail and fire, mixed with blood, which fell on the earth; and a third of the earth was burnt up, and a third of the trees were burnt up, and all green grass was burnt up.

---

is drawn from the Jerusalem temple worship. He then **filled a censer with fire** from the altar **and threw it on the earth**. This led to **thunder, noises, lightning, and an earthquake**. This evidently symbolizes the whole action of God as coming in response to the prayers of the saints (cf. comments on 6:10).

The First Four Trumpets: Natural Disasters, 8:6-12. The **seven trumpets** occur in two groups of four and three. The division is reflected in the announcement by an eagle that three "woes" upon earth's inhabitants would accompany the last three trumpets (8:13). In contradistinction, the first four disasters hurt only the natural world. These four plagues represent God's judgments on the world, warning men to repent. They are partial, affecting only one-third of the world, thus not making human life impossible. God uses natural disasters and social upheavals as warnings; yet they are not final judgments. Only after the end comes with the seventh trumpet (11:18 cf. 22:11) will the final condition of life based upon repentance or lack of it have been determined.

[6, 7] When **the first angel blew his trumpet**, a series of disasters resembling the plagues on Egypt (Ex. 7-11) occurred. The plague here includes **hail** with **fire, mixed with blood**. Egypt's seventh plague was "hail and fire flashing continually in the midst of the hail" (Ex. 9:24; cf. Ps. 105:32). This describes a severe thunderstorm, but **blood** is mixed with the **hail and fire**. Blood could signify the fire color but is usually thought to be a combining of the first Egyptian (blood) and the ninth (hail-fire) plagues. When the disaster **fell** (literally, "was cast") **on the earth, one-third of the earth and trees and all green grass were burned up.** This would, of course, effect men but being partial would not destroy life.

⁸The second angel blew his trumpet, and something like a great mountain, burning with fire, was thrown into the sea; ⁹and a third of the sea became blood, a third of the living creatures in the sea died, and a third of the ships were destroyed.

¹⁰The third angel blew his trumpet, and a great star fell from heaven, blazing like a torch, and it fell on a third of the rivers and on the fountains of water. ¹¹The name of the star is Wormwood. A third of the waters became wormwood, and many men died of the water, because it was made bitter.

The reason for the imitation of the plagues of Egypt is the interweaving of the Old Testament Exodus typology into the visions of Revelation. These symbols of judgment upon Egypt were also worked into later Old Testament judgment passages, especially Ezekiel 38:22 and Joel 3:3.

[8, 9] When **the second angel blew his trumpet**, there was **something like a great mountain, burning with fire, thrown into the sea**. The removal of mountains, as in Old Testament language signifying overthrow of social institutions and governments (see 6:14), was to strike terror into the hearts of the earth dwellers. In Jeremiah's vision of the destruction of Israel's enemy Babylon, the Lord said, "I am against you, O destroying Mountain . . . which destroys the whole earth; I will stretch out my hand against you and roll you down from the crags, and make you a burnt mountain" (Jer. 51:25). This symbolizes God's wrath and the uncertainty of wordly structure in the vicissitudes of history. When the mountain fell into the sea, **one-third** of it **became blood, one-third of the creatures of the sea died, and one-third of the ships were destroyed**. Again, the stroke is partial, hurting only things —not men.

[10, 11] When the **third** trumpet sounded, **a great star, blazing like a torch, fell**, this time affecting the rivers and the fountains of water. This is reminiscent of the scene of premonition of judgment and its accompanying terror in 6:13. There the imagery was similar to such Old Testament passages as Isaiah 24:21, 22 and 34:4, where

Partial Eclipses REV. 8:10-12

¹² **The fourth angel blew his trumpet, and a third of the sun was struck, and a third of the moon, and a third of the stars, so that a third of their light was darkened; a third of the day was kept from shining, and likewise a third of the night.**

---

the removal of a heavenly star signified the overthrow of his earthly counterpart (king). In Daniel 8:10 Jewish leaders of Antiochus Epiphanes' time are called stars, whose deaths are symbolized by stars falling. Another possible reference is Lucifer in Isaiah 14:12. What was seen before as a premonition is now seen as a reality. In the continued partial judgment only **one-third of** the fresh **water** sources are affected.

But the picture is here heightened by the statement that **the star's name is Wormwood**. The Greek word signified a **bitter** plant, and this was the effect it had on the water. Compare Exodus 15:23, but here the matter is more serious because the affected **water is** wholly **turned to wormwood**. Several Old Testament passages predict the downfall of corrupt governments under this term (e.g., Jer. 9:15; 23:15).

[12] After **the angel blew** the fourth **trumpet**, there were partial eclipses of the light **of the sun, the moon, and the stars, one-third** in each case. The eclipse is another of the repetitions from the premonitions of judgment in the fifth seal, where the sun and moon became black and red (6:12). The darkening of the sun is the ninth plague of Egypt (Ex. 10:21), and the judgments of God's wrath are often portrayed in the Old Testament by this sign (Joel 2:28ff. and Jer. 4:23, for example).

The First Two Woes, 8:13—9:21. The announcement that three "woes" will accompany the last three trumpets divides the seven trumpets into the groups of four and three. As distinct from the first plagues, which hurt only natural phenomena, the last three are to bring affliction "to those who dwell on the earth." The three woes are also a programmatic device by which the reader is to observe the development of the climax of the first series of visions (9:12; 10:7; 10:14; 11:15).

REV. 8:13–9:1   *Fallen Star*

¹³ **Then I looked, and I heard an eagle crying with a loud voice, as it flew in midheaven, "Woe, woe, woe to those who dwell on the earth, at the blasts of the other trumpets which the three angels are about to blow!"**

¹ **And the fifth angel blew his trumpet, and I saw a star fallen from heaven to earth, and he was given the key of the shaft of the bottomless pit;**

---

[13] The succession of trumpet blasts begun in verse 7 is interrupted from midheaven by **an eagle crying** aloud. In the Old Testament the eagle played a part in the symbolism of the exodus as a type of God's repeated deliverance of his people (Ex. 19:4). From this point of view the eagle would symbolize God's protecting care over the church amidst the woes to be brought upon the world. More likely, however, is the suggestion that eagle here, as often in the Greek Bible (cf. Luke 17:37) should be translated "vulture" and is a symbol of terrible doom to come (cf. Hos. 8:1). The woes are to come upon **those who dwell on the earth.** This phrase is used throughout the Revelation to signify God's enemies, those who worship the beast (3:10; 6:10; 11:10; 13:8, 12, 14; 17:2, 8).

[1] As **the fifth angel** sounded. John **saw a star fallen from heaven to earth.** The **star** signifies an angel such as in 8:10 (cf. Isa. 14:12; Dan. 8:10), which in turn represents the heavenly defeat of an earthly counterpart (cf. 12:7-9). The fallen angel thus depicts, in a way familiar to first-century Jewish readers, the corporate life of men in its opposition to God. This angel **was given the keys of the shaft of the bottomless pit.** The use of the word **given** (cf. 6:2, 4, 8, etc.) signifies this angel—in contrast to the angel of 20:1, who acts as God's agent—is an evil force whose action is tolerated or permitted in God's overruling providence. The demonic creatures loosed from the abyss are not willed by God, but he permits their ravage because he can overrule their actions for the good of his creation, while at the same time their evil influences become the seed of the destruction of evil.

Locusts REV. 9:2-6

²he opened the shaft of the bottomless pit, and from the shaft rose smoke like the smoke of a great furnace, and the sun and the air were darkened with the smoke from the shaft. ³Then from the smoke came locusts on the earth, and they were given power like the power of scorpions of the earth; ⁴they were told not to harm the grass of the earth or any green growth or any tree, but only those of mankind who have not the seal of God upon their foreheads; ⁵they were allowed to torture them for five months, but not to kill them, and their torture was like the torture of a scorpion, when it stings a man. ⁶And in those days men will seek death and will not find it; they will long to die and death flies from them.

[2-6] The **pit** ("abyss") which **opened** is a familiar Old Testament (Septuagint) designation for the deep (*tehom*). To the Hebrews the abyss represented the forces who were still rebellious to God's sovereign will. From this hadean deep the earthly forces of evil are continuously encouraged and reinforced in their rebellion. The effect created by the forces let loose from beneath is the plague which is part of the self-destroying power of evil.

The **smoke rose from the shaft of the bottomless pit**, like that of **a great furnace** which **darkened the sun and the air**. This description is to be connected with the phenomen of **locusts** which appear. They swarm in the sky as smoke, obscuring the whole heaven. The description resembles the locust plague of Joel (1:4ff.), which likewise produced "a day of darkness and gloom, a day of clouds and thick darkness" in which "sun and moon are darkened and the stars withdrew their shining" (2:2, 10).

Unlike the literal plague of locusts in which Joel saw the judgment or day of the Lord typified, these of John's vision were unnatural. Instead of eating the **grass of the earth or any green growth or any tree**, they preyed upon **those of mankind who have not the seal of God upon their foreheads**. This scourging against human beings is symbolized by power given to them **like the power of scorpions**. Later features (**human hair and faces**, vss. 7,8) show that the imagery is concerned with human beings inspired by evil forces to inflict torture **as when a scorpion stings a man**. Notice that it is only

REV. 9:2-12 *Locusts*

⁷In appearance the locusts were like horses arrayed for battle; on their heads were what looked like crowns of gold; their faces were like human faces, ⁸their hair like women's hair, and their teeth like lions' teeth; ⁹they had scales like iron breastplates, and the noise of their wings was like the noise of many chariots with horses rushing into battle; ¹⁰they have tails like scorpions, and stings, and their power of hurting men for five months lies in their tails. ¹¹They have as king over them the angel of the bottomless pit; his name in Hebrew is Abaddon, and in Greek he is called Apollyon.*ᵇ*

¹²The first woe has passed; behold, two woes are still to come.

ᵇ Or *Destroyer*

---

that part of **mankind who do not have the seal of God** (see comment on 7:1ff.) **upon their foreheads** who are tortured (cf. 8:18, where the woes are to come upon the earth-dwellers). The consequences of such evil come only on men who do not serve God.

But the judgments portrayed as rising from the pit are not the final and universal judgment. The locusts were **allowed to torture them for five months** only. The demonically inspired evil, though so torturous that men **seek death and long to die**, still is controlled by God and limited in its effect upon the world. Even it serves God's purpose.

[7-10] Joel's portrayal of the **locust** swarm had their **like**ness to **horses arrayed for battle**, and the noise of their wings like many chariots rushing into battle (cf. 2:4,5). Here the locusts' antennae seem **like women's hair**; their heads and breasts were covered with **scales** which resemble **crowns of gold** and **iron breastplates** respectively. **Their teeth** resemble **lions' teeth**. Joel's army devoured everything before it, like "lions' teeth" or the "fangs of a lioness" (1:6). But John's vision differs from Joel's in that his were **like human faces**. It is repeated that the monsters' **sting** lasts only **five months**.

[11, 12] The evidence mounts that John's vision here is a symbol for the earthly forces of evil inspired from Hades and indicates, not a temporal event which can be placed chronologically into a historical scheme, but the self-inflicting torment of a sinful world. The final indication given

Golden Altar REV. 9:11-15

¹³ Then the sixth angel blew his trumpet, and I heard a voice from the four horns of the golden altar before God, ¹⁴ saying to the sixth angel who had the trumpet, "Release the four angels who are bound at the great river Euphrates." ¹⁵ So the four angels were released, who had been held ready for the hour, the day, the month, and the year, to kill a third of mankind.

---

is the personification of these forces as Destruction. Death and Hades have already been personified (riders on the fourth horse, 6:8). Now the **locusts** are said to **have as** their **king the angel of the bottomless pit** (cf. vs. 1). The **name** of this angel is **Destroyer**, which is given in both the **Hebrew** (**Abaddon**) and the **Greek** (**Apollyon**). *Abaddon* transliterates a Hebrew term for Sheol, the region of the dead—in general—but also often, as in this passage, the home of evil forces (Job 26:6; 31:12; Prov. 15:11; 27:20). Later John will speak of all forces of earthly injury, torment, and judgment, which are to be destroyed at the final trumpet, as the "destroyers of the earth" (11:18).

[13] There is no interruption; the second **woe** follows immediately. When **the sixth angel** sounded, John **heard a voice from the four horns of the golden altar before God**. This **altar** is the altar of burnt incense (Ex. 30:1-3), a symbol already familiar as the answer to the prayers of God's children (8:3, 5; cf. 16:7). Such prayers are not merely prayers of vengeance in retaliation for persecution and injury (see on 6:10) but are prayers for vindication from the sentence passed upon them by the society of the Destroyer. Such prayers were seen as righteous, even as God's judgment upon the evil Destroyer will be seen as righteous (11:18; 19:2), because in the very nature of God's universe those forces which determine to remain evil must be destroyed before God's complete sovereignty can be proclaimed. Only with this in mind can one understand why the forces from beyond the **Euphrates** must be unloosed.

[14, 15] **The voice from the altar** calls for the **release** of **four angels**. These are different from the four angels of 7:1ff. who are holding back the four winds of judgments. These are bound themselves; that is; they are restrained until the time

REV. 9:14-19 *Euphrates*

¹⁶ The number of the troops of cavalry was twice ten thousand times ten thousand; I heard their number. ¹⁷ And this was how I saw the horses in my vision: the riders wore breastplates the color of fire and of sapphire[c] and of sulphur, and the heads of the horses were like lions' heads, and fire and smoke and sulphur issued from their mouths. ¹⁸ By these three plagues a third of mankind was killed, by the fire and smoke and sulphur issuing from their mouths. ¹⁹ For the power of the horses is in their mouths and in their tails; their tails are like serpents, with heads, and by means of them they wound.

[c] Greek *hyacinth*

---

determined by God. They are the angels representing the wrath of God upon men, of whom they are to kill a third. The angels are **bound at the great river Euphrates**.

The **Euphrates** held dark forebodings for Old Testament prophets. It was the northern boundary of the land promised to Israel (Gen. 15:18; Deut. 1:7; Josh. 1:4). But it was also the border between Israel and the countries to the north against whose invading armies the prophets had repeatedly warned (Isa. 14:31; Jer. 1:14f.; 6:1; 10:22; 13:20; 25:9, 26; 46:20, 24; 47:2; Ezek. 26:7; Hab. 1:6-9). In New Testament times **the Euphrates** separated the Roman Empire from the Parthians, who had several times defeated the Romans in their attempts to stabilize their eastern boundary. Even the mention of that dread enemy struck terror after the defeat of Crassus at Carrhae in 53 B.C. and the more recent encounter in A.D. 62. Undoubtedly these passages lay in the background of what the vision should mean to its first-century readers.

[16-19] But John's angels with their armies were of a different sort. Their immensity is signified by their number, **twice ten thousand times ten thousand** (two hundred million). But they were an extraordinary cavalry—wearing **breastplates** fiery **red and sapphire and sulphur**. Their **horses' heads were like lions' heads. From their mouths issued** three plagues of **fire and smoke and sulphur**. Moreover, the horses' hurt was **in their mouths and tails**, the latter of which were **like** deadly **serpents**. The latter reference may identify these **horses** as akin to the old serpent, the Devil (12:4).

Idolatry REV. 9:16–10:2

[20] The rest of mankind, who were not killed by these plagues, did not repent of the works of their hands nor give up worshiping demons and idols of gold and silver and bronze and stone and wood, which cannot either see or hear or walk; [21] nor did they repent of their murders or their sorceries or their fornication or their thefts.

[1] Then I saw another mighty angel coming down from heaven, wrapped in a cloud, with a rainbow over his head, and his face was like the sun, and his legs like pillars of fire. [2] He had a little scroll open in his hand. And he set his right foot on the sea, and his left foot on the land,

---

The correct background is probably Ezekiel's picture of Gog and Magog (Ezek. 38, 39). The former prophet's vision of invading armies had been fulfilled by the Assyrian and Babylonian invasions, but Ezekiel had seen the hordes of King Gog of the land of Magog invading a returned and resettled Israel who dwelt securely and who would be protected by God's "great shaking," as God would enter into judgment with him with pestilence and bloodshed, and with torrential rains and hailstones, fire and brimstone (Ezek. 38:19-23).

[20, 21] Even the terrors of the fifth and sixth trumpets (the first two woes) did not cause men to **repent** of their idolatry, which is described in terms of Old Testament polemic (cf. Pss. 115:4-7; 135: 15-17). Before the third woe is unleashed, two visions concerning God's faithful are recorded.

The Vision of the Little Book, 10:1-11. [1, 2] This vision and the one following in chapter 11 are usually taken as programmatic or theme sections. The present vision telling John that he must prophesy a second time thus prepares for the new section of the book in chapter 12. The vision in chapter 11 reassures the prospective martyrs that their witness is important to the fulfillment of God's redemptive purposes. The appearance of the **mighty angel** provides a cross reference to 5:1 and 18:21. He comes **with** the **rainbow** of divine mercy (4:3) and attributes of Christ (1:15, 16). His **little scroll**, unlike the one of chapter 5, is **open**.

³ **and called out with a loud voice, like a lion roaring; when he called out, the seven thunders sounded.** ⁴ **And when the seven thunders had sounded, I was about to write, but I heard a voice from heaven saying, "Seal up what the seven thunders have said, and do not write it down."**

---

[3] The angel uttered his message **with a loud voice**. At the same time **the seven thunders sounded**. Once again the import may be a summing up of Old Testament ideas. The **voice** speaking like **a lion** is a familiar figure for God's message, especially that of doom upon the disobedient (Jer. 25:30; Hos. 11:10; Amos 1:2; 3:4, 8). Likewise in Psalm 29:3-9 (and see also Ps. 18:13; 1 Sam. 2:10; 7:10): "the voice of the Lord is upon the waters; the God of glory thunders, the Lord, upon many waters." That voice then threatened disaster upon even the cedars of Lebanon. Thus **the seven thunders** may imply that John could perceive the voice of the angel announcing the judgments of God, which the previous trumpets have implied would surely come.

[4] This message John heard and understood. He was **about to write it down** when he was told not to do so but to **seal up what the seven thunders have said**. Commentators generally see in this a prohibition due to the ineffable nature of divine things. But there must be something more than this in John's not being permitted to reveal the meaning of the utterance of **the seven thunders**. That meaning is suggested by the sequence as interpreted below. The agents of divine judgment which have been symbolized by the trumpet series might certainly be expected to destroy the ungodly alien world opposed to God's people. Perhaps that is exactly what the **lion**like **voice** of the angel and **the seven thunders** imply. But they are sealed and not written down—not because the divine wrath cannot be told, but because other events prevent their happening. The judgment in its total effect is cancelled by the longsuffering of God, who does not will that any should perish but that all should come to repentance (2 Peter 3:9). But God's patience can be effective only if there is something else besides these cosmic forces of judgment to bring repentance. The suffering of God's witnesses is the factor which is to do this. Thus the angel proceeds to the oath

No More Delay REV. 10:4-7

⁵And the angel whom I saw standing on sea and land lifted up his right hand to heaven ⁶and swore by him who lives for ever and ever, who created heaven and what is in it, the earth and what is in it, and the sea and what is in it, that there should be no more delay, ⁷but that in the days of the trumpet call to be sounded by the seventh angel, the mystery of God, as he announced to his servants the prophets, should be fulfilled.

---

that this crisis is to begin without delay. Then follows the story of the testimony and death of the witnesses, their resurrection, and the resultant penitence of the world (11:3-13).

[5, 6] After the sealing up of the pronouncements of the seven thunders, **the angel** who had been **standing** with his right foot **on the sea and** his left on the **land** now utters a solemn oath. The oath is taken with the **lifting up of his right hand to heaven** and swearing **by** the one **who lives for ever**—a very solemn oath (for Old Testament oaths see Gen. 14:22; Ex. 6:8; Ezek. 20:15).

The point of the oath is that there should **be no more delay**. The word for **delay** here is *chronos*, which literally means "time." But the angel is not predicting the end of time; the literal meaning is "extension of time." There is precedent for this meaning **delay** (Hab. 2:3; Heb. 10:37). One may well ask, "No delay before what?" The background source provides the answer: the Greek quotes Daniel 12:7, and the interpretation which this suggests is that contrary to Daniel's time (in which there was to be a long delay before the three and one-half years of persecution began) in John's day there would be **no delay**; the crisis was upon the church. This was not the parousia; it was what must "soon take place" (see comments on 1:1). The next vision (11:2, 3) will reveal the three and one-half years (forty-two months) of the testimony of the witnesses to be followed by their death. But their death will not be final; their enemies will still be around to rejoice, and they themselves will be raised.

[7] John has been assured (by the angel's oath) that there would "be no more delay" before the beginning of the persecution. The vision also interprets the words in Daniel in their

REV. 10:7-10 *Mystery of God*

⁸ Then the voice which I had heard from heaven spoke to me again, saying, "Go, take the scroll which is open in the hand of the angel who is standing on the sea and on the land." ⁹ So I went to the angel and told him to give me the little scroll; and he said to me, "Take it and eat; it will be bitter to your stomach, but sweet as honey in your mouth." ¹⁰ And I took the little scroll from the hand of the angel and ate it; it was sweet as honey in my mouth, but when I had eaten it my stomach was made bitter.

---

new fulfillment to mean that with the end of the persecution and the triumph of the cause of the martyrs would come the days of the trumpet call to be sounded by the seventh angel. This is the third woe, or the seventh **trumpet** which will follow (11:15-19); and, when this happens, the **mystery of God** will **be fulfilled** or finished. This corresponds to the announcement in 11:15 that "the kingdom of the world has become the kingdom of our Lord," who should "reign for ever and ever." Similarly, in Daniel the fulfillment of "time, two times, and half a time" would see the accomplishment of "all these things" which Daniel had foreseen (Dan. 12:7). Thus the **mystery of God** seems to refer to the problem which is the subject of the revelation; that is, when the persecution would come and why it was necessary. God's servants the prophets had the gospel preached to them ("announced," in Greek, *euangelizesthai*), and in this gospel the certainty and purpose of such suffering had been made known (cf. Acts 14:22), as it is now being reemphasized in the Apocalypse. When **the seventh angel** sounds, the whole **mystery** will become plain.

That this sequence in the Revelation (just as in Daniel) seems to telescope the end of the persecution with "the end" is not to be taken as a literal identification of events.

[8] After the prediction that there would be no delay and that the **mystery** would be finished, John is **told** to **go** to the angel and **take the scroll** he had **in his hand**.

[9, 10] After John responds to the command, he is **told** "**Take it and eat.**" The background here is Ezekiel 2:9, 10; 3:3, 14. The **sweet**ness of John's **little scroll** probably signifies that the contents of the book would gladden his heart by its

Prophesy Again REV. 10:9–11:2

[11] And I was told, "You must again prophesy about many peoples and nations and tongues and kings."

[1] Then I was given a measuring rod like a staff, and I was told: "Rise and measure the temple of God and the altar and those who worship there, [2] but do not measure the court outside the temple; leave that out, for it is given over to the nations, and they will trample over the holy city for forty-two months.

---

message; at the same time it would be **bitter** news in that it would disclose the terribleness of the suffering of God's people in the conflict with the dragon and the beast.

[11] One might assume that when **the seventh angel** sounded and **the mystery of God** was finished (according to the word just spoken, vs. 7) John's mission would be over. Not so. John **must again prophesy to many peoples**. This obviously explains the meaning of the **little scroll** and the finishing of the **mystery**. Clearly it means that the Revelation is divided into two grand divisions. The first concerns the great closed book which had been in the hand of God and which only Jesus Christ had been able to open. It is with this that the visions of chapters 6-11 are concerned. That part of the vision is now drawing to a close, but the whole of the revelation is not over. The second part (the little book open in the angel's hand) is a second prophecy and will consist of chapters 12-16.

The Measuring Scene and the Two Witnesses, 11:1-14. Chapters 10 and 11 contain incidents which intervene before the last of the three woes was pronounced (see 8:13; 9:12; 11:4). The little book and the measuring scene, with that of two witnesses, are intended to show the persecuted church how suffering and martyrdom serve the redeeming purpose of God. Fitting into this, the present scene climaxes the theme of the book: the church must suffer persecution, but it is protected; the witnesses are killed and their resurrection is in itself redemptive; their suffering causes "the rest" to give God glory.

[1, 2] John has now become an actor in the drama. By some one unnamed he is **given a measuring rod like a staff.**

REV. 11:1-3 *Measuring the Temple*

> ³ **And I will grant my two witnesses power to prophesy for one thousand two hundred and sixty days, clothed in sackcloth."**

Symbols here have been adapted from Ezekiel's measuring of the ruined temple before its restoration (Ezek. 40:3) and from Zechariah's vision of an angel measuring Jerusalem before it was rebuilt (Zech. 2:1ff.). The old Jerusalem and its temple were surveyed to insure their rebuilding. John is told to **rise and measure the temple**, and it is obvious from the context that the purpose is for its preservation. The temple, the **altar**, and **those who worship there** are to be measured; the court outside is not to be measured, and as a consequence, **it is given over to the nations, and they will trample over the holy city**. Who are the ones measured? Not the Jewish temple and its worshipers (as though this were a prophecy written before A.D. 70), because Titus' soldiers did not preserve the temple but destroyed it as they did the rest of the city (the story is told in Josephus' *Wars* by an eyewitness). Surely in such a symbolic book John would not have spoken so literally of a material city. The temple, then, and **the court** and **the holy city** represent the church as the spiritual temple and the city of God (as in Rev. 3:12; 1 Cor. 3:16; 2 Cor. 6:16; Eph. 2:20; 1 Peter 2:5). Nor is the court the worldly elements in the church (such as the compromisers of the seven letters), for when the persecution came, this element did not receive the opposition while the godly element was spared. The fact that **the court** and **holy city were trampled forty-two months** shows that this refers to the suffering and martyrdom of the church. This time is borrowed from Daniel's prediction of the limitation placed on the suffering of the saints of God. John uses the symbol as the typical time of persecution (vs. 3; 12:14; 13:5). The measuring is parallel with the sealing of the saints in chapter 7. It represents the spiritual security of the church in its faith in the risen Christ, but it leaves the church at the same time exposed to suffering. To suffer is to witness; to witness is to prophesy. The church is free to give its testimony. The church's counterpart, the heavenly temple, is measured in 21:15.

[3] The temple had been measured to guarantee that the **two witnesses had power to prophesy**. Their witness extends

Two Witnesses REV. 11:3-5

⁴ These are the two olive trees and the two lampstands which stand before the Lord of the earth. ⁵ And if any one would harm them, fire pours from their mouth and consumes their foes; if any one would harm them, thus he is doomed to be killed.

---

over a period of one thousand two hundred and sixty days, which is the same as the forty-two months of the trampling of the holy city—again the typical period of persecution.

[4] John now proceeds to identify the two witnesses, but his explanation is puzzling. Its interpretation depends, as often, partly on the overall meaning given to the visions. The best interpretation is that John referred to the contemporary scene and that the vision is meant to explain the meaning of the persecution the church was suffering and was to suffer. The two witnesses who were to prophesy **are the two olive trees and the two lampstands which stand before the Lord**. Here John picks up again the imagery of Zechariah's vision of a lampstand with a bowl on top, with seven lamps and beside it "two olive trees" (4:1ff.).

The Spirit had already appropriated the lampstand or candelabrum to represent the churches (Rev. 1:12, 20). The two witnesses, then, are not the whole church, but a part of it. But they are also like their Old Testament counterparts, the two olive trees. In Zechariah the olive trees are identified as Zerubbabel and Joshua, leaders of the movement to restore Zion; they are "the two anointed ones of the Lord" (Zech. 4:14). But whom would John have thought of as such a parallel? Not two individuals, as there is no "king" or "priest"singled out in the church. All Christians are priests and kings (1:6 and 5:10). John has transformed Zechariah's vision into a Christian vision of the martyrs (witnesses) testifying to Christ. Doubtless, the two olive trees symbolize the saints, especially those who bear witness as is now described.

[5] That the vision does not intend the witnesses to be taken as specific individuals is further indicated by identifying them with the power possessed in their day by Elijah and Moses. The power of the witnesses is such that they cannot be silenced or destroyed so long as their testimony is

REV. 11:5-7 *Elijah and Moses*

⁶ They have power to shut the sky, that no rain may fall during the days of their prophesying, and they have power over the waters to turn them into blood, and to smite the earth with every plague, as often as they desire. ⁷ And when they have finished their testimony, the beast that ascends from the bottomless pit will make war upon them and conquer them and kill them,

---

unfulfilled: **if any one would harm them** (just as Elijah treated Ahaziah's messengers, 2 Kings 1:10ff.), he is destroyed by fire. Only the fire is not literal from heaven this time; the **fire pours from their mouth** so that the witnesses **consume their foes.** This is tantamount to the witnesses' slaying their adversaries by the word which comes from their mouth (see Jer. 5:14).

[6] Elijah had still another power: **to shut up the sky so that no rain might fall** during the days of his prophecy (see 1 Kings 17:1; Luke 4:25; James 5:17). The two witnesses have such a power, and it lasts **during the days of their prophesying** (three and one-half years, vs. 3, as in Elijah's case).

Moses' image enters in that the two witnesses have **power over the waters to turn them into blood** (as in Ex. 7:28), with Moses' similar ability to **smite the earth with every plague, as often as they desire** (1 Sam. 4:8).

One should not think of the witnesses as being able to perform these miracles literally. Notice that in the sequel "those who dwell on the earth" rejoice over the death of the witnesses because they "had been a torment" to them (11:10).

[7] The two witnesses cannot be harmed until **they have finished their testimony.** Like Moses and Elijah they were protected and indeed had divine powers of afflicting the enemy. This we have seen refers to the power inherent in their message, which tormented the disbelieving hearers. Nothing can stop their testimony—not even death. Then **the beast that ascends from the bottomless pit** enters the picture. Previously the abyss or **bottomless pit** (9:2) was described as the abode of evil whence comes the first great woe. Here the

Worldly City

⁸ **and their dead bodies will lie in the street of the great city which is allegorically**[d] **called Sodom and Egypt, where their Lord was crucified.** ⁹**For three days and a half men from the peoples and tribes and tongues and nations gaze at their dead bodies and refuse to let them be placed in a tomb,**

[d] Greek *spiritually*

---

beast is connected with the abode of evil (cf. 13:4, where the beast receives his power from the dragon). The **beast** has not heretofore been mentioned; he is introduced in chapter 13. He is mentioned here by anticipation or prolepsis. The statement that the beast will **make war** on the witnesses and **kill them** signifies the seeming defeat of the witnesses and the silencing of their voices.

[8] After the witnesses are killed, **their dead bodies will lie in the street of the great city.** Their martyrdom will be an open fact, and their defeat will be one which the world beholds. Most significant is the place where the witnesses are said to **lie** after they were killed. **The great city** is that one **where the** witnesses' **Lord was crucified,** that is, Jerusalem. But Jerusalem is no longer the mere literal city of Palestine. It has **allegorically** or figuratively (the Greek has "spiritually") become one with the ancient cities of **Sodom and Egypt.** These cities are taken typically as the epitome of sin (**Sodom**) and opposition to God (**Egypt**). By rejecting and crucifying their Messiah and opposing his people, Jerusalem lost the right to the name "city of God" and becomes one with the city of the world. So Paul, too, talked of the temporal Jerusalem as the "present Jerusalem, who is in slavery with her children" set over against the "Jerusalem from above" (Gal. 4:25, 26). Jerusalem, by reason of the crucifixion, has taken on a new symbolism, different from that which it carries in most of the Bible.

[9] But John sees the victory of the evil forces as short-lived. For **three and a half days** the witnesses' bodies lie in the street, because the **peoples and tribes and tongues and nations** (a designation of the breadth of the evil combination of powers) will not allow them to be **placed in a tomb.** The short period probably signifies that the victory of the beast lasted only a short time.

REV. 11:10-12 *Resurrection*

¹⁰ **and those who dwell on the earth will rejoice over them and make merry and exchange presents, because these two prophets had been a torment to those who dwell on the earth.**
¹¹ **But after the three and a half days a breath of life from God entered them, and they stood up on their feet, and great fear fell on those who saw them.** ¹² **Then they heard a loud voice from heaven saying to them, "Come up hither!" And in the sight of their foes they went up to heaven in a cloud.**

---

[10] But during that short time the people **who dwell on the earth** (another designation of the worldly people who are allied with the beast and who reject Christ; cf. 3:10; 6:10; 8:13; 13:8, 12, 14;17:8) **will rejoice over** the witnesses and **make merry and exchange presents.** The reason for their happiness and merrymaking is that they are no longer **tormented** by the two witnesses.

[11] The joy of those who dwell on the earth did not last long. After **three and a half days** the two dead witnesses came to life; **a breath of life from God entered them, and they stood upon their feet.** The resurrection is told in the exact words of Ezekiel 37:5-10, where Ezekiel had seen the bones representing dead Israel come to life. Thus John symbolized the revival of the church after a seeming death through the silencing of her voice of preaching. The witnesses' resurrection caused **great fear.** This is reminiscent of the ancient fear of Israel's enemies at the news of the strength of God's people (Ex. 15:16; Deut. 2:25).

[12] The resurrection of the witnesses was followed by their being caught up to heaven. The symbolism may recall the ascension of Elijah (2 Kings 2:11). The spectators hear **a loud voice from heaven** like the voice of God calling (cf. John 12:28), **saying, "Come up hither."** This resurrection represented the vindication of the martrys' cause after its seeming hopelessness. The whole world saw the vindication, just as they had viewed the dead bodies. Here, then, is Revelation's answer to the cry of the martyrs from beneath the altar ("How long before thou wilt judge and avenge our blood on those who dwell upon the earth?"). The vision of the two witnesses was in reality the prediction of the ultimate

Earthquake REV. 11:12, 13

¹³ **And at that hour there was a great earthquake, and a tenth of the city fell; seven thousand people were killed in the earthquake, and the rest were terrified and gave glory to the God of heaven.**

---

end of the period of persecution of the church with its vindication (cf. 20:1ff.).

[13] In the Old Testament prophets, the **earthquake** is a familiar symbol of changes and upheavals in the social or spiritual order (see Ezek. 38:19; Hag. 2:6; Isa. 2:10-21; Jer. 4:24). The Revelation used this Old Testament symbolism at the sixth seal (6:12-17) in terms of the ultimate overthrow of the powers arrayed against God's people. So now there is **a great earthquake.** The meaning seems to be the downfall of the pagan order and the triumph of the martyr's cause. In history this occurred in the downfall of Rome after the triumph of the church under Constantine. But it may further symbolize the constant defeat of forces which oppose God in any age.

There is moderation, however, in the disaster suffered by the church's enemies. Only **a tenth of the city** fell and **seven thousand were killed** by the church's enemies. These are conventional symbols for a partial judgment. The city here probably means the symbolic Jerusalem of verse 8, which represents Rome. The more detailed description of that destruction will be given in the second part of the Revelation (chs. 17-19).

The final effect of the earthquake following the martyrs' death and resurrection is different from anything else in the visions thus far: **The rest were terrified and gave glory to God** (contrast 9:21). To fear and do homage or "give glory" to God is equivalent in John's language to repentance and worship (14:7; 15:4; 16:9). This was the effect of the witness of the martyrs and the vindication of their cause.

This in effect answers the question "Why does God allow his saints to suffer?" If evil men are to oppose God's people and cause and if in such a case God is to show longsuffering (2 Peter 3:9), it is inevitable that his people suffer. But that suffering is also redemptive. The witness of the ones beheaded for the testimony of God is added to the witness

REV. 11:13-18 — *Seventh Trumpet*

¹⁴ **The second woe has passed; behold, the third woe is soon to come.**

¹⁵ **Then the seventh angel blew his trumpet, and there were loud voices in heaven, saying, "The kingdom of the world has become the kingdom of our Lord and of his Christ, and he shall reign for ever and ever." ¹⁶ And the twenty-four elders who sit on their thrones before God fell on their faces and worshiped God, ¹⁷ saying,**

> **"We give thanks to thee, Lord God almighty, who
>   art and who wast,
>   that thou hast taken thy great power and begun to reign.**
> ¹⁸ **The nations raged, but thy wrath came,
>   and the time for the dead to be judged,
> for rewarding thy servants, the prophets and saints,
>   and those who fear thy name, both small and great,
> and for destroying the destroyers of the earth."**

---

borne by God and by His Son Jesus Christ in confirmation of the faith of the gospel. The Christians' suffering, as Paul said to the Colossians, "completes what is lacking in the suffering of Christ for the sake of his body" (Col. 1:24).

[14] The two scenes of the little book (ch. 10) and the two witnesses (ch. 11) have brought to an end the event of the sixth trumpet (9:12, 13). The sixth trumpet was also the **second woe** and now it **has passed.** Thus the **third woe**, with which "the mystery of God . . . will be fulfilled," is soon to come.

The Seventh Trumpet: The Third Woe, 11:15-19. [15] The sounding of the **seventh trumpet** warns of the third woe and the finishing of the mystery of God. This section brings to an end the vision of the trumpets. When the **trumpet** of the seventh angel sounded, **loud voices** were heard. Some have thought these were the four living creatures, since the refrain in verse 16 is taken up by the twenty-four elders. There are similar instances of indefiniteness in 12:10 and 19:1, 6. It suffices that the information comes from heavenly voices acclaiming the kingdom.

[16-18] In these verses is celebrated the triumph of the gospel: **thou hast taken thy great power and begun to reign.**

Temple Opened REV. 11:16-19

¹⁹ **Then God's temple in heaven was opened, and the ark of his covenant was seen within his temple; and there were flashes of lightning, voices, peals of thunder, an earthquake, and heavy hail.**

Now comes the end: **the time for the dead to be judged, for rewarding . . . for destroying the destroyers** (9:11).

[19] **God's temple in heaven was opened**—an anticipation of chapters 21 and 22. There was also a **great earthquake**, again John's symbol of Rome's overthrow. See further comments on 15:5, 6.

Verses 15-19 present one of the great difficulties of the book of Revelation. John telescopes the prediction of the downfall of Rome, the triumph of God's kingdom, and the end of the world. Taking this juxtaposition literally, many commentators have held that John expected all of these events to occur soon, in his own day, which, of course, they did not. On the other hand, this combining of great national and worldly disasters with the eschatological "end" is characteristic of biblical and Jewish eschatology (cf. Joel 1:15; Amos 8:2, 9; Jer. 4:12, 18, 23, 27). The prophet, as is evident elsewhere in the book, did not in fact necessarily expect the end of the world with the destruction of Rome. Temporal judgments were typical of and of the same character as the final cosmic judgment.

With one brief anticipation of these verses, John breaks off to begin a new section of his book, to lead later into a fuller description of what has been here declared.

The War in Heaven, 12:1—16:21

With the twelfth chapter the second division of the central part of Revelation begins. Just as the material of 6:1–11:19 constitutes the book that the Lamb was worthy to open (5:1ff.), so 12:1–16:21 constitutes the "little book" containing what John was to "prophesy again" (10:11). The "mystery of God" was to be finished by the sounding of the seventh trumpet (10:7) and the third woe. The revealing of that woe, then, (11:14-19) is followed by chapter 12.

The theme of the first section was God's judgment on an evil world; the new series of visions pictures in more detail the struggle which the church faces. It repeats the theme of the first series, but it gives a smaller picture and details the specific nature of that struggle.

First in chapter 12 a radiant woman is seen to give birth to a child (the Christ), but Satan is waiting to destroy it. When he is foiled, he goes away to make war on the rest of the woman's seed. He calls upon two allies (ch. 13), the beast of the sea and the beast of the land, to make war on the saints who will not worship the first beast. On the opposite side of the struggle (ch. 14) John sees the Lamb with the church militant making war on the beast, while a series of proclamations make clear the nature and issues of the conflict which ends in the harvest vintage of God. With the stage thus set John sees seven angels pour out bowls of God's wrath upon the earth, concluding with the destruction of the mystical city of Babylon (chs. 15, 16). The next vision gives a more detailed picture of the judgment on Rome and the triumph of God's people (chs. 17–19).

The struggle pictured in this section was the contemporary struggle between the Lord and his church on the one side and, on the other, the persecuting Roman Empire (of which the expected persecution under Domitian was to be the immediate manifestation), represented by the first beast, along with the imperial cult (the priesthood of the emperor cult), which is symbolized by the second beast or the false prophet. Babylon is the picture of the corruption and idolatry which Rome as the visible head of the beast represented.

The Woman and Her Child, 12:1-6. The story of the conflict of the church and its enemies begins with the revelation of the principal characters. On the one side there is the picture of the incarnation of the Messiah, and on the other the great red dragon, the Devil, who tries to destroy him. The purpose of the visions is to reveal that Satan's wrath against the Christ is the real cause of the Christian's suffering. The fact that he is unable to prevent the man-child's birth and that he is defeated and cast from his seat of power is intended to presage his ultimate defeat.

Woman with Child REV. 12:1, 2

¹ And a great portent appeared in heaven, a woman clothed with the sun, with the moon under her feet, and on her head a crown of twelve stars; ² she was with child and she cried out in her pangs of birth, in anguish for delivery.

---

[1] John sees **a great portent,** or sign, **in heaven.** This is the first time John uses the term "sign" (*semeion*) in the book. Other things to be called "signs" are the great red dragon (12:3) and the seven angels with the seven plagues (15:1). Otherwise the term is used of miracles or wonders wrought by different ones (13:13f; 16:14, 20). Here the term seems to be used as in Matthew 24:3, 30 (cf. Mark 8:11; Matt. 16:1) of some visible phenomenon "from heaven" as an indication or proof of some power or truth, thus the translation **portent.**

This sign was a **woman clothed with the sun.** In Psalm 104:2 this is divine apparel, along with honor and majesty; compare the appearance of Christ (1:16), and the angels (10:1; 19:17). In contrast notice that earthly creatures are clothed with clouds (7:9), sackcloth (11:1), purple and scarlet (17:4), fine linen (19:8) or a robe dipped in blood (19:13). The woman also had **the moon** (in Song of Solomon 6:10 a sign of "fairness") **under her feet** and had a wreath of **twelve stars** (possibly a reference to the twelve patriarchs/apostles in the symbolism of Israel, cf. 21:12, 14) **upon her head.** As in the story of Joseph's dream (Gen. 37:9), where the "sun, moon, and stars" (all heavenly lights) bow down to Joseph, so here the **woman** is clothed with all three.

[2] This woman **was with child and cried out in her pangs of birth, in anguish for delivery.** If the wording is based upon Isaiah 7:14, to which it bears a resemblance, the association is not specific, for "virgin" is exchanged for woman. This leads to the question of who the woman and the child are. The offspring is clearly identified in verse 5 as the Christ. But it is unlikely that the Virgin Mary is the woman. Though Christ is the son of Mary, the church ("the rest of her seed") is not. It is more likely that those who see her as the Jewish church—or more specifically, the people of God (having both Old and New Testament manifestations) from whom the Christ

REV. 12:2-4 *Red Dragon*

³And another portent appeared in heaven: behold a great red dragon, with seven heads and ten horns, and seven diadems upon his heads. ⁴His tail swept down a third of the stars of heaven, and cast them to the earth. And the dragon stood before the woman who was about to bear a child, that he might devour her child when she brought it forth;

---

was to come—are correct. Jerusalem, the capital of Judaism, is often described in the Old Testament as a woman in child labor because of her spiritual travail (see Isa. 26:17 and 66:7-9, the language of which is echoed here). Also compare the same figure used by Jesus of the apostles (John 16:21) and by Paul of his concern for the maturing of his converts (Gal. 4:19). Paul referred to the church ("the Jerusalem which is from above") as "the mother of us all" (Gal. 4:26), and in John's vision here the same **woman** who gives birth to Christ is afterwards persecuted (12:13) along with her seed (vs. 17).

It has been suggested that the use of the **woman** clothed in light to represent the church may have been an intentional correction of the current Roman custom of identifying the emperor with the goddess Roma (deity of the city) as her son and representing her (on coins, etc.) as clothed in the sun, and the emperor himself as the sun or moon. John will portray the personification of Rome, not as the mother of the emperor savior-god, the queen of the earth (17:7), but as the great whore, a travesty on the virgin mother.

[3, 4] The second **portent**, or sign, which John saw was a **great red dragon**, who is plainly identified in verse 9 as "the old serpent," or "the Devil and Satan." But the symbolism under which he is further described is less plain. The fact that he had ten horns relates him to the fourth beast of Daniel's famous vision, where the ten horns are said to be ten kings who should arise to "wear out the saints of the Most High" (Dan. 7). These same seven heads and ten horns will later appear on the beast which comes out of the sea (13:1; 17:3, 7). There the seven heads will definitely be identified with the seven hills of Rome, where the scarlet woman sits; at the same time the seven kings in some fashion are to be identified with Rome (see on 17:9, 10), and the ten kings are still to

Old Testament Imagery REV. 12:3, 4

arise. The fact that they are attributed to Satan signifies that ultimately their powers are derived from the Devil, who is "the ruler of this world" (John 12:31; 14:30; 16:11). It will be remembered that the Devil in tempting Jesus said that the kingdoms of the world "have been delivered to me" (Luke 4:6). That he is **red** signifies his murderous work; while the fact that **his tail swept down a third of the stars of heaven** which were **cast to the earth** is another reference to Daniel, where the same is said of the little horn (18:10). The Daniel passage is usually thought of as referring to the killing of leaders of Israel, the people of God (cf. Jer. 33:22). In John's vision the **dragon stood before the woman about to bear a child, that he might devour her child**.

The Old Testament background must be examined to explain why the symbol of the **dragon** is chosen. The **seven heads** symbol (unlike the ten horns) is not drawn from Daniel. Instead, it is taken from the "many-headed" dragon of Old Testament usage, in which numerous passages speak of the serpent or **dragon** under various names—Leviathan or Lotan or Rahab (a variant of *Tiamat*, an allied form of which, *tehom*, is the Hebrew word for "deep" or abyss): Psalms 74:14; 89:10; 104:5-9; Proverbs 8:27-29; Job 26:13. This language undoubtedly is drawn from the ancient Semitic myth of creation. But among the Hebrews the myth has been replaced by the revelation of creation by the power of the living God, and the language survives as merely figurative or demythologized language. From this it has been historicized; that is, it is used in typological language to identify the historical enemies of Israel with the ancient enemy (the chaos monster) which Jehovah had "slain and cut to pieces at creation." Thus Jeremiah had compared Nebuchadrezzar to the sea monster (*tannin*) who had swallowed Israel (Jer. 51:34, 44), and Ezekiel had identified Pharaoh, king of Egypt, as "the great monster (*tannim*) that lieth in the midst of his rivers" (Ezek. 29:3), and as the dragon *Rahab* (Isa. 30:7). The slaying of the **dragon** was (typically) repeated as God overcame Babylon once more and prepared a way in the waters for Israel's return to Zion (Isa. 27:1; 51:9-11.) The intertestamental Jewish book Psalms of Solomon continues the figure by calling Pompey, the Roman commander and

REV. 12:3-6 *Male Child*

⁵she brought forth a male child, one who is to rule all the nations with a rod of iron, but her child was caught up to God and to his throne, ⁶and the woman fled into the wilderness, where she has a place prepared by God, in which to be nourished for one thousand two hundred and sixty days.

---

conqueror of Palestine, by the same title (2:29). Thus for proud earthly rulers such as Egypt, Babylon, or now Rome, who tend to deify themselves and oppress the people of God, to be identified with the old serpent or **dragon**, and with the understanding that as such they were merely the tools of the ancient enemy of God, the Devil, John is following in a literary tradition deep in Old Testament thought and still current in Jewish apocalyptic literature.

[5] By **brought forth** John does not mean precisely the birth of Jesus (thus passing over the earthly life of Jesus and going directly to his ascension), but rather his death, resurrection, and ascension. This seems sure from the fact that John pictures the struggle in verse 5 by quoting the second Psalm. There sonship ("Thou art my son, this day I have begotten thee") follows the Messiah's death and the begetting spoken of is the resurrection, the begetting from death. So Paul interpreted Psalm 2 in his speech at Antioch (Acts 13:33), and so he writes in Romans 1:4. This was a familiar theme in the preaching of the early church.

The term **male child** in Greek emphasizes the child's masculinity and again echoes Isaiah's prediction of Jerusalem giving birth to a son (Isa. 66:7-9). But the **male** here is the Christ, seen specifically in his enthronement following his resurrection. This is made clear by the quotation of Psalm 2:7-9 that he is the one "**who is to rule all the nations with a rod of iron.**" The **child caught up to God and to his throne** clearly has the ascension in mind.

[6] A result of the ascension of Jesus was that he had won the victory over death and the elemental spirits or principalities and powers (Col. 2:15). During his (earthly) life he could be tempted and could have succumbed to the tempting power of the Devil and his angels. In fact, the cause of his death inheres in the fact that he would not yield to those

Wilderness REV. 12:6-8

⁷ Now war arose in heaven, Michael and his angels fighting against the dragon; and the dragon and his angels fought, ⁸ but they were defeated and there was no longer any place for them in heaven.

---

forces. But by his death he both won the victory over them and removed himself from the possibility of their power. Christians by sharing his death also escape from the power of the forces of evil. This truth is what John symbolizes by saying that **the woman fled into the wilderness, where she has a place prepared by God**. The **wilderness** or desert here refers in biblical typology to the exodus experience of Israel. This is one feature of the "dragon" terminology for Satan, since the **dragon** had been used to symbolize Egypt, and in chapters 15 and 16 this symbolism of the exodus story (the crossing of the sea, the new song, the plagues) will be continued. In that experience God bore Israel on eagle's wings and protected her during the years of wandering (Ex. 19:4). So here the **wilderness** symbolizes the security and protection of the woman during the years of her persecution.

In her **prepared place** the **woman was nourished for one thousand two hundred and sixty days**. This, like the time of prophesying of the two witnesses in 11:3, is borrowed from the literalizing of the "time, times, and half a time" of the persecution of the saints of the Most High by the little horn of Daniel 7:25 (see on 11:3). God would protect his community during the period of persecution.

The War in Heaven, 12:7-12. [7, 8] The scene shifts from the opposition of the dragon against the woman and her seed to the **war** that **arose in heaven**. Taking the lead in **fighting against the dragon** in this heavenly battle are **Michael and his angels**. The archangel Michael is presented in the book of Daniel as the special patron angel of Israel, and as such he is their "prince" (Dan. 10:21) and "the one who has charge" of Daniel's people to defend and deliver them (12:1). **The dragon and his angels were defeated**. The **war** is said to have been **in heaven**, by which most students think is meant the lower parts of the many (seven) heavens, for this is where Jewish literature assigns the Devil's place (Slavonic Enoch 7 and 18; Ascension of Isaiah 10:29). This idea seems reflected in Ephesians 2:2, where Satan is called "the prince of the power of the air." Jesus himself saw in the victory of his disciples over Satan's demonic allies a signal of Satan's fall from the sky (Luke 10:18). But a second biblical concept is also a part of the scene. In his heavenly connection Satan is presented as the "accuser of the people of God" (as in Job 1:6ff.; Zech. 3:1; and similarly in Jewish literature, e. g., Jubilees 1:20; Enoch 40:7). This "battle" in reality concerns the culmination—really, the termination—of this power of Satan to accuse the saints in heaven's court (whence the biblical name "devil," Greek *diabolos*, accuser or slanderer), as indicated by his title "the accuser of our brethren" (vs. 10). It is hardly necessary to stress that this battle has nothing to do with any real or imaginary pre-creation expulsion of Satan and his angels from heaven (e.g., as in Milton's *Paradise Lost*). Verse 11 makes this quite plain.

It is not clear when this battle is located in time and what its relation is to the attempt to devour the woman's child (12:1-6). It is in some way attendant upon the previous story and probably parallel with it. When John wrote, he seemed to think of this event as past and as the occasion for Satan's fury in the Christian persecutions which the church was then facing (vss. 13ff.). Once Satan's host was conquered, **there was no longer any place for them in heaven**. The prosecuting attorney loses his right to practice in the heavenly court. Verse 10 seems (though there are difficulties) to indicate that the victory occurred at the crucifixion (the time of salvation, etc.).

This disbarment of Satan is reflected in other language in John's Gospel. Jesus was innocent, as his judges declared, but he had no illusions about who the real accuser was. "The ruler of this world is coming," he said, "He has no power over me" (John 14:30). Satan, however, was blind, not seeing that his unjust victory over Christ would be his own downfall. For though Satan won the verdict in Pilate's court, God reversed the decision in the resurrection. The prince of the world was judged (16:11; cf. Heb. 2:14). Furthermore, in that trial Jesus was representing all men: his judgment was that of all the world; his victory the world's victory and

The Devil, the Deceiver REV. 12:7-11

⁹ And the great dragon was thrown down, that ancient serpent, who is called the Devil and Satan, the deceiver of the whole world—he was thrown down to the earth, and his angels were thrown down with him. ¹⁰ And I heard a loud voice in heaven, saying, "Now the salvation and the power and the kingdom of our God and the authority of his Christ have come, for the accuser of our brethren has been thrown down, who accuses them day and night before our God. ¹¹ And they have conquered him by the blood of the Lamb and by the word of their testimony, for they loved not their lives even unto death.

Satan's defeat. "Now is the judgment of this world, now shall the ruler of this world be cast out" (12:31). Hereafter, the saints "in Christ Jesus" have no condemnation (Rom. 8:1) with such an advocate as Jesus (1 John 2:1ff.). Satan has no chance as accuser. There is **no longer any place found in heaven for him** and his work.

[9] After his defeat in heaven **the great dragon was thrown down to earth**. Although he had already been decisively defeated, he was allowed to carry on his work for a season on earth. **The dragon** is identified as **the ancient serpent** (cf. Old Testament occurrences given at vs. 3). The Old Testament does not make too clear the way in which references to the many-headed monster of chaos are to be taken, but here he is identified as the **Devil and Satan, the deceiver of the whole world**. Serpent, of course, is meant to connect him with the deception of Adam and Eve in the Garden of Eden (Gen. 3:1ff.). Satan's two principal works are as deceiver or beguiler (cf. 20:3, 8, 10; 2 Cor. 2:11; 11:3; 1 Tim. 2:14) and accuser of the saints (Job 1:6ff.; Zech. 3:1ff.; and later literature—Jubilees 1:20; Enoch 40:7). With him are also thrown down his angels (cf. Matt. 25:41).

[10, 11] At the point where the Devil is cast out of heaven, **a great voice in heaven** proclaims praise in a manner so characteristic of the Apocalypse. The voice, probably belonging to one of the heavenly creatures, proclaims the beginning of the **salvation and the power and the kingdom of our God and the authority of Christ**. The reason assigned is

¹² Rejoice then, O heaven and you that dwell therein! But woe to you, O earth and sea, for the devil has come down to you in great wrath, because he knows that his time is short!"

that the **accuser of the brethren has been thrown down** or expelled from heaven. It is most likely that the defeat of Satan is the triumph and ascension of Christ ("caught up to God and to his throne," vs. 5). This is in accord with verse 11 of the hymn of praise, which attributes the victory over Satan to **the blood of the Lamb**. However, there is a difficulty. The victory is also accomplished by the martyrs' death—and by **the word of their** (not his) **testimony**. This is one of the central theological affirmations of the Revelation—that the purpose of martyrdom is to contribute to the ultimate triumph of the gospel. It, like the cross, was an exercise in the love of God. But this would mean that the bringing in of the kingdom of God would take place only after the period of martyrdom was over and the universal recognition of Christ took place. There is a sense in which this is taught in the Apocalypse. In 11:15ff. after the martyrdom was accomplished the announcement was given out that "the kingdom of the world has become the kingdom of our Lord and of his Christ." But this was a future event at the time of this hymn, and the song John hears in 12:10f. seems to celebrate it as an accomplished fact. At this point the martyrdom has not occurred. Actually this chapter makes it plain that the persecution facing the church grew out of the wrath of the Devil, angered by the victory of Christ at his ascension. The great persecution was still to come, and it was a prelude to the final destruction of Satan. The problem must then be solved either (1) by considering the song as an anticipation of the ultimate triumph when the victory of the cross will be ratified by the victory won through martyrdom, or (2) by pointing to the union which the Christian has with the cross of Christ and the fact that he already shares in the "tribulation, and the kingdom, and the patient endurance" (1:9), so that the ultimate victory is already anticipated, and can thus be so described, in the victory of Christ on Calvary.

[12] The departure of the Devil from heaven is the occasion for joy in heaven. On the other hand, a **woe** is forecast for

Persecution by the Dragon   REV. 12:12-14

[13] **And when the dragon saw that he had been thrown down to the earth, he pursued the woman who had borne the male child.** [14] **But the woman was given the two wings of the great eagle that she might fly from the serpent into the wilderness, to the place where she is to be nourished for a time, and times, and half a time.**

---

the **earth and sea** (terms for the whole of the terrestrial world) because **the devil has come down to you**. Henceforth Satan's area of operation will be limited to the human inhabitants of this planet. The **woe** is compounded because the dragon is in great wrath. The occasion, of course, for his anger is his defeat at the hands of Christ and his knowledge that **his time is short**. The time of persecution (e.g., the time of the persecution of the two witnesses, 11:3) is limited. It is described in terms of Daniel's three and one-half years. Satan, too, already knew this. He will do his best in this period to destroy the church.

The War on Earth, 12:13-17. [13] In verse 6 John had described the flight of the **woman into the wilderness to a place prepared for her**, in which she would be **nourished for one thousand, two hundred and sixty days**. Now this scene is taken up and elaborated. It should be remembered that the **woman** has been interpreted, not literally as the Jewish church (the Christians are not strictly its seed) nor as the church of Christ (the Messiah was not out of her), but as the people of God in an ideal sense—the messianic community conceived in its continuity from Old Testament to New. When **the dragon** saw that he had been thrown down to earth, he pursued the woman who had borne the male child (the Christ, vs. 5). The word **pursued** is the ordinary word in the New Testament for hostile pursuit (Matt. 10:23; Acts 26:11) and then for "persecute" (Matt. 5:10ff.; Acts 7:52; Rom. 12:14). It is probably correct to see this persecution of the woman as the beginning of persecution of the church by the Roman Empire.

[14] Divine help protects the woman, though the story is told in the passive voice so that God is not named. She is given **the two wings of the great eagle that she might fly from the serpent into the wilderness**. The imagery here is connected

REV. 12:14-17 — *Exodus Typology*

¹⁵ The serpent poured water like a river out of his mouth after the woman, to sweep her away with the flood. ¹⁶ But the earth came to the help of the woman, and the earth opened its mouth and swallowed the river which the dragon had poured from his mouth. ¹⁷ Then the dragon was angry with the woman, and went off to make war on the rest of her offspring, on those who keep the commandments of God and bear testimony to Jesus. And he stood* on the sand of the sea.

_* Other ancient authorities read *And I stood*, connecting the sentence with 13:1

---

with an exodus typology which runs throughout the book. The Revelation begins with the renewal of the covenant promises of Israel (1:6; cf. Ex. 19:6) made at the exodus. The plagues of the trumpet series and the bowls are adaptations of the plagues of Egypt. Numerous other sections are understood similarly, including the crossing of the sea and the song of Moses (15:2f.). Even the typology of the dragon has obvious connections with this most important experience of the first Israel. Thus the eagle and the flight into the wilderness are based upon the statement of Exodus 19:4. In her place of safety the woman was nourished for **a time, and times, and half a time**. The period of time here is in the same form as in the book of Daniel, from which it is taken over (Dan. 7:25; 12:7). The expression in Hebrew means three and one-half years and is convertible to the expressions forty-two months and twelve hundred sixty days (11:2, 3). Here, as in chapter 11 (see notes there), it is the time of the persecution or martyrdom of the church, but **the earth** protects her.

[15-17] **The dragon** was angry and continued his assault on the **woman**, but he was unable to destroy God's people. The woman's **offspring** is an allusion to Genesis 3:15, with its assurance of triumph over the Tempter. The RSV's **bear testimony to Jesus** perhaps should be rendered "hold to the testimony borne by Jesus." This is more strictly parallel to the commandments of God and accords with other uses of the phrase in Revelation (1:2, 9; 19:10; but see 6:9 and 12:11 for testimony to Jesus).

The Two Great Beasts, 13:1-18. The next episode in the new drama of the little book reveals the worldly enemy of the

Beast from the Sea — REV. 13:1, 2

¹And I saw a beast rising out of the sea, with ten horns and seven heads, with ten diadems upon its horns and a blasphemous name upon its heads. ²And the beast that I saw was like a leopard, its feet were like a bear's, and its mouth was like a lion's mouth. And to it the dragon gave his power and his throne and great authority.

---

woman's seed. In the attempt to destroy the woman's seed the real enemy is Satan, the ancient dragon. But the visible earthly agent who carries on Satan's war against the saints now emerges. The student should remember that a proleptic vision of the work of this beast has already been seen. It was "the beast which rises out of the abyss" that killed the two witnesses in the vision of the measuring of the temple (11:7).

[1, 2] When the dragon was frustrated in his attempt to harm the woman in the wilderness, he went away to make war with the rest of her seed, and he stood on the sea to call up reinforcements. John then **saw a beast rising out of the sea**. The sea here should be equated with the great deep or the primeval ocean of the creation story, which (cf. Isa. 51:10; Job. 26:12; Hab. 3:8) is specifically identified with the monster Rahab. John intends the same identification here, as he has already forewarned by describing the beast in 11:7 as "rising out of the bottomless deep" (or the abyss). The further indication is that the monster has **seven heads**; for, while other features of the beast are reminiscent of Daniel's beasts, it is only in the description of the Old Testament monster Rahab or Leviathan that the seven or "many heads" are depicted (see comments on 12:3). But on the other hand, the seven heads stand for Roman emperors (17:10), and there was a local setting for the reference to the sea, because the representative of Rome, the proconsul, came to his province from the sea.

The beast is further described in deliberate imitation of Daniel's vision (7:2ff.). But there are also definite differences. John's vision contained one beast which is a composite of Daniel's first three. Daniel was told definitely that his beasts represented four empires (Dan. 7:17), and the fourth beast had ten horns, which represented ten kings who should arise as a part of the fourth kingdom.

REV. 13:1-3 *Blasphemous Name*

³ One of its heads seemed to have a mortal wound, but its mortal wound was healed, and the whole earth followed the beast with wonder.

The combining of the descriptive elements of the primeval monster, who is a personification of Satan, with those of the beast of Daniel's world empires seems to signify that the world force of John's day which was "to make war on the saints and overcome them" (vs. 7) was the reappearance (in type) of the ancient political antagonists of God's people. At the same time it affirms that such opposition is spiritual alignment with Satan, God's ancient enemy. John later (17:9, 12) identifies the seven heads as the seven kings (emperors) and the ten horns as ten kings. The seven heads also represented the seven hills of Rome. It seems clear that the first beast represents Imperial Rome, the ten diadems the allied subject kings through which the worldwide power was exercised (see comments on 16:14). Each of the beast's heads had a blasphemous name upon it, and this is likely a reference to the title *divus* or *theos* (the Latin and Greek titles for "God") placed upon the image of the emperors' heads on coins. Julius, Augustus, Claudius, Vespasian, and Titus had all been deified by the Roman Senate after their death, and some emperors used the titles during their lives. According to Suetonius (*Domitian* 13) Domitian had asked to be addressed as Lord and God (*Dominus et Deus*).

To this beast **the dragon gave his power and his throne and great authority.** Satan had claimed all the kingdoms of the world as his (Luke 4:6) and this was true, to the extent that world rulers apostatized from their divinely given purpose (Rom. 13:1ff.) and served Satan's aims. So he was called the ruler of this world (John 12:31; 14:30; 16:11). With this one may contrast the fact that Christ by right is declared the "ruler of the kings of the earth" (1:5) and ultimately is shown crowned with his "many diadems" (19:12). Here the war against the saints was of the Devil, but was waged through such agents as Nero and Domitian.

[3] If the **heads** represent the emperors, this does not mean that they were all bestial. John later will be told that in the person of the one ruling when he saw the vision of 17:1ff.

Nero Redivivus REV. 13:3

that "the beast is not." It was through **one of its heads** that the monster is typified. That head **seemed to have a mortal wound**. Its appearance (5:6) is something of a parody of Christ, "as though it had been slain." The beast had experienced, too, a kind of resurrection, having been "wounded by a sword and yet lived" (vs. 14). John could hardly be speaking merely of the death of this one head, for at the time of the vision of chapter 17 "five have fallen." Hence it is usually thought that the description refers to the head which exemplified the trait of the monster to make war on the saints (vs. 7). There had already been one head (or emperor), Nero, who did so. He had received his mortal wound (in his suicide) and had so ceased to represent the beast. Nor did his immediate successors do so. There was soon to come another beast (the eighth, of 17:11) who would so represent the beast once more. So John perceived the mortal wound as healed, so that the beast was able to persecute the church once more. Undoubtedly this referred to Domitian.

Many commentators see back of this figurative description the legend of *Nero redivivus*. After Nero died in A.D. 68, his body was given a state funeral, but many people refused to believe that he was dead. The legend became current that he had gone among the Parthians and was soon to return at the head of a Parthian army to destroy Rome. Tacitus reports that three imposters claimed to be Nero; two of these were received by the Parthians (*Hist*. 1:2; 2:8; see also Suetonius *Nero* 57). Dio Chrysostom (*Orat*. 21:9) knew of the myth and ridiculed it. But the myth was given currency among the Jews, some of whom took comfort that Nero's return would be the way in which Rome would be punished for the fall of Jerusalem (Ascension of Isaiah 4:2f.; Sibylline Oracles, 4:119, 138; 5:143ff., 362ff.). Whether (as seems likely) this idea furnished the imagery employed in John's vision or not, it is plain that John expects the persecuting policy of Nero to be revived by another head or emperor, as it was under Domitian. So Tertullian, "Consult your histories; you will there find that Nero was the first who assailed with the imperial sword the Christian sect ... Domitian, too, a man of Nero's type in cruelty, tried his hand at persecution" (*Apology*, ch. 5).

REV. 13:3-6 *Emperor Worship*

⁴Men worshiped the dragon, for he had given his authority to the beast, and they worshiped the beast, saying, "Who is like the beast, and who can fight against it?"

⁵And the beast was given a mouth uttering haughty and blasphemous words, and it was allowed to exercise authority for forty-two months; ⁶it opened its mouth to utter blasphemies against God, blaspheming his name and his dwelling, that is, those who dwell in heaven.

The whole earth followed the beast with wonder. In the earlier years the Caesars were given divine honors only after their death. The recognition of their deity in the provinces such as Asia represented the adoration of weary citizens for the peace and prosperity which the *pax romana* had brought. The inscriptions furnish many illustrations of thanks to the god Caesar for this safety. Cities vied with each other in erecting temples to Roma and the emperors and in assuming the title of "temple keeper" (*neokoros*) of the imperial gods. With the exception of the mad Caligula, Domitian seems to have been the first to demand the honor. In it all was a note of genuine wonder.

[4] But John wants it known that when the world **worshiped the dragon, they worshiped the beast**. The evil power behind this worship was the monster Satan himself. The exultation of the wondering multitude **Who is like the beast, and who can fight against it**? is an echo, probably an intentional parody, of the praise ascribed to God in the Old Testament (Ex. 15:11; Isa. 40:25; 46:15; Pss. 89:6-8; 113:5). Worship of such a depraved individual as a Nero or a Caligula or Domitian was indeed a travesty.

[5, 6] Daniel's picture of Antiochus Epiphanes, king of Syria who was to make war on the saints of Israel, has influenced John's description of his visions. Daniel said, "I looked then because of the sounds of the great words which the horn was speaking" and he "shall speak astonishing things against the God of gods" (Dan. 7:11; 11:36; cf. 7:8, 20), and the Roman emperors did the same. The **blasphemous words** are probably the titles and claims of deity. The beast was **allowed to exercise authority for forty-two months**. John expected a termination to the work of persecution as surely

Persecution Allowed REV. 13:5-8

⁷ Also it was allowed to make war on the saints and to conquer them.ᶠ **And authority was given it over every tribe and people and tongue and nation, ⁸ and all who dwell on earth will worship it, every one whose name has not been written before the foundation of the world in the book of life of the Lamb that was slain.**

ᶠ Other ancient authorities omit this sentence.

---

as he expected the persecution itself=the forty-two months=the three and one-half years=twelve hundred sixty days. The period of the beast's domination was the same as the woman's stay in the wilderness (12:6, 14), the prophesying with sackcloth of the two witnesses (11:3), or the trampling of the holy city (11:2; cf. Dan. 8:10f.).

[**7, 8**] John had been told that the Devil's rage at being cast out of heaven prompted him to go away **to make war on the saints** (12:17). This war, which is the persecution of the church, is one of the principal themes of Revelation. The imagery is based partly upon the second Psalm (the son who is to break the enemies with the rod of iron). Daniel 7:21 is also in view. The beast John sees **also was allowed to make war on the saints and to conquer them**. The people of Israel were overrun by Antiochus (as foreseen by Daniel); the saints of the new Israel as enemies of the emperor may expect to fall. In a similar way, the war was anticipated in the vision of the two witnesses (11:7), and here the second beast caused those who would not worship the image of the beast to be slain (13:15).

One important aspect here is that war was **allowed** and that the beast's apparent victory is given; that is, war and victory take place within the framework of God's control of the universe (cf. 6:4, 8, 11; 9:1-5; 13:5, 15; 16:8). God had his own purpose in permitting the persecution, just as he did the crucifixion of Christ. It has already been observed that part of that purpose was the conversion of the world (see comments on 11:13). This permission extended to giving the beast authority **over every tribe and people and tongue and nation** (the fourth time this phrase is used), which signifies that the Roman power was worldwide. **All who dwell on the earth** (cf. comments on 11:10; and use of this expression in

REV. 13:7-12 *Endurance and Faith*

⁹If any one has an ear, let him hear:
¹⁰If any one is to be taken captive,
to captivity he goes;
if any one slays with the sword,
with the sword must he be slain.
Here is a call for the endurance and faith of the saints.
¹¹Then I saw another beast which rose out of the earth; it had two horns like a lamb and it spoke like a dragon. ¹²It exercises all the authority of the first beast in its presence, and makes the earth and its inhabitants worship the first beast, whose mortal wound was healed.

3:10; 6:10; 8:13; 13:14; 17:2, 8) are identified as worshipers of the beast—those **whose names have not been written in the book of life**. For the significance of the latter, see 3:5.

[9, 10] If any one has an ear, let him hear serves as a serious call to attention and of warning to Christians (cf. the formula in the letters to the seven churches, chs. 2, 3). The warning is modeled after Jeremiah 15:2. Jesus added: **If any one slays with the sword, with the sword must he be slain** (Matt. 26:52). This is a warning against resisting the persecutor. God himself, who had given the beast power and who had his own purpose to be served in the persecution, saw resistance other than with the force of arms. In this crisis of persecution lay the **call for the endurance and faith of the saints**. In this struggle the church had its opportunity to work out its salvation through faithful endurance and submission to God's will (cf. 14:9-12, esp. vs. 12).

[11, 12] The second aspect of the dragon's helpers is now revealed: John **saw another beast which rose out of the earth**. It parodies the Lamb, for **it had two horns like a lamb**, suggesting innocence, if not actually weakness. However, from John's point of view, its real character is revealed when it **spoke like a dragon**. Just as the first beast was an ally to whom the dragon gave authority, so this beast was subordinate to the first. The beast received the authority, held it, and exercised it before the beast from the sea. This beast, then, was some one to whom the power or authority of the emperor was delegated. One candidate for this would be the proconsul sent yearly by the emperor to govern the province. But

Worship the Beast REV. 13:11-14

¹³It works great signs, even making fire come down from heaven to earth in the sight of men; ¹⁴and by the signs which it is allowed to work in the presence of the beast, it deceives those who dwell on earth, bidding them make an image for the beast which was wounded by the sword and yet lived;

another characteristic was that it **makes the earth and its inhabitants worship the first beast, whose mortal wound was healed**. This sponsorship of the deity of the emperor was rarely a role of the proconsuls.

One group that does come to mind was the provincial council, a group consisting of representatives from the important cities of Asia. The council was taken over by Augustus and became a model as a liaison governing group in other provinces. It should be remembered that in the first century religion was often a function of the state, and state officials usually doubled as priests or cult officials. The Asiarchs of Acts 19:31 were members of the provincial council and were probably priests in the cult of the emperor. This group, accustomed to honoring their former Greek kings as deity, led the way to deifying the emperor and are the group most likely to have taken it as their duty **to make the earth's inhabitants worship the first beast**.

[13] Another evidence of the character of the second beast was its involvement in prophetic wonder-working. It should be noted that the second beast is always referred to from this point in the book as the false prophet (16:2, 10, 13; 17:3ff.; 19:19, 20; 20:4, 10) because, in all probability, of its role in simulating the miracles wrought by true prophets (cf. Ex. 7:11f.; Mark 13:22; 2 Thess. 2:9; 2 Tim. 3:8). Such deceptive miracles were a characteristic of the power of Satan himself (12:9). One way of describing this power was to liken these priestly wonder-workers to Elijah, who had made **fire come down from heaven to earth**.

[14] The signs were done **in the presence of the beast**, that is, at the official state functions, with the Roman representatives, present and probably assisting. The result was that **it deceives those who dwell on earth** (see on 11:10). Any representation of the reigning Caesar which placed him before the people was an **image** (*eikon*). The representation might

REV. 13:14-17 *Mark of the Beast*

¹⁵ and it was allowed to give breath to the image of the beast so that the image of the beast should even speak, and to cause those who will not worship the image of the beast to be slain. ¹⁶ Also it causes all, both small and great, both rich and poor, both free and slave, to be marked on the right hand or the forehead, ¹⁷ so that no one can buy or sell unless he has the mark, that is, the name of the beast or the number of its name.

take the form of the head on coins, the image on a standard, or a statue. Busts or statues are probably intended here.

[15] A further description of the land beast's work was that it was allowed to make **the image of the beast speak**, a reference probably to ventriloquism or to the device, the means of which have been discovered by modern archaeologists, of piping the human voice beneath the altars bearing the statues of the gods. These and other forms of magic were widespread in the ancient world. Their purpose is explicitly stated as to cause those who will not worship the image of the beast to be slain.

[16, 17] The famous "mark of the beast" is next mentioned. The word **mark** (*charagma*) had a variety of meanings all including a symbol (in later writings, such as the sign of the cross); a letter of the alphabet so used; any mark, engraved, printed or branded; a letter of the alphabet or an impress of such, made by a stamp; an impress, as on coins. The practice of official stamping with the emperor's abbreviated name has been documented. The branding of slaves by ordinary owners, as well as by the emperors, is also documented. If the reference here were to coinage or to some sort of document certifying that the bearer had participated in worship at the emperor's shrine, the statement that the mark was necessary **to buy or sell** would be understood. But John refers to the mark put on the right hand or forehead of the worshiper, a practice for which there is no illustration besides the present mention. What the mark was is plain enough; this is shown by the appositive statement **the name or number of the beast**.

Most commentators doubt that John meant that the worshiper was literally stamped with the initials of the reigning emperor (or the numerical equivalent of it) and that this

REV. 13:16-18

¹⁸ This calls for wisdom: let him who has understanding reckon the number of the beast, for it is a human number, its number is six hundred and sixty-six.[g]

[g] Other ancient authorities read *six hundred and sixteen*.

---

stamp was required for trading in the markets of Asia. It is more likely that John's language is symbolic, the counterpart of the sealing or marking of the saints in chapter 7, which would hardly be taken literally. As the saints have the name of their God written on them (3:12), so those guilty of obeisance to the image of the emperor are marked before God and before the world. The text implies that any who were known to have refused so to worship may have been refused trade in the pagan markets. Certainly one who refused to use the money with the title of Caesar as a god on it would be effectively cut off from such trade. Thus the limitation on Christian participation may not have come from governmental decree so much as from Christian refusal to participate in the circumstances or requirements of such activities.

[18] John cryptically calls for the attention of the reader as if this is a special point around which the understanding of his message turns. **This calls for wisdom** (cf. 17:9). **The number of the beast . . . is a human number . . . six hundred and sixty-six.** John makes it plain by the combination of verses 17 and 18 that he is speaking of the name of a man; and, since it is clear that the beast represents the persecuting emperor, it seems equally clear that one of the Caesars is meant. Since he has already used the *Nero redivivus* symbol, implicating Nero and Domitian, the obvious question to ask, in interpretation, is whether either of these names will give the correct number. By number here is meant the practice of taking the letters of a name and giving them their numerical value, since both Greek and Hebrew used the letters of the alphabet as numerals. In Greek, for example, the letters *alpha* (a) through *iota* (i) stand for 1 through 10; the next letter, *kappa* (k), being 20; *lambda* (l) being 30, and so on. To each of these decimal numbers the first ten letters are added for the interdecimal numbers: ka=21, lg=33, etc. We can reckon the number of any name by putting down and adding the numerical values of its letters. It was a favorite game in

REV. 13:18–14:1 *Mount Zion*

¹ **Then I looked, and lo, on Mount Zion stood the Lamb, and with him a hundred and forty-four thousand who had his name and his Father's name written on their foreheads.**

---

ancient times to guess the name behind certain numbers. The reference here is complicated by the existence from early times of a textual variant reading six hundred sixteen instead of six hundred sixty-six. Either 666 or 616 may equal Nero Caesar (666 if the name is spelled from Hebrew or Aramaic; 616 from the Latin, with the *n* left off the *Neron*). The recent discovery of an Aramaic illustration of Nero Caesar spelled so as to equal 666 at Qumran gives credence to this as a solution. Given a Jewish background for many Christians and Greek Godfearers, it is not surprising that John should have adopted this riddle.

The Forces of the Lamb, 14:1-20. Opposite to the two beasts, the allies of the dragon, is now seen the army of God with its captain, the Lamb. A part of this picture is a series of announcements which reveal the eternal interests of mankind in the war. Three angels proclaim successively (vss. 6-13) the nearness of judgment, the fall of the great city Babylon, and the final destiny of eternal punishment for the worshipers of the beast. Two important corollaries are their summons to worship the Creator and the assurance of God's care for the faithful. Finally, there are the scenes of reaping and vintage (vss. 14-20), which many consider to be the judgment of Rome but which may represent the great martyrdom of the church.

[1] **Mount Zion** was the temple mount in Jerusalem and had become in the Old Testament a symbol of God's blessings and the security of God's people (Pss. 2:6; 48:1ff.; 78:54, 68; 87:1; 125:1; Isa. 28:16; 59:20; Micah 4:7; Obad. 17, 21). In the New Testament it is the city of the living God, representing the strong foundations of the unshakable kingdom (Heb. 12:22). As a prepared place, it is the counterpart of the place of safety in 12:6, 14.

The **Lamb** picks up references at 5:6; 7:17; 12:11 and 13:8 and contrasts with "like a lamb" in 13:11. The **one hundred and forty-four thousand** are the same as in 7:4 except the

Voice from Heaven REV. 14:1-4

²And I heard a voice from heaven like the sound of many waters and like the sound of loud thunder; the voice I heard was like the sound of harpers playing on their harps, ³and they sing a new song before the throne and before the four living creatures and before the elders. No one could learn that song except the hundred and forty-four thousand who had been redeemed from the earth. ⁴It is these who have not defiled themselves with women, for they are chaste;[h] it is these who follow the Lamb wherever he goes; these have been redeemed from mankind as first fruits for God and the Lamb,

[h] Greek *virgins*

---

tribal distinctions are no longer in view. They are the martyrs out of the total number of the redeemed (7:9). In direct contrast to the mark of the beast (13:17) they have the **name** of the Lamb and of the Father **on their foreheads** (cf. Ezek. 9:4; Rev. 3:12; 22:4). The divine name on **the forehead** suggests at once the imparting of a character which corresponds to the mind of God and a consecration to his service.

[2, 3] The description of the sound is found again in 19:6 and is based on Ezekiel 1:24 and 43:2. For the great thunder, compare Revelation 1:15 and for the harps, 5:8. The sound was like **many** (rushing) **waters** in volume, **loud thunder** in its intensity, and harp music in its melody. The **new song** was a common phrase in the Old Testament to celebrate God's ever-new acts of salvation (Pss. 33:3; 40:3; 96:1; 98:1; 144:9; 149:1; Isa. 42:10). It is used for the song of the **four creatures** and twenty-four **elders** in 5:9 (cf. the song of the martyrs in 15:3).

[4] The description of the hundred and forty-four thousand which follows is meant partly to identify them in terms of their role in the continuing narrative and partly to admonish the readers concerning the character of those who are to attain to the promises. Despite the addition of the term **with women** after they **have not defiled themselves,** it seems strange that some commentators take this as referring to their being literally virgins. In the Old Testament sexual intercourse did leave one ceremonially unfit for certain kinds of service to God for certain periods of time (Ex. 19:15; Lev.

⁵ **and in their mouth no lie was found, for they are spotless.**

15:16; 1 Sam. 21:4), and especially was this true for waging a holy war (Deut. 23:9, 10). If the passage is taken literally, it should be seen as referring to violations of God's ordinances concerning marriage so prevalent in pagan society rather than as a repudiation of marriage. But it is probably more nearly correct to take the passage figuratively and refer to 2 Corinthians 11:2, where Christians are described as a chaste virgin espoused to one husband (Christ).

Furthermore, they **follow the Lamb wherever he goes.** Jesus' call to discipleship was "follow me" (Mark 2:14; 10:21; Luke 9:59; John 1:43; 21; 19). This involved a total self-commitment even to breaking normal ties (Matt. 8:22; Luke 9:61f.) and involved a participation in Christ's salvation (Mark 10:17, 21) or eternal life (John 8:12). Jesus further said in Mark 8:34 that anyone who wished to come after him must deny himself and take his cross and follow him. Probably the words here indicate participation in Jesus' suffering by a martyr's death (see John 12:25f.).

Next, the hundred and forty-four thousand were redeemed (or purchased) **from mankind as first fruits**, interpreting the **redeemed** of verse 3 and reflecting the earlier praise ascribed to Jesus as the one who purchased men with his blood (5:9). It is the Lamb's great achievement that his death (blood) ransomed those destined to become his own. But this purchase merges into the thought of full dedication to God and Christ—they are redeemed as **first fruits**. In Numbers 15:20f. Israel was to take the common bread of the land and eat, provided a portion of it was offered as a wave offering to God, thus consecrating the whole to him. This figure is frequently caught up by New Testament writers (Rom. 11:16; 1 Cor. 16:15; James 1:18). John may here be anticipating the picture of the harvest in verses 14-20.

[**5**] Finally, they are those in whose mouth **no lie was found.** This pictures another facet of the righteous man who is to dwell in God's holy mount (Ps. 15:1ff.; cf. Zeph. 3:13, a passage describing the faithful remnant of Israel). Like purity (vs. 4), truthfulness is a distinctive characteristic of the fol-

Eternal Gospel REV. 14:5-8

⁶Then I saw another angel flying in midheaven, with an eternal gospel to proclaim to those who dwell on earth, to every nation and tribe and tongue and people; ⁷and he said with a loud voice, "Fear God and give him glory, for the hour of his judgment has come; and worship him who made heaven and earth, the sea and the fountains of water."

⁸Another angel, a second, followed, saying, "Fallen, fallen is Babylon the great, she who made all nations drink the wine of her impure passion."

---

lowers of Christ, but refers here, more specifically perhaps, to the absence of compromise by those who become martyrs. The vision of the Lamb's followers ties in with the suffering servant concept of Isaiah 53:7 (cf. use made in 1 Peter 2:23). **Spotless** refers to the absence of blemishes which would render a sacrifice unfit. John may also be saying that the Lamb's followers share not only the character of their Lord, but also his fate.

[6, 7] The **eternal gospel** is not some new gospel or latter-day revelation. It is the same gospel of the death and resurrection of Christ (1 Cor. 15:1-4) which the one hundred and forty-four thousand had received and which was to be preached to all men (Luke 24:47). Here it is addressed **to those who dwell on earth** (cf. 8:13; 13:7f.). These are they who have opposed God and his people, for the redeemed are to come from **every nation, tribe, tongue, and people** (7:9). They are called upon to **fear God and give him glory,** words used by John to express response to the gospel in repentance and **worship** to God (11:13; 15:4; contrast 16:9). The need for obedience to the gospel is seen in the fact that **the hour of** God's **judgment has come.** John's Gospel uses the phrase "the hour is coming" or "has come" in reference to the judgment of Jesus' death and resurrection (John 12:23, 31f.; 13:1; 16:32; 17:1; cf. 5:24f.). Even so, the **judgment** here may refer to the death of the martyrs (John 16:2) as a time of decision for men.

[8] The fall of **Babylon** is announced in words adopted from Isaiah 21:9 (cf. Jer. 51:6-10; Isa. 51:21-23; Rev. 17:2). The far-reaching effect of Babylon's (Rome's) vileness and corruption is recalled in the figure that she made **all nations**

REV. 14:8-13 *Cup of Wrath*

⁹And another angel, a third, followed, saying with a loud voice, "If any one worships the beast and its image, and receives a mark on his forehead or on his hand, ¹⁰he also shall drink the wine of God's wrath, poured unmixed into the cup of his anger, and he shall be tormented with fire and sulphur in the presence of the holy angels and in the presence of the Lamb. ¹¹And the smoke of their torment goes up for ever and ever; and they have no rest, day or night, these worshipers of the beast and its image, and whoever receives the mark of its name."

¹²Here is a call for the endurance of the saints, those who keep the commandments of God and the faith of Jesus.

¹³And I heard a voice from heaven saying, "Write this: Blessed are the dead who die in the Lord henceforth." "Blessed indeed," says the Spirit, "that they may rest from their labors, for their deeds will follow them!"

---

drink the wine of impure passion. It becomes, however, for those who partake the "wine of God's wrath" and "the cup of his anger" (vs. 10). Verse 8 anticipates the fuller account of chapter 18.

[9-11] The **third angel** of the present series pronounces **torment** to those who do not respond to the gospel (vss. 6, 7) but continue to **worship the beast and its image** (13:4, 12, 15, 16). **To drink the cup of God's wrath** is a frequent Old Testament figure for punishment (Ps. 75:8; Isa. 51:17; Jer. 25:15; cf. Matt. 20:22; 26:39). Since wine was served as a table drink mixed with water, unmixed wine refers to God's anger in its full strength, or undiluted. **Fire and sulphur** alludes to the destruction of Sodom and Gomorrah (Gen. 19:24; cf. Ezek. 38:22; Isa. 34:9f.; Matt. 25:41). The fate of those who worship the beast is described further: torment . . . for ever and ever . . . no rest, . . .

[12, 13] Parallels to chapter 13 continue in the **call for the endurance of the saints** (13:10), who **keep the commandments** and **the faith** (2:13; 12:17). Unlike the worshipers of the beast (vs. 11), these shall have **rest.** They may **die in the Lord** as martyrs in the upcoming persectuion, **but their deeds follow them.**

Harvest REV. 14:14-20

[14] Then I looked, and lo, a white cloud, and seated on the cloud one like a son of man, with a golden crown on his head, and a sharp sickle in his hand. [15] And another angel came out of the temple, calling with a loud voice to him who sat upon the cloud, "Put in your sickle, and reap, for the hour to reap has come, for the harvest of the earth is fully ripe." [16] So he who sat upon the cloud swung his sickle on the earth, and the earth was reaped.

[17] And another angel came out of the temple in heaven, and he too had a sharp sickle. [18] Then another angel came out from the altar, the angel who has power over fire, and he called with a loud voice to him who had the sharp sickle, "Put in your sickle, and gather the clusters of the vine of the earth, for its grapes are ripe." [19] So the angel swung his sickle on the earth and gathered the vintage of the earth, and threw it into the great wine press of the wrath of God; [20] and the wine press was trodden outside the city, and blood flowed from the wine press, as high as a horse's bridle, for one thousand six hundred stadia.[j]

[j] About two hundred miles.

[**14-20**] The present scene represents one of the most difficult of all to interpret. The **harvest** of the wheat and the **vintage** of the grape are widely used in the Old Testament as symbols of God's judgment or destruction, either of Israel or her enemies (Joel 3:9-14; Hos. 6:11; Lam. 1:15; Jer. 51:33; Isa. 63:1-6). Thus many commentators see this as a double of the apocalyptic announcement of the impending doom of the beast. Others see the visions as portraying the end, with the **harvest** the ingathering of the righteous, and the **vintage** the wicked.

On the other hand, it has been suggested that the scenes really portray the beginning of the great martyrdom which John had predicted would soon come upon the whole earth. That persecution had been depicted in the first half of the Revelation by the death of the two witnesses, followed by the judgment scene at the seventh trumpet in which the "destroyers of the earth" were destroyed (11:3-13, 18). The harvest scene would parallel these events in the second half of the visions. Considerations of order have some bearing on the question. If the interpretation of martyrdom is not true, then the martyrdom, which is one of the main subjects of the Apocalypse, is passed over in the second half. Too, the martyrdom's being described here would put it in the proper place in the sequence of the visions: In chapter 13 the battle lines are drawn up between the dragon and his beastly helpers on the one hand, the Lamb and his followers on the other (ch. 14). The harvest scene comes just after this array and just before the victory song by the martyrs in heaven (ch. 15), which victory precedes the judgment on the beast in the bowls of wrath and the destruction of the city (ch. 16). The greatest difficulty in this interpretation lies with the **wine press** viewed as **the wrath of God** (vs. 19). The item which seems to make the view possible is the reference to the event as transpiring **outside the city** (vs. 20) of the world where the Lord was crucified (11:8; 14:8); on the other hand, if the city is Zion (vs. 1), then the judgment interpretation would be correct. With some hesitation, the view that the great martyrdom is being described is adopted here.

The scene opens with John seeing a white cloud with Jesus seated like a son of man (cf. Dan. 7:13). On Jesus' head is a golden crown, probably emphasizing that the martyrdom is a sovereign decision of the Lord himself. It has been emphasized throughout that whatever happens, it is because it has been "given" or "permitted." References to the death of the saints have made it plain that their death will also take place according to his plan and that it will take place for a purpose.

It is strange that an angel gives to the one **on the cloud** the command **"Put in your sickle, and reap . . ."** This probably implies that the signal comes from the Father, who is at one with the Son in what is to happen. So he who sat upon the cloud **swung his sickle on the earth, and the earth was reaped.** The words **harvest** and **reap** are not used of **judgment** in the Old Testament. Jesus uses them for an earthly ingathering of men (Matt. 9:31f.; Mark 4:29; Luke 10:2; John 4:35-38). Added weight is given to the great martyrdom interpretation by the mention of the "first fruits" in 14:4. This identifies the faithful with God's **harvest** (in the Old Testament the first fruits of both grain and wine were offered to God, Ex. 22:29).

Seven Plagues REV. 15:1

¹ **Then I saw another portent in heaven, great and wonderful, seven angels with seven plagues, which are the last, for with them the wrath of God is ended.**

The Song of Moses and the Lamb, 15:1-8. Although the theme of this section of the Revelation is the war of the Lamb with the beast (12:7, 17; 13:7; 16:14; cf. 11:7), there is no prolonged description of such a war. The martyrdom of the saints is referred to along with the declaration that that martyrdom is the means, together with the previous death of Christ, of the victory over the beast (12:11). The martyrdom is probably pictured, as we have seen, in the reaping scene (14:14-20). Now to be shown are the judgments meted out by God upon the beast. This is climaxed in 16:19 with the destruction of "the great city" (Rome). Before the judgments, a prelude is given—the martyrs are seen singing the song of Moses and the Lamb.

[1] The visions of 12:1—16:21 are held together by the use of the word **portent** ("sign" or "wonder"), which in this sense is limited to this section of Revelation (12:1, 3; 15:1). The other (*allo*) similar sign was **seven angels with seven plagues.** The plagues are the judgments to be visited upon the city. They are called plagues because the entire section is seen as the antitype of the exodus of Israel (cf. plagues, crossing the sea, engulfing [conquering] the beast, cf. Isa. 51:10; Ezek. 29:3, the song of Moses, tent of testimony, smoke of Sinai). The plagues are symbolically seven, because they are the last (cf. 21:9). The term **last** marks these plagues as the concluding series upon Rome in contrast to former partial judgments intended as a call to repentance. It does not mean that they are the final cosmic display of God's wrath in the age. John's visions do telescope the judgment upon the beast with the end time (see comment on 11:18), but John does not expect the world to end with Rome. Her spectators will survive her (18:15, 20), and John's visions contemplate an additional span of time before the end (see comment on 20:4, 8). The time was to come when all hope of repentance by those who defiantly blasphemed God was gone. These are the last plagues upon the pagan city of Rome.

REV. 15:2-4 *New Exodus*

²And I saw what appeared to be a sea of glass mingled with fire, and those who had conquered the beast and its image and the number of its name, standing beside the sea of glass with harps of God in their hands. ³And they sing the song of Moses, the servant of God, and the song of the Lamb, saying,
"Great and wonderful are thy deeds,
  O Lord God the Almighty!
  Just and true are thy ways,
  O king of the ages!ʲ
⁴Who shall not fear and glorify thy name, O Lord?
  For thou alone art holy.
  All nations shall come and worship thee,
  for thy judgments have been revealed."

ʲ Other ancient authorities read *the nations*.

---

[2] Before the **seven angels** delivered their plagues, the martyrs who had conquered the beast and its image are seen **standing beside the sea of glass.** This is certainly the pavement sea extending before the heavenly throne, which has been interpreted as the cosmic reservoir of evil, the habitation of the dragon (4:6). The martyrs have passed through this sea, and it is **red (mingled with fire)** from their blood. Their death represents their exodus from spiritual Egypt (11:8), as the following song shows. They stand with **harps,** probably identifying them with the hundred and forty-four thousand of the Lamb's army (14:2). Their names are "the conquering ones" (cf. the recurring designation in chapters 2 and 3), indicative of their abiding character.

This in some way is the answer to the cry of the martyrs under the altar (ch. 6). There they were told to await the full number of the victims. Now that their number is complete, the martyrs see the eternal outcome of their faith. They are here also seen to have fulfilled the role outlined for them by the angel of the proclamation (14:4-7). By their lives they have preached the eternal gospel.

[3, 4] After the Old Testament exodus from the Red Sea, "Then Moses and the people of Israel sang this song to the Lord" (Ex. 15:1ff.). Israel had long since learned to use this incident to construct a theology of God's continuing

Song of the Lamb REV. 15:3-6

⁵ After this I looked, and the temple of the tent of witness in heaven was opened, ⁶ and out of the temple came the seven angels with the seven plagues, robed in pure bright linen, and their breasts girded with golden girdles.

---

salvation (Ps. 106:6-12, 47). That song of Moses (with different words to suit the present circumstances) is now sung by the martyrs who have passed through their sea. The conquerors by their martyrdom have overcome Domitian and have their share of the victory of Christ over the beast (12:11); hence the song they sing is also **the song of the Lamb.** The song which extols the **great and wonderful deeds of the Lord God the Almighty** is a chain of quotations from several Old Testament passages constructed as a joyful anthem predicting the future universal dominion of the Lord: **all nations shall come and worship thee.** The resurrection of the witness/prophets (the triumph through their death?) has previously been seen as the occasion for the "giving of glory to the God of heaven" (11:13). God is praised as the rightful king of the nations, the one whose ways are just and true, who alone is holy. The martyrs see God as ultimately enjoying his rightful sovereignty as he is universally acknowledged. One may ask what **ways** and **judgments** are in view. This justification of the ways of God to men refers to God's decree that the victory being heralded was to be won by the death of the saints. Only after the martyrs are beyond the pale of existence and see the purpose of God could they sing this song.

[5, 6] The exodus typology is continued by the reference to the opening of **the temple of the tent of witness,** which was built by the Israelites at Sinai after the crossing of the Red Sea. Once before (11:19) at the end of the judgments the ark of the covenant had appeared. In that case the symbolism probably is connected with the Old Testament custom of assuring victory to the hosts of Israel by preceding the army with the ark and the seven trumpets, thus signifying the presence of the Lord. Now the **testimony** (the law hid in the ark within the holy of holies) is featured. God's righteous judgments and ordinances are to have their way. The

REV. 15:5-8 *Seven Bowls*

⁷And one of the four living creatures gave the seven angels seven golden bowls full of the wrath of God who lives for ever and ever; ⁸and the temple was filled with smoke from the glory of God and from his power, and no one could enter the temple until the seven plagues of the seven angels were ended.

---

holiness of the agents of divine wrath is emphasized by their being robed in linen and girt about with gold girdles.

[7, 8] The signal for the judgments to begin is the traditional dramatic technique of handing over the instruments to the agents of destruction. **One of the four living creatures gave to the seven angels the seven bowls full of the wrath of the eternal God.**

The **smoke** recalls that of the divine presence at the dedication of the tent of meeting in the wilderness (Ex. 40:34; cf. Ezek. 44:4). The determined council of God which has decreed the great city's destruction is probably represented by the fact that **no one could enter the temple until the seven plagues were ended.**

The Plagues upon the Great City, 16:1-21. The preparation over, the time for pouring out the seven bowls of the wrath of God upon the earth has come. The series of bowls closely resembles that of the seven trumpets of the first section of the Revelation (chs. 8 and 9), where the same natural elements are affected. The exodus typology is carried further. The number of the plagues is reduced to seven to preserve the symbolism of these bowls as the "last" (15:1) plagues on Rome. But there are significant differences from the trumpet series. In the former series the plagues were mostly upon the natural world and did not hurt men, nor were they universal. But these are the last plagues upon Rome, and men are attacked from the outset. The punishments are punitive and final, not merely calling men to repentance. The blows increase in intensity and climax in the dethronement of the emperor, the invasion of the empire from beyond its borders, and the final earthquake signifying the dividing and fall of the city and its allies.

Plagues REV. 16:1-6

¹ Then I heard a loud voice from the temple telling the seven angels, "Go and pour out on the earth the seven bowls of the wrath of God."

² So the first angel went and poured his bowl on the earth, and foul and evil sores came upon the men who bore the mark of the beast and worshiped its image.

³ The second angel poured his bowl into the sea, and it became like the blood of a dead man, and every living thing died that was in the sea.

⁴ The third angel poured his bowl into the rivers and the fountains of water, and they became blood. ⁵ And I heard the angel of water say,

"Just art thou in these thy judgments,
thou who art and wast, O Holy One.
⁶ For men have shed the blood of saints
    and prophets,
and thou hast given them blood to drink.
It is their due!"

[1, 2] **The loud voice from the temple** commanding **the seven angels** to go and **pour out on the earth the seven bowls of the wrath of God** is presumably the voice of God himself. When the first angel does so, **foul and evil sores,** the counterpart of the plague of boils in the Egyptian plagues, come upon men. Thus men are affected in this series from the start. The judgments are particularly to Rome, and not general natural disasters in which all suffer, because the boils come **upon the men who bore the mark of the beast and worshiped its image** (cf. vs. 6).

[3, 4] The **second** and **third angels** affect the water, first of **the sea** and then the fresh water **rivers and fountains** of waters, by turning them to blood (cf. 8:8f.). This again resembles the plagues of Egypt (the first, turning the water of the Nile to blood, Ex. 7:20). Probably the plagues symbolize the disasters which would befall the citizens of the empire just before and during the destruction of the great city. There is precedent in the Old Testament (Ps. 78:39ff.) for use of the plagues of Egypt as typical reminders of the way God deals with his enemies.

[5, 6] It was a common idea in Jewish thought that all

REV. 16:5-11 *God's Judgments*

⁷And I heard the altar cry,
"Yea, Lord God the Almighty,
true and just are thy judgments!"

⁸The fourth angel poured his bowl on the sun, and it was allowed to scorch men with fire; ⁹men were scorched by the fierce heat, and they cursed the name of God who had power over these plagues, and they did not repent and give him glory.

¹⁰The fifth angel poured his bowl on the throne of the beast, and its kingdom was in darkness; men gnawed their tongues in anguish ¹¹and cursed the God of heaven for their pain and sores, and did not repent of their deeds.

---

the natural elements had their guardian angels (1 Enoch 60:17, 19, 21; 61:10), an idea which John had utilized before (7:1; 14:18). Now one of the angels, **the angel of water,** becomes the spokesman for the others to approve as just the sentence which is administered to Rome. Rome is being repaid in kind. She has shed the **blood of saints and prophets.** Thus the men responsible for the shedding of the blood of the martyrs are to receive their due in the rebellious wars which will precede the end of the city. It is plainly predicted that such wars were to be the means of the destruction of the city (16:12ff; 17:15-16). The expression **saints and prophets** (11:18; 18:24) refers to the loyal Christians and their leaders of the prophetic order (for the latter, see Acts 11:27, 13:1; 1 Cor. 12:28f.; 14:3; Eph. 2:20; 3:5; 4:11).

[7] The **altar** joins in the proclamation of God's true and just judgments, thus reinforcing the approval given by the angels of the natural forces.

[8, 9] The pouring out of the **fourth bowl on the sun** sees a new plague—one not a part of the exodus plagues. While the followers of the beast are **scorched by the fierce heat** so that **they curse God,** John describes the condition of the righteous martyrs as one in which "the sun shall not strike them, nor any scorching heat" (17:16; cf. 21:23; 22:5). At any point along the line of destructive events, men could have repented, had they not taken on themselves the nature of the beast to the extent that repentance was impossible.

[10, 11] The other plagues had affected the people of the empire as a whole. Now the **fifth** plague afflicts **the throne of**

Babylon REV. 16:10-14

¹² **The sixth angel poured his bowl on the great river Euphrates, and its water was dried up, to prepare the way for the kings from the east. ¹³ And I saw, issuing from the mouth of the dragon and from the mouth of the beast and from the mouth of the false prophet, three foul spirits like frogs; ¹⁴ for they are demonic spirits, performing signs, who go abroad to the kings of the whole world, to assemble them for battle on the great day of God the Almighty.**

---

the beast, that is, the very seat and center of the empire, the city of Rome, and plunges it into darkness like that of Egypt's ninth plague (Ex. 10:21ff.). This is a premonition of the end reached in verse 19. The plague was severe; **men gnawed their tongues in anguish and cursed God**. As in the previous plague men **did not repent**.

[12] With the pouring out of the **sixth bowl** the great **river Euphrates** is **dried up**. Again the Old Testament typology of Babylon is brought into play. The prophet Jeremiah had foreseen that the waters of Babylon would dry up and cause her downfall (Jer. 50:38). This plague is parallel to the sixth trumpet (9:13ff.) in which armies from beyond the river invade the empire. Ultimately the imagery is probably dependent, as in other places, on the very real dread in the Roman world of the eastern Parthian forces. But it is connected also with the expectation based upon Ezekiel 38-39 of the invasion of the kings of the earth. Jewish apocalyptic literature had expressed the expectation of these kings as the means of punishing Rome. The ensuing battle is the same as that of 14:14; 19:11-21 and resembles that of 20:7-10.

[13, 14] That Rome, the latter-day Egypt, is the object of these plagues is indicated by **the frogs** which John saw **issuing from the mouth of the dragon and from the mouth of the beast and from the mouth of the false prophet**. There is no mention of **frogs** in any of the imagery of the Old Testament background of the passages on the war. It is a part of the vision to maintain the typology of the exodus, as the frogs constituted the second plague (Ex. 8:2). This is the first mention of the **false prophet**, but by his association with the **beast** he is most certainly the same as the second or land beast of 13:11ff. The **frogs** may represent the false claims, and the propaganda

¹⁵ ("Lo, I am coming like a thief! Blessed is he who is awake, keeping his garments that he may not go naked and be seen exposed!")

---

of the empire and its cult, which were destined to flood the world and eventually provoke the kings of the earth into hatred and destruction of Rome. It needs to be remembered that a part of the expectation of Rome's coming troubles was the belief in the *Nero redivivus* myth (see comments on 13:3). Though this was legend (Nero was not alive), John was utilizing the fear and prophesying the eventual downfall of Rome through the spirit represented by this apprehension.

Here, as elsewhere in the New Testament, the impluse and manifestation of false worship and false doctrine have their origin in unclean spirits or demons (1 Tim. 4:1). The frogs, representing such evil influences, manifested themselves outwardly in signs (false miracles, trickery such as ventriloquy and sleight of hand). The kings were gathered for the final battle to decide the fate of Rome. John will later explain that the ten kings, (probably representing Rome's allies and subject kings, 13:3) will come to "hate the harlot; they will make her desolate and naked, and devour her flesh and burn her up with fire" (17:7-16).

The battle which the vision foretells is brought about by the sovereignty of God. "For God has put it in their hearts to carry out his purpose" (17:17). Similarly, the great battle is that of the great day of God the Almighty. Here is one of the real keys to John's expectations. The destruction of Rome is an event of such cosmic importance that it can be spoken of in terms of the "day of God (Yahweh)" (cf. also 6:17). Although this term is sometimes used of the eschatological end of the world, it is also applied to events in Israel's history which, though of supreme importance, did not imply the inauguration of the last time. In these cases there was simply a prophecy of a catastrophe or a deliverance which would take place in a conceivable time (cf. Lam. 1:21). The overthrow of Jerusalem, for example, was such a day (Ezek. 34:12).

[15] It is in keeping with the context—as a warning of the approaching doom to interpose a blessing upon the one **who**

Armageddon REV. 16:15, 16

¹⁶ **And they assembled them at the place which is called in Hebrew Armageddon.**

---

is awake and prepared for the judgment on Rome, likened to the Lord's final coming as a thief (1 Thess. 5:2-10; Matt. 24:42-44; 2 Peter 3:10).

[16] This symbolic reference to **Armageddon** is not easily explained. Either "city" or "mount" Mageddon is possible, with "mountain" probably preferred. John has used symbols before which presuppose some knowledge of Hebrew (e.g., "abaddon" in 11:11 and the number of the name of the beast in 13:18). He could surely expect his readers also to know something of the history of the region near Megiddo. The plain (Esdraelon) stretching out from this city had been the scene of many major battles (Judges 4, 5; 2 Kings 9:27; 23:29ff.; 2 Chron. 35:22). This plain had already been associated with the war of the Day of God (Zech. 12:1ff.). In this passage, elements of which are based upon the Gog and Magog invasion of Ezekiel 38-39, Zechariah had also seen the nations round about lay siege to Jerusalem only to be laid waste by God. Following this, Zechariah spoke of God's salvation of Israel and the mourning for one "who has been pierced." In that day says the prophet, "There shall be a great mourning in Jerusalem, as the mourning of Hadadrimmon in the valley of Megiddon." Thus Megiddo is associated in prophecy with a great mourning and lamentation of Jerusalem in the days of the great battle of the end time. Remembering that Jerusalem, in the eyes of the Revelation, has become a symbolic name for Rome (11:8) may give the key to this obscure symbolic name for the place of the decisive battle. The only thing not entirely straight is the mention here of the "mountain" of Megiddo, whereas in Zechariah and elsewhere it is "plain." Megiddo is actually a city at the entrance to the plain in the foothills of the Carmel range. The switch may have been made because of the Old Testament viewpoint which places the final battle upon a mountain (Ezek. 39:2, 4; cf. the destroying mountain of Jer. 51:25, where the enemy was to be defeated). At any rate, the name is an apocalyptic symbol—the battle is to take place at Rome and result in her downfall (see also 19:11-21).

REV. 16:17-19　　　　　　　　　　　　　　　*Earthquakes*

¹⁷ **The seventh angel poured his bowl into the air, and a loud voice came out of the temple, from the throne, saying, "It is done!"** ¹⁸ **And there were flashes of lightning, voices, peals of thunder, and a great earthquake such as had never been since men were on the earth, so great was that earthquake.** ¹⁹ **The great city was split into three parts, and the cities of the nations fell, and God remembered great Babylon, to make her drain the cup of the fury of his wrath.**

---

[17] When the **seventh angel poured** out **his bowl**, a **voice**, evidently the voice of God himself, from the throne announced, **"It is done!"** The bowl series had begun with the announcement that these seven bowls would finish the wrath of God. John had seen the forces gathered against Rome. The battle itself is never shown, but the climax is reached. The prophecy of the angel flying in midheaven—"Babylon is fallen" (14:8)—is now complete. The tense of the verb refers to an accomplished fact which abides (cf. 21:6).

[18] Though John is speaking of a political disaster, the fall of Rome, he uses the customary prophetic cosmic natural figures to describe it. Thus there are **lightning, voices, and peals of thunder** (cf. 8:5; 11:19), **and the great earthquake** (compare on 6:12-17). The term **earthquake** has been one of John's favorite symbols for the overthrow of Rome (6:12 and esp. the parallel climax with 11:13, 19), as it had been for the prophets of Israel in their announcements of doom for Israel's enemies (Isa. 13:13; 24:20; Jer. 51:29) and even for Israel itself (Amos 8:8). But the familiar has here individual distinctiveness. Not even the fall of Babylon had the repercussions of that of Rome!

[19] The earthquake opened great fissures or holes in the earth; the great city (Rome) was split into three parts. This is a way of spelling out the complete disruption of the city. But along with Rome, the cities of the nations (her allies) fell. Babylon is remembered for her deed (cf. 18:3), and she is made to **drain the cup of the fury of his wrath** (cf. 14:10; 18:3, 6, as well as the Old Testament passages like Jer. 25:15; Isa. 51:17, 22, whence the concept is derived).

Hailstones REV. 16:20, 21

[20] And every island fled away, and no mountains were to be found; [21] and great hailstones, heavy as a hundredweight, dropped on men from heaven, till men cursed God for the plague of the hail, so fearful was that plague.

---

[20] After the statement of the fall of the city and her allies, John resumes the description in figures of natural convulsion. **Every island fled away, and no mountains were to be found.** These had figured in the vision of premonition of ruin at the opening of the sixth seal (6:12-17). They are the natural results of earthquakes. Again this is symbolic, but there may have been reasons for the choice of figures. Besides the fact that the mountain was a long-used symbol for a government, there is the association of idolatrous worship with mountain tops or "high places"; and lastly, Rome was well known for her place atop the seven hills (17:9).

[21] Finally, **great hailstones** were rained upon men. This element of natural calamity is included evidently to complete the sevenfold application of the plagues of Egypt (Ex. 9:22). Though Babylon falls, men on whom the plagues fall survive to curse God. One may assume that the end of the world follows here as it did in 11:15ff. after the seventh trumpet and as it certainly does in 19:5-10 following the more detailed destruction of the city. Although John thus telescoped the destruction of Rome with the end, it is equally clear that he did not expect the end with that event (Rome's survivors "curse God for the plague," 16:11; her spectators mourn her passing, 18:11ff.). Such is conventional apocalyptic language. Cosmic end-time language was the usual prophetic way of such picturing of the destruction of a city or nation (end of Israel, Amos 8:2; end of Jerusalem, Jer. 5:31; end of Babylon, Jer. 51:13; end of Antiochus, Dan 12:7; 11:40). Thus John is in the prophetic tradition when he uses such cosmic apocalyptic language to convey the significance of the great historical crisis which the church of his day faced. John simply believed that Rome, in allowing herself to become the tool of the dragon and changing herself into the beast which demanded divine honors, was preparing her own doom.

REV. 17:1, 2 *Third Major Vision*

¹ **Then one of the seven angels who had the seven bowls came and said to me, "Come, I will show you the judgment of the great harlot who is seated upon many waters, ² with whom the kings of the earth have committed fornication, and with the wine of whose fornication the dwellers on earth have become drunk."**

THE VISION OF JUDGMENT OF THE GREAT HARLOT
17:1—21:8

The third major division of the book of Revelation, like the first and second (cf. 1:10 and 4:1), is set off by the phrase "in the Spirit" (17:3). John is invited by one of the angels of the seven bowls to view "the judgment of the great harlot." As the first vision disclosed the condition of the seven churches for the great tribulation and as the second has given an explanation of martyrdom by revealing the nature and purpose of the church's suffering, so the present section will explain the cause of the fall of the mythical Babylon (Rome) and will give a detailed picture of its destruction (17:1–19:4).

The section is not exhausted, however, by the fall of Rome. Several other stories follow that further reveal the future of the church. Some of the major themes are the marriage supper of the Lamb (19:5-10), the war between Christ and the Beast (repeated, 19:11-21), the binding of Satan and the thousand-year reign (20:1-6), Gog and Magog (20:7-10), the last judgment (20:11-15), and the heavenly city (21:1-9). This division culminates in the end, though it repeats, in greater detail, Rome's fall (6:12-17; 11:15-19; 15:5–16:21).

Identity of the Woman and the Beast, 17:1-18

The first section of the vision of judgment on the woman consists of material intended to make clear the identification of the city of Rome, the center of the empire, as the woman and the empire as the beast.

John Carried into the Wilderness, 17:1-6. [1, 2] That the vision of the destruction of the great harlot (chs. 17, 18) is a greater elaboration of the fall of Babylon, just

Identity of the Great Harlot REV. 17:1, 2

announced by means of the seven bowls of wrath, seems to be indicated by the fact that **one of the seven angels who had the seven bowls** now comes to John and says, "**Come, I will show you the judgment of** (that is, upon) **the great harlot.**" Here, then, is introduced the woman, the great whore, whose destruction is described in the next chapter.

What impressions does one get as to the basic identity of the woman? Many commentators begin with one of two assumptions: that she is either (1) the city of Jerusalem or (2) some apostate of the woman of splendor already seen in chapter 12, leading some commentators to the conclusion that she is the Roman Catholic Church of the Middle Ages. There is no hint in the present vision to identify the woman with Jerusalem; much points to pagan Rome. The **dwellers on earth** is one of John's stock epithets for the pagan opposition to Christianity (13:8, 12, 14; 6:10; 8:13; 11:10). The term **fornication** used here in a figurative sense to describe the immorality of the woman's traffic, is not necessarily used for spiritual adultery or for the apostasy of one who has been in covenant relations with God. Such passages as Isaiah 23:17, Isaiah 47:10 (Greek), and Nahum 3:4 depict great heathen cities like Tyre, Nineveh, and Babylon, where idolatry and vice were rampant as women of whoredom.

It is much better to start with the text itself and weigh John's own hints and identifications and draw a conclusion from them. Among the clues are these: (1) The Old Testament usage of "Babylon" as a symbol of pagan and idolatrous wantonness and opposition to God's people, represented in the great cities of Babylon, Nineveh, and Tyre. This term had already been applied symbolically in the contemporary world to the city of Rome (Sibylline Oracles III.75). (2) The woman is closely allied with the land beast of chapter 13, for she "sits enthroned" (17:3) upon the beast and is "borne" by the beast (17:7). The Jewish capital, which was in perpetual hostility to her captor Rome, was never in this relationship to the empire. The woman's destruction and that of the beast in the present vision coincide. (3) The description of the extensive trade of the woman represented as a city (18:12ff.) is obviously that of Rome. (4) The worldwide dominion and influence of the woman is indicated

³ And he carried me away in the Spirit into a wilderness, and I saw a woman sitting on a scarlet beast which was full of blasphemous names, and it had seven heads and ten horns. ⁴ The woman was arrayed in purple and scarlet, and bedecked with gold and jewels and pearls, holding in her hand a golden cup full of abominations and the impurities of her fornication;

---

by the fact that she **is seated upon many waters**. This means, according to verse 15, the many peoples and multitudes and nations and tongues which she ruled. This, like her affiliation with the kings of the earth, could not be said of Jerusalem. (5) Her extensive persecution of the saints (17:6; 18:24) is such as could hardly characterize Jerusalem or any known apostate church. (6) **The wine of whose fornication** is surely a description of idolatry, whether one thinks literally of temple prostitution (which was carried out usually in connection with idolatrous worship) or of fornication as a metaphor for idolatry. (7) Finally, John says plainly, "The woman which you saw is the great city having rulership over the kings of the earth" (17:18) and that she sits on "seven hills" (17:9). No other conclusion seems possible than that John is shown the predicted destruction of the powerful agent whom the church feared—the city and empire of Rome.

[3] The details of the vision begin with John's being **carried away in the Spirit** (cf. 1:10 and 4:3) **into a wilderness**. Here, as in 12:14, the wilderness is a place of safety where John can view the scene of destruction without fear. Since so many saving actions of God had occurred for Israel in the wilderness wanderings of the nation, later Israel expected the Messiah to be revealed from the desert, and her writers glorified the desert. John saw the **woman sitting** (here the meaning is "enthroned or seated with authority") **on a scarlet beast**. Like the beast of chapter 13 this beast is **full of blasphemous names** (claims of deity, etc.) and has **seven heads and ten horns** (cf. 13:1, 6). This is the same beast as the sea beast of 13:1ff. John's guide makes this clear by his subsequent revelations about it. It is here termed **scarlet** to call attention to the clothing of luxury characteristic of the empire.

[4] In like manner **the woman**, who is supported by the beast, is clothed luxuriously: she is **arrayed in** the royal

Babylon the Great REV. 17:4, 5

⁵ and on her forehead was written a name of mystery: "**Babylon the great, mother of harlots and of earth's abominations.**"

---

colors of **purple and scarlet** (Luke 16:19) **and is bedecked with gold and jewels and pearls**. Many other indications of the wordly and vain trappings of the rich and wanton Rome will be hereafter described.

The woman holds **in her hand** (as did her Old Testament counterpart Babylon, Jer. 51:7) **a golden cup full of abominations and** the **impurities of her fornication**. The terms in the original generally are used in the Old Testament to designate ceremonial or moral impurities, especially rites and ceremonies accompanying idolatrous worship. It has been conjectured that John is thinking of the voluptuous dress and finery, along with the impurities of the priestesses, of the idolatrous worship of Rome. But included in the description are the traffic and commerce which lay behind her wealth and vanity.

[5] Several ancient writers (e.g., Seneca *Rhet. Contro.* x.2; Juvenal vi. 123) mention the custom of a prostitute wearing a headband on which was written her name or some descriptive phrase showing her occupation. John sees the woman representing the great city with such a name on her **forehead**. It is a **name of mystery**; there is something about the name which cannot be known until it is divinely disclosed. To reveal that mystery is the purpose of this vision. The name is **Babylon**, the name of the great Mesopotamian city on the Euphrates, where God's people were carried into exile (2 Kings 24:10ff.). That earthly city still remained in New Testament times, though she no longer ruled the world. John, however, does not mean the literal city of Babylon. Like the Jerusalem of 11:8, the city is "spiritually" Babylon. The ancient Babylon, which God had used to punish Israel (Jer. 25:8-11; Acts 7:43), had become an archetype of the contemporary evil world. As the realm of Satan, it was full of **abominations**, blasphemies, and idolatries, the bastion of opposition to God and his realm (see Isa. 47:8-15). One of the most interesting symbols for predicting the overthrow of Babylon in the Old Testament is that of lumping her together with Egypt as a kind of reincarnation of the primeval

REV. 17:5-7

⁶And I saw the woman, **drunk with the blood of the saints and the blood of the martyrs of Jesus.**

When I saw her I marveled greatly. ⁷But the angel said to me, "Why marvel? I will tell you **the mystery of the woman, and of the beast with seven heads and ten horns that carries her.**

"dragon" (*Rahab*), whom God had overcome in bringing order to his creation out of *chaos* (Isa. 30:7; Ezek. 29:3; Isa. 51:9-11). So Babylon became an ageless reality, standing not only for the city so named but also as a covert name for whatever pagan nation threatened God's people. When Rome arose to take the place of Babylon as the mistress of the world, including the land of Palestine, the Jews readily perceived Rome as the successor to Babylon and at least by the middle of the first century A.D. applied the mystic name to her (2 Baruch 11:1; Sibylline Oracles V, 143 and *passim*). Thus in giving the city this name a long tradition is being followed.

It is doubtful that the pseudonym is used merely to conceal the name of Rome and avoid trouble with the authorities. The motive is theological; Rome, however alluring she might seem with her ordered empire, her wealth, and finery, is not what she seems. She is the reincarnation of the ancient mystic Babylon: **mother of harlots and of earth's abominations.** She is not only the mother city of the empire with its far-flung provinces; she is also the fountainhead of its impurities and idolatries.

[6] There is the added factor of the city's oppression of God's people. As ancient Babylon—used of God to punish Israel—reveled in the blood of the Jews (Jer. 51:6, 7), so John sees **the woman drunk with the blood of the saints and the blood of the martyrs of Jesus.** From the days of Nero, she deserved this title. But John is being shown the lady at a period when the cup is full and when she is reeling, drunken from this blood.

The Secret Revealed by the Angel, 17:7-18. [7] John's angel guide asks, **Why marvel?** And he promises to unfold **the mystery of** both **the woman and the beast that carries her.** The beast is brought into the description of the woman because it

Beast from the Pit REV. 17:7, 8

⁸ **The beast that you saw was, and is not, and is to ascend from the bottomless pit and go to perdition; and the dwellers on earth whose names have not been written in the book of life from the foundation of the world, will marvel to behold the beast, because it was and is not and is to come.**

---

is to become the instrument of God's judgment upon the city (17:16). The beast bore the marks of slaughter (an imitation of Christ as the Lamb, 13:3), and he had been "wounded by the sword and yet lived" (another imitation of the one who died and was "alive for evermore," 1:18). All this was connected with the *Nero redivivus* myth.

[8] Another parody is now presented when it is said that **the beast was, and is not, and is to ascend from the bottomless pit and go to perdition**. This imitates the description of the Almighty, who "is and who was and who is to come" (1:4). "Was" probably means that the beast had persecuted the saints at a former time (Nero); "is not" signifies that active persecution was not going on at the time of the vision (see comment on 17:10). The other descriptions of the beast concern its origin and destiny. Though he imitates God who "is and was," the beast is not eternal as is the Almighty. The actual source of the imperial persecution is Satan, from whose place in the bottomless pit the beast ascends. Like its mentor, Satan, the ultimate destiny of the beast is perdition, the lake of fire and brimstone (20:10).

This commentary has assumed that such titles for the opponents of God's people as "the beast from the bottomless pit" or "from the sea," "the city of Babylon," "the city of Jerusalem," and "the great harlot" are symbols of the contemporary embodiment of civil power in opposition to God, that is, Rome. The explanations which John's vision gives further (vss. 9, 15, 18) seem to remove all doubt. It is true that symbolical language is mixed into the account: the dragon, the abyss, the sea, the cities of Babylon and Jerusalem. But that mixture is appropriate because the current temporal power which usurps divine honors and persecutes the people of God is a reembodiment of the ancient power of spiritual darkness already subsumed in the Old Testament under

REV. 17:8-11　　　　　　　　　　　　　　*Seven Mountains*

⁹ **This calls for a mind with wisdom: the seven heads are seven mountains on which the woman is seated;** ¹⁰ **they are also seven kings, five of whom have fallen, one is, the other has not yet come, and when he comes he must remain only a little while.** ¹¹ **As for the beast that was and is not, it is an eighth but it belongs to the seven, and it goes to perdition.**

---

these very terms. The way had been prepared for John by the prophets who had historicized the legend of the dragon monster and used it as a typology for (1) creation, (2) Egypt at the exodus, (3) Babylon at the exile and return (Isa. 51:9ff.), and as a prediction of what God would do for Israel in the "last days" (Isa. 27:1).

[9] Through a series of riddlelike statements John is given the key to the identity of the woman and the beast. The **heads** of the beasts represent the Roman kings (emperors), and the woman is the city on **seven mountains**, who rules over the kings of the earth. John stresses the clues which he will give by saying that they **call for a mind with wisdom** (cf. 13:18). Those who seek to know the identity of the beast need the intelligence of careful reading and study. **The seven heads are the seven mountains on which the woman is seated.** The seven mountains of Rome were a commonplace with Latin writers (Vergil, *Aeneid* 11.784; Horace, *Carmen saeculare* 1.8; Ovid, *Tristia* 1.5.68-70; Martial, *Epigrams* LXIV.20). This clue makes most unlikely the common assumption that Revelation is given in the form of an apocalypse as a ruse to hide its content from the authorities. Such a clue is not very subtle.

[10, 11] The next clue attempts to identify the woman by enabling the reader to pick the king or emperor under whom the visions were seen and with whose action and character the visions were concerned: **The seven heads** (of the beast) **also are seven kings**. John's meaning is fairly clear, though there are problems. It is not certain how John intended his readers to count the emperors and thus identify "the one who now is."

The emperors with their dates are:

Julius Caesar	died 44 B.C.
Augustus (Octavius)	31 B.C.-14 A.D.

Roman Emperors REV. 17:10, 11

Tiberius	A.D. 14-37
Gaius (Caligula)	A.D. 37-41
Claudius	A.D. 41-54
Nero	A.D. 54-68
Galba, Otho, Vitellius	A.D. 68-69
Vespasian	A.D. 69-79
Titus	A.D. 79-81
Domitian	A.D. 81-96

The principal key to applying the list is the repeated use of the *Nero redivivus* imagery (13:3, 12, 14). Since Nero is the emperor who formerly persecuted the church, he is the head or king who was, and he is also the one of the **five** who **have fallen** (that is, died or perished from the scene). The king who **is** must therefore be Vespasian; the one who **has not yet come** and who will **remain only** for **a little while** is Titus, who ruled only one full year and parts of two others (79-81); Domitian is an eighth, but he was the first emperor since Nero actively to persecute the church. Every emperor is not envisioned as a part of the beast in one sense; that is, not all of them show the beastly characteristics borrowed from the dragon. Some do not persecute the people of God. Thus since Nero **the beast** has not existed: he **was and is not.** But also Domitian, the **eighth, belongs to** (or is one of) **the seven.** This last phrase is difficult in Greek and probably means "he is equivalent to one of the seven" (cf. Acts 21:8; Matt. 26:73). Domitian is the reincarnate Nero. If this is correct, John omits in his counting Julius Caesar, who was a dictator and not Imperator in the later sense of the term. Nor does he include the short-termed claimants to the throne (Galba, Otho, and Vitellius) between the death of Nero and the enthronement of the Flavian Emperor Vespasian (68/69). This way of listing is natural from the view of the time of the Flavian dynasty.

The main difficulty with this interpretation is that it places the vision in the reign of Vespasian, whereas the early tradition of the church (Irenaeus) said that "the vision was seen no long time since in the reign of Domitian." There are no patent solutions to this difficulty, only some possibilities. If John had been banished to Patmos (as he seems to be saying) during Vespasian's reign, his banishment could have extended through the short reign of Titus and on into the reign

REV. 17:10-12

¹² And the ten horns that you saw are ten kings who have not yet received royal power, but they are to receive authority as kings for one hour, together with the beast.

of Domitian, thus giving rise to the later tradition that the vision was seen in Domitian's time. Under such conditions the book would not have been published until John's return to the mainland, anyway. The fact that there was a king not yet come who was to remain only a little while (Titus) makes it possible to postulate the time of the visions near the end of Vespasian's time and thus on the threshold of the reign of Domitian. Although there is no record of persecution of Christians under Vespasian which would have accounted for John's being banished "on account of the word of God and the testimony of Jesus" (1:9), little is actually known of the history of these years. John does not say he was banished by the emperor himself; it could have been by the action of a local official. There was no uniform Roman policy concerning such matters, and local affairs were under local jurisdiction. This also accords with the numerous indications given in the book that the trial of persecution which John expected (cf. 3:10) had not yet begun. John's main point is that the line of Roman emperors has only a little time remaining until a reincarnation of Nero was to emerge, one who (as Nero) would best be described in terms of the ancient Rahab, the dragon of Old Testament prophecy.

[12] The next feature of the beast is that it had ten horns. This was a feature of Daniel's vision (Dan. 7:7, 20, 24); it was interpreted to Daniel as meaning ten kings who would rise out of his fourth beast. The beast from the sea (Rev. 13:1) also had ten horns that were crowned, and in the present vision this is explained as ten kings **who have not yet received** authority. When they do become manifest, they will remain **for** only **one hour**—a short time. Also they will **receive authority together with the beast.** It is most likely that in this vision the number ten is merely symbolic—that John has no definite number in mind but uses Daniel's number to represent the role which the subordinate rulers and subject kings would play in the drama of the future. They are the kings of the earth with whom the harlot commits fornication (17:2;

[13] **These are of one mind and give over their power and authority to the beast;** **[14]** **they will make war on the Lamb, and the Lamb will conquer them, for he is Lord of lords and King of kings, and those with him are called and chosen and faithful."**

18:3, 9); they join the beast from the abyss in making war on the saints (16:12-14; 19:19); and at the last they are the ones who are to turn against Rome, hate her, and become the instruments of her destruction (17:16, 17). The role that the local rulers and officials played in the persecution of Christians is illustrated in many stories of martyrdom.

[13, 14] In the course of her conquests and in the consolidation of her empire Rome had taken in many provinces and kingdoms. The usual policy was to allow local rulers (e.g., the Herods in Palestine) to continue ruling under the watchful eye of the provincial proconsuls. Obstinate rulers were, of course, not tolerated. Those who remained and prospered were naturally **of one mind** and gave **over their power and authority to the beast**; that is, they supported and carried out his policy. **They will make war on the Lamb** by joining the beast in the great persecution (Rev. 12:17; 13:7; 11:7). John would prepare the church to meet this grim reality. Although he has no illusion about the outcome being martyrdom (13:7, 15), he assures his readers of the ultimate victory of their cause. This victory from the standpoint of the Christian witnesses has already been proclaimed: "They have conquered him by the blood of the Lamb and by the word of their testimony, for they loved not their lives unto death" (12:11). The Lamb secured victory on the cross, the tragedy/triumph which ended the incarnation (1:5; 3:21; 5:5). But that triumph must be secured by the reenactment of the victory in the lives of the martyrs, who are willing to commit their lives to the cause even to death. Here the victory is attributed to two factors: first, their leader. The Lamb is given the titles attributed to God in the Old Testament; he is **Lord of lords and King of kings** (Deut. 10:17; Dan. 2:47; cf. 2 Macc. 13:4 and Paul's use in 1 Tim. 6:15). With such a leader the cause could hardly fail. But in the end John foresaw that it would be the willingness of the saints as the **called and chosen and faithful** army of the Lamb to provide the means of

[15] And he said to me, "The waters that you saw, where the harlot is seated, are peoples and multitudes and nations and tongues. **[16]** And the ten horns that you saw, they and the beast will hate the harlot; they will make her desolate and naked, and devour her flesh and burn her up with fire, **[17]** for God has put it into their hearts to carry out his purpose by being of one mind and giving over their royal power to the beast, until the words of God shall be fulfilled. **[18]** And the woman that you saw is the great city which has dominion over the kings of the earth."

---

the ultimate victory—through martyrdom (cf. "be faithful unto death, and I will give you the crown of life," 2:10). For the enlargement of the theme of the great war of the Lamb compare the notes which accompany the theme through the book: 11:7; 12:17; 13:7, 15; 14:1-5; 16:12-16; 17:14; 19:11-21.

[15] After discussing various aspects of the beast, the angel guide now reverts to the description of the woman. Rome drew what she possessed from the multitudes of her provinces stretching from the Atlantic to the Euphrates. The use of water as the symbol for mighty empires is current in the Old Testament. Babylon was a city which sat by many waters (Jer. 51:12f.), probably a reference to the many canals in the region. The overthrow of the city was likened to the drying up of her waters (Jer. 50:38). Similarly, Rome sat on many waters (vs. 1), and the universality of her subject peoples is thus represented.

[16] These people and multitudes and nations have their own kings, represented by **the ten horns** (vs. 12) of the beast. They were at first to be of one mind and give over their power and authority to the beast and even combine with it to make war on the saints (vs. 14). But ultimately they will rise and become the instruments of Rome's destruction: **They and the beast** (the empire as a whole) **will hate the harlot; they will make her desolate and naked, and devour her flesh and burn her up with fire.** Some would refer this merely to the principle of attrition at work in the history of nations. But, specifically, the prediction is that of the future overthrow of Rome.

[17, 18] All this will take place because of God's lordship over history. In chapter 6, at the revelation of the four horsemen, it is demonstrated that God works in and through

Rome's Dominion REV. 17:17–18:1

¹ **After this I saw another angel coming down from heaven, having great authority; and the earth was made bright with his splendor.**

---

the judgmental forces of nature to accomplish his purpose; so here **God has put it into the hearts** of the kings and peoples **to carry out his purpose by being of one mind and** thus **giving over their royal power to the beast, until the words of God** (as those being uttered by the voice of the prophecies of this book: 17:16; 18:2, 8, 18f.; cf. 19:9; 21:5; 22:6) **shall be fulfilled.**

If there remains any doubt as to whom the woman represents, it is quieted by the final word: **The woman that you saw is the great city which has dominion over the kings of the earth.** Who else but Rome? As many early interpreters, Tertullian says, "Babylon also in our John is a figure of the city of Rome, as being like her great and proud in royal power, and warring down the saints of God" (*Against Marcion* 3, 13).

The Dirge over the Fallen City, 18:1—19:4

From the discussion of the signs by which the identity of the harlot and the beast could be known, the vision now turns to the judgment of God upon the city. This judgment had been promised by the angel guide (17:1). This is the third time that the fall of the city has been dealt with. (See notes on 6:12-17; 11:13; 16:18, 19.) The present vision is a fuller treatment of one of the major themes of the Apocalypse: the future judgment of God upon Rome.

The section consists of four subdivisions. First, there is a dirge or lament of an angel announcing that the city has fallen (18:1-8); next there is an accompanying dirge by the kings and merchants who mourn the loss of her trade (18:9-20); this is followed by an action parable in which an angel casts a great millstone into the sea, symbolizing the city's fall, which it then laments (18:21-24); and finally, voices from heaven and the elders praise the truth and justice of God's judgments upon the city (19:1-4). Much of this is taken over almost verbatim from the dirge and oracle literature of the Old Testament, again stressing the way in which John sees this as a fulfillment of the Old Testament purpose of God.

The Fall of the City Announced, 18:1-8. **[1]** The next

²**And he called out with a mighty voice,**
　"Fallen, fallen is Babylon the great!
　It has become a dwelling place of demons,
　a haunt of every foul spirit,
　a haunt of every foul and hateful bird;

---

part of this vision of the judgment of the city is begun as **another angel** (different from the one at the beginning of the vision, 17:1) was seen **coming down from heaven.** The description stressing the **great authority** of the angel and its **splendor,** which made **the earth bright,** emphasizes the role the angel plays in revealing the downfall of the city. The description of the angel is reminiscent of the beginning of the vision about the restoration of the temple given to Ezekiel (Ezek. 43:1ff.). Here, however, the angel announces the destruction of the city, not the rebuilding of the temple. The parallel may be in the fact that the fall of Rome will be the occasion for ascribing "salvation and glory and power" to God (19:1).

[2] As the angel **called out with a mighty voice,** the lament begins: **"Fallen, fallen is Babylon the great!"** This cry has been heard once before in the Revelation, as one of the angel messengers had anticipated the present passage (14:8). The words echo the cry of the Watchman on Zion's walls who repeated the news of the messengers that Cyrus, the Persian king, had captured Israel's enemy Babylon (Isa. 21:9; cf. Jer. 50:1ff.).

The Old Testament foresaw that the enemy cities of Israel would fall and that they would become desolate and be turned back to the desert, **a dwelling place** of wild birds and beasts, **a haunt of** demons and **foul spirits.** The imagery is part of the locale. People who lived in the ancient Middle East fought a continual battle with the encroaching desert, with its winds and sweeping sands. An abandoned city soon became a haunted place. The words fit the Apocalypse, for the New Testament contention is that there is something demonic in the perverted worship and practices of the pagan religion represented in the city of Rome (9:2, 20). The "desert" in 12:14 and 17:3 is different, for there the typology is drawn

Fornication REV. 18:2, 3

> ³ for all nations have drunk*ᵏ* the wine of her impure passion,
> and the kings of the earth have committed fornication with her,
> and the merchants of the earth have grown rich with the wealth of her wantonness."

ᵏ Other ancient authorities read *fallen by*

---

from the wilderness experience of Israel, to whom it was a haven from the bondage of Egypt and where God revealed himself and made a covenant with them. The ancient language of desolation borrowed here prefigures Rome's destruction.

[3] Any justification needed for God's judgment on the city lies in her sins. She is the mother city, the fountain from which **all nations have drunk the wine of her impure passion.** The Greek literally translated is "the wine of the wrath of her fornication," a very difficult phrase. *Thumos* can mean "passion," but it can also mean "wrath," which is the more likely meaning here. If so, here it is probably a symbol for the retribution or punishment which will finally be visited on the city. The phrase could imply the punishment which God gives to the wicked to drink, but in another sense it could also mean the wrath or rage inherent in the fornication of Babylon. If the latter, it would refer to the "wages of sin," the nemesis which is allowed to work its way until it brings its own penalty. This would be similar to what we have observed about the four horsemen and trumpet series, one emphasis of which is that God allows the natural and demonic forces to work their own self-destruction.

The kings of the earth have committed fornication with her. The Septuagint of Isaiah 47:10 says of Babylon, "Know thou, the understanding of these things and thy harlotry shall be thy shame." The Hebrew of the passage is usually taken another way. This is the only Old Testament passage that mentions the fornication of Babylon. The word, however, is used in this same sense by both Isaiah (23:15-17) and Nahum (3:4) for the sins of Tyre and Nineveh. Tyre "plays the harlot with all the kingdoms of the world upon the face of the earth." This reference to the practice of idolatry is made all

> [4] Then I heard another voice from heaven saying,
> "Come out of her, my people,
> lest you take part in her sins,
> lest you share in her plagues;

---

the more understandable because many pagan cults (Astarte, Isis, Cybele, *et al.*) were connected with sexual debauchery. It was a favorite metaphor of the prophets to describe the apostasy of Israel into idolatry. But, since it was also used to depict the way of life in pagan cities, its use here need not be taken as proof that the woman here is the apostate of the woman in 12:1.

The city's wicked influence is further described: **the merchants of the earth have grown rich with the wealth of her wantonness.** The kings of the earth who have given their power to the harlot have their own allies or underlings, the merchants of the earth. They have grown rich in trade with Rome. The Greek word *dunamis* (literally "power") here means the externals of power, that is, the resources or wealth. "Wantonness" (*strenos*) usually means sensuality but often has a secondary sense of softness or luxury. The idea is that the idolatry and sensuality of the city demanded and consumed an abundance of products so that the merchants who supplied them grew wealthy in the trade (see the list of articles in vs. 12). Here is one of the keys to the hold that Rome had upon the world of her day. The *pax romana* ("Roman peace"), brought about by the all-powerful military arm of the empire, held the world at bay. The vast travel and communication system of the empire provided the means of moving goods and building up of a world trade. The provinces which had long known war, revolution, piracy, and unrest grew rich under Rome's protection and trade. There is evidence of great gratitude to the emperor as the symbol of the government which made this safety and prosperity possible. All of this contributed to a feeling of self-sufficiency and luxury, plus a worship of wealth and lasciviousness, as well as of the state which made it possible.

[4] A second **voice** is heard, this time probably that of God himself (cf. **my people**), calling upon his people to come

Come Out REV. 18:4-6

⁵**for her sins are heaped high as heaven,
and God has remembered her iniquities,**
⁶**Render to her as she herself has rendered,
and repay her double for her deeds;
mix a double draught for her in the cup she mixed.**

---

out of Babylon lest they **take part in her sins** and **share in her plagues** or punishment. That God's voice should issue the warning underscores the certainty of the punishment. The call is patterned on Jeremiah 51:6-9, 45 (in the Hebrew, not in the Septaugint). There the exiles are warned to flee the city to escape the dangers of the judgments coming upon it. Here the call is obviously not addressed to Christians living in the sin of spiritual Babylon. The call comes at a point in time when Rome is about to fall and the church is already in the wilderness of safety (12:14). This, then, is addressed to potential Christians or the people in Babylon who are still amenable to the moral and spiritual issues of the conflict. When Paul came to Corinth, the Lord told him, "I have many people in this city" (Acts 18:10). God's call is ever addressed to "people" who are not his, who are "no people" (Hosea 2:23), to come out before the judgments come and while it is still called "today" (Heb. 4:7).

[5] Like Babylon, her spiritual counterpart has sins **heaped high as heaven** (Jer. 51:9). **God has remembered her iniquities.** God's judgments are not merely vindictive; the book has made it abundantly clear that God wills and has done everything for the salvation of all men. The possibility of taking shelter in God's mercy has just been stressed in the call to come out of the city, but God's judgments are just and true (19:2). Those who are hardened in sin and reject mercy must suffer their rightful penalty, and Rome's sins are multitudinous. It is God's place as creator and judge to exact vengeance.

[6] In this light, the command is given (evidently to the avenging angels) to **render to her as she herself has rendered, and repay her double for her deeds.** The double repayment is traditional language for full recompense (Ex. 22:4, 7, 9; Isa. 40:2; Jer. 16:18).

> ⁷ As she glorified herself and played the wanton,
> so give her a like measure of torment and mourning.
> Since in her heart she says, 'A queen I sit,
> I am no widow, mourning I shall never see,'
> ⁸ so shall her plagues come in a single day,
> pestilence and mourning and famine,
> and she shall be burned with fire;
> for mighty is the Lord God who judges her."
> ⁹ **And the kings of the earth, who committed fornication and were wanton with her, will weep and wail over her when they see the smoke of her burning;**

---

[7] Again it is charged that the city has **glorified herself and played the wanton.** The verb here is the same root as the noun in verse 4 and means to live in sensuality or luxury. The **measure of torment and mourning** to be given her is to equal her glorification and wantonness. The full pride of Rome is reached in her claim (like that of Tyre and Babylon—Isa. 47:7-9; Ezek. 28:2; Zeph. 2:15) that she is higher than God. As a city she claimed to be eternal; her coins proclaimed her the "eternal (*aeternitas*) city."

[8] The city that claimed to live forever without loss of children was told that **in a single day the plagues of pestilence, mourning and famine would come upon her.** Such prophetic language as "in a single day," quoted directly from Isaiah's oracle against Babylon (Isa. 47:9), is not to be taken literally. Like "in one hour" of verses 10, 16, 19 (cf. 17:12), it is a symbol for suddenness.

The city's destiny is **pestilence and mourning and famine.** Note that these expressions, together with "war" (as in 17:8), make up the Apocalyptic forces of punishment (woes). John is connecting here the destruction of the city with the forces of judgment revealed in the beginning of the visions in the seals and the trumpets. From the beginning he has moved toward the revelation about this downfall of Rome. The assurance given to John that this judgment will come to pass is that **the Lord God who judges** the city is **mighty** (cf. the term "The Almighty," 4:8; 11:17; 15:3; 16:17).

Lament for the City, 18:9-20. [9] In verses 2 to 8 the

Weeping for Rome REV. 18:9-13

[10] they will stand far off, in fear of her torment, and say,
"Alas! alas! thou great city,
thou mighty city, Babylon!
In one hour has thy judgment come."
[11] And the merchants of the earth weep and mourn for her, since no one buys their cargo any more, [12] cargo of gold, silver, jewels and pearls, fine linen, purple, silk and scarlet, all kinds of scented wood, all articles of ivory, all articles of costly wood, bronze, iron and marble, [13] cinnamon, spice, incense, myrrh, frankincense, wine, oil, fine flour and wheat, cattle and sheep, horses and chariots, and slaves, that is, human souls.

---

voice speaking is God himself. Now John sees that the earthly allies of the city, **the kings of the earth**, who **were wanton with her**, are destined **to weep and wail when they see the smoke of her burning.** They are the allies in the provinces and are not affected by the judgments themselves, except in the loss of their traffic.

[10] They are represented as standing **far off** after Rome's destruction, **in fear of her torment** (as though they might be next) and lamenting her fate. This is proof enough that John did not expect the end of the world to follow the fall of Rome. Thus in other visions (11:15ff. and 16:17-21), when John pictured the fall of the city and spoke of this in terms of the end, he was using traditional apocalyptic language and was not meaning to intimate that the two events would actually coincide.

[11] Along with the kings, **the merchants of the earth weep and mourn** for the city. The destruction of Rome brought an end to the trade which Rome demanded for her extravagances, leaving no one to buy **their cargo any more.** Not only did the provinces serve as granaries for Rome, but they exported to her rare and expensive items of luxury and ornamentation.

[12, 13] A long list of products, beginning with **gold** and ending with **slaves,** that is, **human souls,** found their way by caravans and by ships to the port of Ostia and thence to Rome. Products came from such distant sources as India, China, Arabia, and Africa. This picture of trade could

REV. 18:12-17 *Alas for Rome*

¹⁴ "The fruit for which thy soul longed has
gone from thee,
and all thy dainties and thy splendor are
lost to thee, never to be found again!"
¹⁵ The merchants of these wares, who gained wealth from her, will stand far off, in fear of her torment, weeping and mourning aloud,
¹⁶ "Alas, alas, for the great city
that was clothed in fine linen, in purple
and scarlet,
bedecked with gold, with jewels, and with
pearls!
¹⁷ In one hour all this wealth has been laid waste."
And all shipmasters and seafaring men, sailors and all whose trade is on the sea stood far off

---

describe (of all cities in the ancient or medieval world) only the Rome of the first Christian centuries. It constitutes one of the strongest arguments for the interpretation of the city as pagan Rome before its fall to the barbarians.

[**14, 15**] In a fitting metaphor the voice likens the fall of the city to ripe summer **fruit** (Jer. 40:10, 12), which at the moment it seemed ripe for picking and enjoying, has vanished. In the eye of the vision the climax to Rome's years of glory would never come. Another summer of harvest is not to be expected. The kings (vs. 10) who thus lament are joined by **the merchants of these wares** (mentioned in vs. 12), **who gained wealth from her.**

[**16**] The dirge of the merchants begins and ends like that of the kings (vs. 10). But while the kings lamented the loss of power of the mighty city, the merchants see the loss of the rich splendor of the city.

[**17**] The verb "laid waste" *(eremoun)* more naturally describes the aftereffects of destroyed and deserted cities. And so it is used in 17:16 and verse 19, below. But it is the great wealth of the city that the merchants see laid waste; that, rather than the city or its population, is more meaningful to them. Joining the merchants in similar lament are the **shipmasters and seafaring men,** sailors and all whose trade is on

Great Mourning REV. 18:18-20

[18] and cried out as they saw the smoke of her burning,
"What city was like the great city?"
[19] And they threw dust on their heads, as they wept
and mourned, crying out,
> "Alas, alas, for the great city
> where all who had ships at sea grew rich by
> her wealth!
> In one hour she has been laid waste.
> [20] Rejoice over her, O heaven,
> O saints and apostles and prophets,
> for God has given judgment for you against
> her!"

---

the sea. They are the ones who have made their living by conveying the goods to satisfy the hunger and tastes of the city to her port.

[18, 19] The Old Testament predecessors of this city had considered themselves as having the ultimate in power and wealth. Babylon had boasted, "I am, and there is no one besides me" (Isa. 47:10). The chief illustration, however, is drawn from Ezekiel's lament over Tyre, which, as a great commercial port, was a more exact parallel to the loss of Rome's trade (Ezek. 27:29ff.). There, too, the mariners and pilots had wailed aloud and cried bitterly and **threw dust on their heads** (a sign of great mourning). The scene is repeated over the New Testament city as **all who had ships at sea and who grew rich by her wealth** and her power to purchase goods brought from the ends of the earth in their ships cried, **"In one hour she has been laid waste."**

No actual description of the destruction is given, even after the readers have been brought so many times to the earthquake and the burning of the city. The description is given principally through the eyes of those who see her in ruin after her destruction and lament their own stakes in the loss of her fortunes. That Rome should perish utterly must have seemed impossible. Her allurement must not have been lost even upon the saints; this was the power of her temptation.

[20] Verse 20 serves as a transition to the next section. There is a change of person from the kings, merchants, and shipowners, who have poured forth their lament. It is probable that these words come from the writer John himself. Too, there is a deliberate reflection in this verse of 12:12, the first court-room scene, where there is an apostrophe (or a turning aside from the subject to address someone directly): **heaven,** who is urged to **rejoice.** There heaven was asked to rejoice because, with the fall of Satan and with the martyrs' willingness to suffer, the defeat of the dragon was assured. John is saying that not only heaven, but also **saints and apostles and prophets,** by whom the victory has now been won, are to rejoice.

The expression **God has given judgment for you against her** has caused much difficulty. The Greek reads literally "God has judged the judgment of you from (or out of) her." *Krima* (judgment) most naturally means "sentence." "Your judgment" would mean "the judgment she has passed on you," that is, the sentence passed on the martyrs in the Roman courts before they were put to death. The phrase "from or out of her" would then mean, as in Genesis 9:5, the person from whom requital is exacted. The sense is expressed in the Old Testament law which said that "if a malicious witness rises against any man, . . . and if the witness is a false witness and has accused his brother falsely, than you shall do to him as he had meant to do to his brother" (Deut. 19:16ff.).

Thus at long last comes the answer to the cry of the martyrs beneath the altar (6:9ff.). Those who have been "slain for the word of God and for the witness they had borne" had been put to death in Rome's courts as "atheists" toward the state god(s) and enemies of truth. But now, as it were, that judgment has been reviewed by the supreme court of heaven and found to be false. Vengeance must be exacted of the malicious witness herself, Rome, who had perpetuated the falsehood, with the same sentence she had unjustly imposed upon the martyrs. She must repay double the cup she has mixed (vs. 6). This helps explain why Revelation from the beginning (1:5) has used the figures and metaphors drawn from the courtroom and why its primary term for the persecuted Christian is "witness" (Greek *martus,* from which the English word "martyr" is derived). It has figured prominently in the theology of suffering developed in the book that

Great Millstone REV. 18:20-23

²¹ Then a mighty angel took up a stone like a great millstone and threw it into the sea, saying,

> "So shall Babylon the great city be thrown
> down with violence,
> and shall be found no more;
> ²² and the sound of harpers and minstrels, of
> flute players and trumpeters,
> shall be heard in thee no more;
> and a craftsman of any craft shall be found in
> thee no more;
> and the sound of the millstone shall be heard
> in thee no more;
> ²³ and the light of a lamp
> shall shine in thee no more;
> and the voice of bridegroom and bride
> shall be heard in thee no more;
> for thy merchants were great men of the earth,
> and all nations were deceived by thy sorcery.

---

the testimony of faith on the part of the "called, chosen, and faithful" witnesses "who love not their souls unto death" would in the reversal of the judgment have a part in the undoing of Rome, the ally of the beast. The city would be "conquered by the blood of the Lamb and the word of their testimony, for they loved not their lives unto death" (12:12).

Stone Cast into the Sea, 18:21-24. [21] The symbolic act (often from the frequent use of this type of illustration in the Old Testament called an "action parable") by which **a mighty angel took up and threw a great millstone into the sea** is suggested by Jeremiah 51:63. The end of Babylon suggests the end of Rome. Of her it is also said, **So shall Babylon the great city be thrown down with violence, and shall be found no more.**

This is another cross reference by which John signifies the paralleling of his sections of the book. This is the third angel to be called "mighty," the first two having introduced the first (5:2) and the second scrolls (10:1). This third "mighty angel" must signify that the fall of the city is connected to the earlier scrolls—probably that it signifies the end or fulfillment of the purposes of the parallel scrolls.

[22, 23] The casting of the stone is followed by another

²⁴ And in her was found the blood of prophets
   and of saints,
and of all who have been slain on earth."
¹ After this I heard what seemed to be the loud voice of a great multitude in heaven, crying,
   "Hallelujah! Salvation and glory and power belong to our God,

---

dirge over the city. This third lament—from the angel of the stone—describes the cessation of the inner actions, the daily life of the city. A list of things which will no longer be heard is **the sound of harpers and minstrels, of flute players and trumpeters,** followed by things which will no more be found in the great city: **craftsmen,** the grinders at the **millstone, and the light of a lamp** shining. The absence of homes is signified by **the voice of the bridegroom and bride** that **shall be heard no more.** Since the city is to be burned, such evidences of life in it will no longer be heard or found. As if in a chorus, such sins of the city as **sorcery** are repeated.

[24] But more telling, **in her was found the blood of prophets and of saints, and of all who have been slain on earth.** Rome had murdered Christians, but she was not guilty of slaying all martyrs, much less all who had been slain on earth. Some emperors had not persecuted the church (under some of them "the beast was not," 17:11). Why, then, should Rome be held accountable for the blood of all **the slain of the earth**? Guilt is often cumulative. Jesus once reminded Jerusalem that she inherited the guilt of the people of Israel's earlier history. They had killed the prophets, and she garnished the tombs of the martyred prophets. Unless the Jewish city and nation repented and dissociated themselves from this bloody history, they would suffer the cumulative guilt. So Rome as the reincarnation of ancient Babylon (as she was also of the beast) would suffer the cumulative guilt of prophets, saints, and martyrs of all time.

Praise for God's Judgments, 19:1-4. **[1]** The song of **a great multitude in heaven** is begun and closed with the Hebrew word **Hallelujah.** This term of worship, meaning "praise Yahweh," is taken over from the Old Testament (cf.

Hallelujah REV. 19:1, 2

²for his judgments are true and just;
he has judged the great harlot who corrupted the
    earth with her fornication,
and he has avenged on her the blood of his
    servants."

---

vs. 4 with Ps. 106:48) and is used in the New Testament only in this chapter. The vision, begun with the promise of judgment upon the harlot city (17:1ff.), now ends with the celebration of that fact: **Salvation and glory and power belong to our God.** Salvation means not only the deliverance of the saints into the eternal kingdom (2 Tim. 4:18) but refers also to the accomplishment of God's purpose. **Glory** comes close to its earlier classical meaning of fame or renown justly due God for what he has done. **Power** implies the fact now established that the Almighty has lordship over his creation. He has destroyed demonic and satanic power and brought his purpose for the world to its intended perfection.

The passage has many similarities with other praise sections of the Revelation, especially chapters 4 and 5. There, however, the praises are partly anticipatory. Only the defeat of forces arrayed against heaven and the Lord's people would make the ascribed virtues absolutely demonstrable. That defeat has now been accomplished. This victory has been anticipated in the destiny of the saints who were sealed (7:11f.), in the story of Satan's being cast out of heaven (12:10ff.), in the song of victory parallel to this at the seventh trumpet (11:15-18), and in the new song of the martyrs in 15:3, 4. In all of these, the reign, kingdom, or authority of the Lord is promised. What has been so often anticipated is now a fact.

[2] God's actions which bring about the fall of the great harlot are here called his **judgments,** and they are declared to be **true and just**. Rome deserved her fate; the sins which led to her fall have been spelled out. These sins are recapitulated in the one statement that **she corrupted the earth with her fornication**, and (since she had shed

REV. 19:2-4 *Smoke for Ever*

³ Once more they cried,
"**Hallelujah! The smoke from her goes up for ever
and ever.**"
⁴ **And the twenty-four elders and the four living creatures fell down and worshiped God who is seated on the throne, saying, "Amen. Hallelujah!"**

---

the blood of prophets and saints) **God has avenged on her the blood of his servants**.

[**3, 4**] Once more the chorus cries, "**Hallelujah**," praising the Lord for his deeds, evidenced by the smoke of the city burned by fire. Like the fire which consumed Sodom and Gomorrah, its **smoke** is said to go **up for ever and ever**. The smoldering of the city calls attention to the eternal judgment of fire that is the fate of those who were found in the city (cf. 11:13; 18:4) who had the name and mark of the beast upon them (19:20). The heavenly chorus is joined by **the twenty-four elders and the four living creatures** who also **worshiped God, saying, "Amen. Hallelujah!"**

The Marriage Supper of the Lamb, 19:5-10

By a series of cross references ("God's servants," "peals of thunder," the verb *ebasileusas*, "the ones who fear him," "great and small," etc.) John indicates that 19:5ff. is parallel to 11:15-19; the fall of the city brings us to the end. It is not that John expected the end of the world with the end of the city. John still expects a thousand-year reign of the saints before the end of the world and the judgment. In 11:15ff., as well as here (vs. 6), God is pictured as reigning or as taking his power and beginning to reign. In the former passage the end of the city is pictured as the time for "destroying the destroyers of the earth and for judging the world and rewarding God's servants." Here the city has already been judged, but the final judgment is put off until the special treatment of the great battle (19:11-21), the thousand years (20:1-6), and the renewal of Gog and Magog (20:7-10). In this passage the invitation to the marriage feast of the Lamb takes the place of

Praise REV. 19:5, 6

⁵And from the throne came a voice crying,
"Praise our God, all you his servants,
you who fear him, small and great."
⁶Then I heard what seemed to be the voice of a great multitude, like the sound of many waters and like the sound of mighty thunderpeals, crying,
"Hallelujah! For the Lord our God the Almighty
reigns.

---

the rewarding of the servants of God. Again it is important to note that John is using traditional apocalyptic in which, for descriptive and theological reasons, a great historical crisis is treated as "the end."

[5, 6] In answer to the heavenly chorus which has praised the judgments of God upon Babylon, another **voice comes from the throne crying, "Praise our God"** and calling upon **his servants, those who fear him, small and great** to praise him. There is an answering voice, this time of a multitude so great that it sounded like the sound of many waters and mighty thunderpeals. This multitude repeats again the **Hallelujah** (vss. 1, 3, 4). The reason assigned this time for the praise is that **the Lord our God the Almighty reigns.** The reign of God is a recurring theme in the Apocalypse, and it is the equivalent to the universal acceptance or triumph of the gospel. John makes no distinction between the sovereignty of the Father and the Son. There are frequent references to the authority, the throne, and right of both to rule (1:5; 4:11; 5:12f.; 17:14; 19:16). Although the kingdom is treated as a reality (1:9), even to the affirmation that the saints participate in the reign of Christ (1:6; 5:10), the Apocalypse treats that reign as not actualized, in one sense, until the powers which prevented its earthly realization are defeated. Repeatedly the great persecution and marytrdom of the church are seen as the means of that realization (12:11; 17:14). Thus when the martyrdom is complete, God is declared the King of the ages and the universal acceptance of the gospel is proclaimed (15:3, 4). And when Rome, the capital city which sits upon the beast is destroyed, the reign of God is declared to be a fact (cf. 11:17 and here, 19:6).

REV. 19:7-8　　　　　　　　　　　　　*Messianic Banquet*

⁷**Let us rejoice and exult and give him the glory,
　for the marriage of the Lamb has come,
　and his Bride has made herself ready;
⁸it was granted her to be clothed with fine linen,
　bright and pure"—
for the fine linen is the righteous deeds of the saints.**

---

[7] The anticipation of the joy of the last age is well known in the Old Testament (Pss. 96:11f.; 97:1, 8; 126:2, 5f.; Isa. 12:6; cf. Test. Levi 18:16; 2 Baruch 29:3ff.; 2 Esdras 6:32). The figure of the messianic banquet upon the mountains of Israel is set forth in Isaiah's so-called "Little Apocalypse" (Isa. 25:6) as the reward for the faithful in the last days. The idea had been taken over by Jesus to describe privileges in the kingdom of God (Matt. 8:11; 22:1ff.; 25:1ff.; 26:29; Mark 2:19; Luke 14:15ff.). In this imagery, frequently combined with that of the marriage, the banquet becomes part of the messianic nuptials. In the Old Testament (Hos. 2:5; Isa. 1:21; Jer. 2:2) the bridal figure is applied to Israel, and it is natural that Paul speaks of the church as betrothed to Christ (2 Cor. 11:2; cf. Eph. 5:32). The heavenly realization of this union is the figure now used: **the marriage of the Lamb has come**. This is still spoken proleptically, similar to the announcement of the fall of Babylon in 14:8, which is not fulfilled until chapters 17-19. Much is yet to intervene before the Bride is revealed at the wedding feast (21:1-5).

[8] The particular feature of the Bride's preparedness is that she is **granted to be clothed with fine linen, bright and pure**. This linen is **the righteous deeds of the saints**. One is reminded of the wedding garments in the parable of Jesus (Matt. 22:11). The clean garment (already used in Rev. 3:4; 6:11; 7:14) as a symbol for sanctity and righteous deeds is again borrowed from the Old Testament (Gen. 35:2; Isa. 52:1; Zech. 3:4). But it should be noted that this clothing is not the Bride's own. Like the robes of the souls under the altar (6:11), **it was granted** (*edothe*) **her to be clothed in fine linen**.

The righteous deeds of the saints thus evidently means something other than the ordinary good deeds of Christians.

Beatitude REV. 19:8-10

⁹ And the angel said to me, "Write this: Blessed are those who are invited to the marriage supper of the Lamb." And he said to me, "These are true words of God." ¹⁰ Then I fell down at his feet to worship him, but he said to me, "You must not do that! I am a fellow servant with you and your brethren who hold the testimony of Jesus. Worship God." For the testimony of Jesus is the spirit of prophecy.

¹ Greek he said

In 7:14 John has shown the martyrs—the church triumphant—clothed in robes "washed and made white in the blood of the Lamb." In the present passage the great martyrdom has prepared the guests for the wedding feast.

[9] John's guide, who may still be the angel of 17:1 and the voice from the throne of verse 5, called on him to write. The beatitude is a recasting of the blessing pronounced in 14:13, "Blessed are the dead who die in the Lord henceforth. Blessed indeed, that they may rest from their labors, for their deeds follow them!" The reward of rest from labor is more specifically identified here under the image of the festival of marriage. The words are a Christian interpretation of the remark introducing Jesus' parable of the Great Supper (Luke 14:15): "Blessed is he who shall eat bread in the Kingdom of God." As in many other symbols, that first anticipated by the prophets for the messianic age is regarded as fulfilled in the church or kingdom of Christ on earth as a foretaste of a greater and more perfect fulfillment in heaven. The angel assures John that "**these words are true words of God**." The reference may be to the beatitude just expressed. But it is also possible that these are the authentication for the entire vision of the judgment upon the harlot, which began in 17:1. The words are followed by John's worshiping the angel. (There is a similar scene and authentication at the end of the vision of the New Jerusalem, 22:6ff.) Probably the angel who has guided John in the vision is at the end of it testifying of its truthfulness.

[10] This scene is duplicated in 22:6ff. and warns against any form of idolatry, including angel worship (Col. 2:18). The angel, whom John would have worshiped, declares that he is only a fellow servant with John and with John's **brethren who hold the testimony of Jesus. Fellow servant** puts the angel and those in the prophetic order to which John belonged on the same plane. Much depends on whether "those who hold the testimony of Jesus" is taken as subjective or objective genitive. The same expression occurs in 1:2, 9 and 12:17. By almost universal agreement the initial use (1:2) is subjective. It is closely related to "the word of God" (1:2 and 6:9) and to "the commandments of God" (12:17). As in 12:17, "those who keep the commandments of God" and who "hold the testimony of Jesus" seem to be complementary statements. Jesus gives his testimony as "the faithful witness" (1:5; 3:14, and in vs. 11, here). The meaning, then, is the testimony or witness which he bore in his life, teaching, and death to the word or commandments of God. For Christians to hold that testimony means to take a stand upon that platform and uphold it by life, by word, or even by death. This is what the martyrs under the altar had done (6:9), as well as the martyrs who are to reign with Christ (20:4). Even in those passages where the meaning "testifying" seems demanded (e.g., the two witnesses "finished their testimony," 11:17), the meaning probably is that they had completed their prophetic preaching of the word of God attested to by Jesus. If this is correct, then **"For the testimony of Jesus is the spirit of prophecy"** means that the Holy Spirit, as the representative of the risen Christ, who works in the churches (2:7, etc.) and inspires the prophets, is also the inspiration behind the testimony of Jesus which the martyrs hold. The same Spirit inspires both the prophets (in giving their inspired testimony, as John is doing here) and the word of God and the testimony which Jesus gave. The martyrs make the word their own testimony by confessing and preaching it.

Sequel to the Fall of Rome, 19:11—21:8

The War between Christ and the Beast, 19:11-21. John is now shown a picture of the great war between Christ and the beast. Each has his army—Christ a heavenly army which followed him (vs. 14), and the beast an army made up of the kings of the earth and their forces (vs. 19). This battle has

Faithful and True — REV. 19:11

> ¹¹ **Then I saw heaven opened, and behold, a white horse! He who sat upon it is called Faithful and True, and in righteousness he judges and makes war.**

often been mentioned in the course of the visions. The imagery and its terminology are drawn primarily from two Old Testament sources. The first is the war hymn of Psalm 2; the second is the numerous prophetic passages describing the holy war of God in the last days (e.g., Isa. 8:9f.; 17:12f., 24; 29:7ff.; 59:15b-20; 63:1-6; Joel 3:9-21; Ezek. 38; 39; cf. 2 Esdras 13:5-50; 2 Baruch 72; Psalms of Solomon 17:23ff.).

John has several indications that this battle is none other than the great martyrdom, the persecution struggle of the church on earth. First, there is the fact that this scene recapitulates the references to the war scattered throughout the book. Secondly, there are specific cross references (vss. 15, 19) to Psalm 2 and the war passages already connected with the persecution struggle.

[11] The battle scene begins as John **saw heaven opened**. This is the third time John has seen heaven opened. The first was in 4:1 at the beginning of the vision in which the great scroll was disclosed. The second was at the seventh trumpet, when the vision of that scroll was completed (11:19). That this description of the great war begins with heaven opened again probably signifies that this battle holds the key to or discloses the climax of that scroll. There is no connection with the **white horse** which the rider sits upon here and that of 6:2; the similarity of color is incidental. It has already been noted that the horse in 6:2 is one of the apocalyptic symbols of disaster. The present summary makes it plain that the rider of this horse is the Lord. **Faithful and True** identifies the rider with the "faithful and true witness" of the message to the church at Laodicea (3:14) as well as the faithful witness of the opening address (1:5). The term "witness" is dropped here, but the judicial function with which it is connected is continued in that **in righteousness he judges and makes war**. The combination of judging and making war is curious, but in various Old Testament apocalyptic passages which foretell of the war of God in the last days the two functions are also united (cf. Joel 3:12; Dan. 7:13, 21, 26; Ezek. 38, 39).

REV. 19:11-13 *Many Crowns*

[12] **His eyes are like a flame of fire, and on his head are many diadems; and he has a name inscribed which no one knows but himself.** [13] **He is clad in a robe dipped in** [m] **blood, and the name by which he is called is The Word of God.**

[m] Other ancient authorities read *sprinkled with*

The rationale for the mixed metaphor (of judgment and war) is that in John's version it is not a battle fought with carnal weapons. It is a war waged spiritually and fought in the courtrooms of the Roman magistrates. This is why the prelude to the battle in heaven (12:7-11) is depicted as a lawsuit in which Satan as the prosecutor is expelled from the scene of the court (heaven). But it is also the reason that the victory of the Lord over the beast and the city is won by the blood of the martyrs, "those who loved not their lives unto death" (12:11) and "because those with him are called chosen and faithful" (17:14).

[12] Further evidence that the one who sat on the horse is Jesus is that **his eyes are like a flame of fire**, a description used before (1:14; 2:18). Here, for the first time in the Apocalypse, he is wearing **many diadems** or crowns. Heretofore only the dragon and the beast have been so crowned. But their crowns are parodies on those of the Lamb, as are other features such "as being dead and coming to life." Now that the Christ is to be revealed as the ultimate victor in the struggle with the beast, he wears the crowns which rightfully belong to him. His having **a name inscribed which no one knows but himself** may be interpreted—even in the face of all things revealed about him—as the ultimate mystery of his being and nature. He is inscrutable, even as his ways and his love are past tracing out.

[13] The rider **is clad in a robe dipped in blood**. But the question is whose blood. In previous accounts of the struggle it has been made plain that the ultimate victory will be won through the martyrdom of Christ's followers (12:11 and 17:13). His clothes, therefore, are red because of his leadership of an army willing to go to the cross in following their master (Mark 8:34-38). There are already many martyrs, but this conflict will add to their number (6:11).

Word of God REV. 19:13-15

[14] **And the armies of heaven, arrayed in fine linen, white and pure, followed him on white horses. **[15]**From his mouth issues a sharp sword with which to smite the nations, and he will rule them with a rod of iron; he will tread the wine press of the fury of the wrath of God the Almighty.**

The concept of Jesus as **The Word of God** is closely associated with the role of Christ. In the Prologue to John's Gospel the term refers to the Son as the divine *logos* who was with the Father, partook of his deity, and was the agent of creation (John 1:1f.). John must have been familiar also with the use of the Word as personified wisdom in the Wisdom of Solomon 18:15-19, which is probably based on the Old Testament references to God's word as fire or a hammer (Jer. 23:29), as that which "runs swiftly" (Ps. 147:15), or that by which those displeasing to God are "slain" (Hos. 6:5). Also close in thought is Hebrews 4:12. For Revelation, the title probably carries the idea of the living Christ who stands behind the message of the book as a representative of the living message of the gospel itself. Thus the contents of the book are called "the testimonies of Jesus" and are equated with the Word of God (1:2). The resurrected Christ who inspires and leads his army cannot be separated from the Jesus of history who was the incarnation of the Word of God.

[14] Though some think of the army as Christ's angels (Matt. 26:53), the army is more likely the same as that of 14:4, that is, the hundred and forty-four thousand, since their adornment is due, not to their angelic splendor, but to the **fine linen, white and pure** (through Christ's blood). They ride victorious **white horses** and have their robes of **fine white linen**. **White** here, as in other places, signifies righteous lives "granted to them" by virtue of their justification through Christ (19:8; 7:14; 6:11).

[15] Further proof that the rider is the Christ and that this scene vitally concerns the major theme of the Apocalypse is the mosaic of references from the Old Testament to the work of the Messiah. The first is to the Davidic king who was to judge the poor with righteousness and decide with equity for the meek of the earth. In this judicial connection he was **to**

smite the nations with the rod of his mouth and with the breath of his lips slay the wicked (Isa. 11:4). **The sharp sword,** then, refers to the judicial power of his verdicts to redress the poor and distressed. In the Roman sense this would mean—if John's reference retains its Old Testament force—that the Christ and not the judge in the Roman court held the *jus gladii* (right of the sword), symbol of the power of life or death. But the figure is changed. Other prophetic references take the "mouth like a sharp sword" (Isa. 49:2) in the sense of Hebrews 4:12 and Ephesians 6:17, that is, the power of the spoken word. Hence the reference is to the proclamation of the word of God, the gospel preached as his word, and the weapon by which the kings of the earth and the beast are to be defeated. The ultimate weapon for the armies is the gospel; they fight with no other weapon than to lay their life upon the altar (cf. the two prophetic witnesses, 11:7).

Further, the rider is **to rule them** (the nations) **with a rod of iron**. This, from Psalm 2:9, has already been used to identify the male child in the story of the woman and the dragon as the Christ (12:5). And the same work is a joint privilege of the conqueror (to the church at Thyatira, 2:27).

The statement **he will tread the wine press** is the same as in the vintage scene of 14:17, drawn from the picture of God's wrath in Isaiah 63. This has already been interpreted as another reference to the great martyrdom. The element added here is that **of the fury of the wrath of God.** John has already commented on this cup, which the woman was made to drink (18:6). The **wine press** and the **cup of fury of wrath** are usually taken as merely symbols of Rome's punishment; but they need not be. If the wine press is the martyrdom, it is also the place where the cup of wrath is prepared, because (as explained at 18:3) the law of retribution demands the penalty double for those who cause an innocent victim to be injured by false witness. The wine press where the martyrs were put to death was also the place where the wine was mixed for the cup on which Babylon became drunk with the blood of the martyrs (17:6).

[16] The rider has three names. He is known to himself by a name unknown to any others; he is the Word of

King of Kings REV. 19:16-18

¹⁶ On his robe and on his thigh he has a name inscribed, King of kings and Lord of lords.

¹⁷ Then I saw an angel standing in the sun, and with a loud voice he called to all the birds that fly in mid-heaven, "Come, gather for the great supper of God, ¹⁸ to eat the flesh of kings, the flesh of captains, the flesh of mighty men, the flesh of horses and their riders, and the flesh of all men, both free and slave, both small and great."

God. Besides these, **on his robe and on his thigh he has the name King of kings and Lord of lords.** His titles are probably predictive of his conquering the kings of the earth; compare 17:14, where his being such a **King** and **Lord** is the reason that his cause will conquer. The term here serves to cinch the identity of Christ as the leader of the army. The cross reference to King of kings, etc., in 17:14 is another sign pointing to the parallel between the war here and in that passage.

[17, 18] Now that the army has been described, the battle is introduced by one of the **angel** guides **standing in the sun.** Why he stands in the sun is not clear. He **called to all the birds that fly in mid-heaven**, recalling the eagle or vulture of 8:13 which pronounced the three woes. The "woe" forecast by the cries of that bird never was actually disclosed when the seventh trumpet sounded (11:15). It is possible, then, that John means that the outcome of this battle depicts the third woe on "those who dwell on the earth." The call of the birds is to **"Come, gather for the great supper of God, to eat the flesh of kings."** One is reminded immediately of the similar call in the Gog and Magog battle scene of Ezekiel 39:17ff. John sees this passage as having a double fulfillment, for it is applied again in 20:7-11 in the attack of Gog and Magog which follows the thousand-year reign. The different classes of men and their horses probably signify the fullness of the earthly agents of the beast and false prophet, who beguile the kings and their allies into attacking the armies of the Lord. They will be overcome and their flesh eaten by the birds. In Ezekiel the Lord calls the supper "my table," which is reflected here in the **supper of God.**

REV. 19:19-21 — *Beast Captured*

[19] And I saw the beast and the kings of the earth with their armies gathered to make war against him who sits upon the horse and against his army. [20] And the beast was captured, and with it the false prophet who in its presence had worked the signs by which he deceived those who had received the mark of the beast and those who worshiped its image. These two were thrown alive into the lake of fire that burns with sulphur. [21] And the rest were slain by the sword of him who sits upon the horse, the sword that issues from his mouth; and all the birds were gorged with their flesh.

---

[19] The actual battle is described briefly. There is little effort to keep separate the relationship between the beast, the woman, and the kings. The woman is the city, the capital of the empire; the beast is the empire itself; and the kings are the horns of the beast, the rulers of the provinces which were to aid the beast and finally turn against the harlot city (17:14-16). John is clear that the line from kings to city to empire to the dragon, Satan, is one combination. All are involved in the war. Already through the invitation to the birds it has been revealed that the army is to be killed and its flesh eaten. This is, of course, symbolic of their defeat. This is no carnal battle, but a struggle over God's word (vss. 13f.).

[20] John is more interested here to disclose that **the beast is captured,** along with **the false prophet** (the second beast of 13:11; cf. 16:13; 20:10), who had worked signs (13:13ff.) and deceived those who succumbed to the **worship of the beast**'s image **and received its mark.** They were **thrown alive into** hell, **the lake that burns with sulphur.** The end is suggested by the fate of Daniel's fourth beast, whose body was given into the burning fire (Dan. 7:11). In both instances the meaning is the end of the beastly phase of the empire and the priestcraft of the emperor cult, together with the eternal punishment of those participating in its sins.

[21] **And the rest** (the kings and their armies, vs. 19), unlike the personified leadership, were not cast into the lake of fire but **were slain by the** word of God, **the sword** of the rider, **that issues from his mouth** (vss. 13f.). For the figure of

Millennium REV. 19:21–20:1

the Word of God as a sword, see the statements of Hebrews 4:12 (the word is a double-edged sword) and Ephesians 6:17 (the sword of the spirit, the word of God). The slaughter is thus spiritual, or figurative, as is the consumption of the **flesh** by the birds.

John's understanding of the messianic war is now plain. John viewed the battle as the struggle between the early church and the Roman empire, in which Rome (as the embodiment of the ancient beast) attacked the Lamb by attacking his followers. The battle was not fought with carnal weapons on an earthly battlefield. It was fought with the gospel of Jesus Christ, as that gospel was proclaimed, lived, confessed, and witnessed in death by the followers of Jesus Christ.

The Thousand-Year Reign, 20:1-6. The triumph of the martyrs' cause is symbolized by the binding of Satan and the thousand-year reign (the millennium). The visions thus far have shown John the defeat of Rome and her allies, including the destruction of the city. Repeatedly the question has been raised concerning whether John expected the world to end with the destruction of Rome. The most certain evidence that John expected a long period of the history of the church stretching beyond the history of Rome is the present vision of the thousand-year reign. Here is another vision of hope for the martyrs that the victory won by their witness was to last for a time indefinitely longer than the period of their trial. This concept is expressed by a traditional apocalyptic idea of the triumphant reign of God after the enthronement of the Messiah and before the end of time. This thousand-year reign is usually called the millennium, from the Latin word for "one thousand years."

This scene is certainly one of the most diversely explained of all Scripture. A correct interpretation can be made only by keeping the exegesis within the framework of the Apocalypse and noting John's own readaptation of apocalyptic ideas. This is what is missing in both the literalistic futurist interpretation of the premillennialists, or dispensationalists, and the more figurative Augustinian view associated with both the continuous historical and philosophy of history interpretations. These explanations take the passage out of

REV. 20:1, 2 *Satan Bound*

> ¹ Then I saw an angel coming down from heaven, holding in his hand the key of the bottomless pit and a great chain. ² And he seized the dragon, that ancient serpent, who is the Devil and Satan, and bound him for a thousand years,

---

John's scheme and make it either a physical return of Christ to reign in Jerusalem (elements not even mentioned in the text) or an allegory of the victory of the church in her struggles throughout the Christian dispensation.

[1] John saw **an angel coming down from heaven.** The angel is to be seen as another heavenly messenger charged with a special mission in the revelations (cf. 18:1; 19:1). It is hardly likely that he is the Christ. He is **holding in his hand the key of the bottomless pit.** By **pit** (Greek, *abussos*) is meant the spiritual underworld, the abode or stronghold of Satan (9:1; 11:7; 17:8). That a messenger of God held **the key** of the door to this realm shows that even this part of the creation is ultimately under divine control. The angel had **a great chain.** The Greek word signifies a manacle or handcuff such as was used to chain the demoniac (Mark 5:4) or ordinarily used to restrain Roman prisoners (Acts 12:7; 28:20). The Apocalypse has already described Satan's being cast out of heaven and limited in his activity to earth (12:7-17), the occasion of the great persecution. The picture of the war just given (19:11-21) has shown the defeat of Satan's allies, the beast and kings of the earth.

[2] Now Satan's limitation (not yet his destruction, 20:10) is shown: The angel **seized the dragon, that ancient serpent, who is the Devil and Satan, and bound him for a thousand years**. The manacle or chain is not meant to imply that Satan is tied up hand and foot immovable; rather he is limited or restrained, as one chained to a soldier or (using somewhat the same figure) as Satan himself had for eighteen years bound a sick woman, whom Jesus healed (Luke 13:16; see also Matt. 12:29). John had developed the idea that the Satanic war against the saints was "allowed" by God (cf. use of the verb "it was given to him," 13:7). The binding of Satan means the withdrawal of that power; the great persecution, having accomplished its purpose, is brought to an end.

Thrown into the Pit REV. 20:3

³ **and threw him into the pit, and shut it and sealed it over him, that he should deceive the nations no more, till the thousand years were ended. After that he must be loosed for a little while.**

---

[3] The restraint of Satan is further described as the angel **threw him into the pit, and shut it and sealed it over him.** What Isaiah, in his apocalyptic vision of the last times, had predicted for the opposing kings on earth (Isa. 24:21f.) is here transferred to their leader. For the figure of a spirit being bound or fettered, see Tobit 8:3. Jewish apocalyptic writers were familiar with the idea of the limitation of Satan's work by binding (see Testament of Levi 18:2-18; Enoch 18:12-16; and Similitudes of Enoch 53:3; 54:5).

The binding of Satan was for **a thousand years.** This is an obvious contrast to the period of martyrdom which was to be three and one-half years (or forty-two months, or one thousand two hundred and sixty days). The thousand years probably represents the longer period of the triumph of the gospel after the destruction of Rome and the limitation of Satan's power to persecute. The dragon is bound that he may **deceive the nations no more till the thousand years were ended.** Satan's deception of "those who dwell upon the earth" through the two beasts is what John has pictured as the cause of the idolatry or worship of the beast and the leading cause of the war against the saints, with "all who do not worship the image of the beast to be slain" (13:14, cf. further 12:9; 18:23; 19:20). John says that the binding of Satan will be the cessation of that deception, and thus of the war of persecution.

It is not explained why after the thousand years Satan must **be loosed for a little while.** The period of binding is followed by the time of Gog and Magog's attack (20:7-10). What is meant by this partly determines what is meant by the loosing of Satan. The most logical meaning within the context is that another period or dimension of persecution follows the binding and loosing. It may be that God foresees the need of a final sifting of the saints grown weak in faith without the testing of persecution.

The term **a thousand years** is John's adaptation of an apocalyptic image for the messianic era. He evidently found

REV. 20:3, 4 — *Messianic Age*

> [4] Then I saw thrones, and seated on them were those to whom judgment was committed. Also I saw the souls of those who had been beheaded for their testimony to Jesus and for the word of God, and who had not worshiped the beast or its image and had not received its mark on their foreheads or their hands. They came to life again, and reigned with Christ a thousand years.

that symbol expressive of the future of the cause of the gospel beyond the fall of the harlot city. There existed in Jewish apocalyptic circles a well-documented idea that the Messiah would come without fanfare, be revealed, for example, in the desert, and make his manifestation to Israel. It was believed that the perfect keeping of the Law for one day, or a day of perfect repentance by Israel, would bring the kingdom in. Following the Messiah's appearance, some believed, the eternal period of time would begin; that is, the resurrection and judgment would occur and the rule would be forever. Others believed that the Messiah would establish his rule among men and would rule during a set or limited period of years as an interim kingdom between his coming and the judgment. It is an adaptation of this type of understanding of the kingdom that the New Testament church adopted, as expressed in the Gospels. The Jewish apocalyptists who envisioned such a period following the Messiah's appearance differed as to how long it would be. In 2 Esdras 7:23-30 the rule is taken to be four hundred years.

[4] After the binding of Satan, John saw the reign of the martyred saints. The seer **saw thrones, and seated on them were those to whom judgment was committed.** The use of specific language (cf. Dan. 7:9, 22, 27) makes plain that this scene is meant to be the fulfillment of Daniel's vision of the Ancient of Days (God) giving "dominion and glory and kingdom" to "one like a son of man" (Dan. 7:13f.) jointly with "the saints of the Most High." In the same vision the saints were also to possess the kingdom (Dan. 7:18), and it was said of them, "judgment was given for the saints of the Most High, and the time came when the saints received the kingdom" (Dan. 7:22). That prediction had long been interpreted within the Christian tradition as signifying not only the

Reign with Christ REV. 20:4

enthronement of Christ at his ascension (Mark 14:62), but also the enthronement of Christ's disciples, "who will sit on twelve thrones judging the twelve tribes of Israel" (Matt. 19:28; Luke 22:29, 30; 1 Cor. 6:2, 3). The Apocalypse has already given several hints of this same interpretation (cf. 5:10, 11; 11:15). The defeat of the beast and the restraining of the Dragon means the saints' reign with Christ; the saints are now to assume the empire of the now-defeated monster. Part of Daniel's vision was that those seated on the thrones were given judgment, as here. Again, this has been frequently alluded to, as when John has connected the war of the beast and the Lamb's followers with this judgment (3:21; 14:7; 16:5; 19:11).

But this place of judgment upon the thrones is given only to the marytred saints, to those **who had been beheaded for their testimony to Jesus and for the word of God, and who had not worshiped the beast or its image and had not received its mark.** The Spirit had promised the church at Laodicea, "He who conquers, I will grant him to sit with me on my throne, as I myself conquered and sat down with my Father on his throne" (3:21), a passage which more than any other seems to show that John uses "conqueror" in the sense of the faithful martyr's death. The descriptive clause "and who had not worshiped the beast or its image and had not received its mark" is thus not meant to include a larger and more general group than the martyrs. This is no universal reign; only the martyrs take part in it.

These martyrs **came to life again and reigned with Christ.** The expectation of Daniel (Dan. 12:1f.) was that many of the dead would be raised to participate in the Messiah's reign. How John saw the fulfillment of this in connection with the reign of Christ has already been indicated. If it is correct to see the two witnesses' death (11:3) as fulfilling the victory of the beast over the saints (13:7), then their coming to life was their resurrection, as it was also the beginning of the expected reign of God (11:17). The martyrs participate in that reign because their witness won the victory which made it possible. Their death was the death of the cause they represented; what is their resurrection but the resurrection of their cause?

REV. 20:4-6 — *First Resurrection*

⁵ **The rest of the dead did not come to life again until the thousand years were ended. This is the first resurrection.** ⁶ **Blessed and holy is he who shares in the first resurrection! Over such the second death has no power, but they shall be priests of God and of Christ, and they shall reign with him a thousand years.**

The contention that this figurative use of resurrection cannot be maintained, because the two resurrections implied in the passage must be of the same kind, does not necessarily follow. The Gospel of John could use the literal bodily resurrection (5:28) to illustrate his use of resurrection as a figure of entering from spiritual death to eternal life (5:24). There are few who would argue that the resurrection of the witnesses in 11:11 was literal; there are many reasons to consider these two passages (11:1-14 and 20:1-6) as parallel.

[5] The martyrs' reign with Christ is the first resurrection. Daniel had prophesied the resurrection of the righteous to share the new age (Dan. 12:2, 3). John had seen the resurrection of the two martyred prophets and their rapture to heaven after their martyrdom by the beast (11:11); the raising of the martyrs here is surely the same. Neither is it an earthly bodily resurrection to an earthly millennial reign in Jerusalem with a reincarnated Jesus. It is the resurrection of their cause. John calls it **the first resurrection** to differentiate it from the general resurrection at the end prior to the great judgment of the last day (20:12, 13). It is a limited and unique event: **the rest of the dead** (even the saints not martyred for the testimony of the word of God) **lived not until the thousand years were ended**. The witnesses' death has brought about the victory. When the cause for which they were killed was triumphant, they are thus said to be raised or **come to life;** and, because their death brought it about, they alone reign in the period of triumph. After this, there will be a time when "the dead, great and small" will be raised to stand at the judgment (20:11ff.).

[6] God's approval of the part played by the martyrs in the final triumph of the gospel of Christ is indicated by his

Satan Loosed REV. 20:6, 7

⁷ **And when the thousand years are ended, Satan will be loosed from his prison**

---

blessing upon them: they are **blessed and holy.** They need have no fear of the eternal torment which threatened those tempted to compromise with idolatry (14:9-11). Over such **the second death has no power** (cf. 2:11; 21:8). Furthermore, their work continues in the mediation of the blessings of Christ during the thousand years: **They shall be priests of God and Christ, and they shall reign with him a thousand years.** On this, see comments on 1:9; 5:10. John's conviction is that the martyrs' death will contribute to the greater acceptance of the gospel when their cause is victorious (15:4). They being dead will yet speak. By them the nations will be offered up as a priestly sacrifice (cf. Rom. 15:16).

Satan Loosed, 20:7-10. [7] This sequel to the preceding passages shows that John has in mind some sort of revival of Satan's work of deception before the final end of the world. Gog and Magog are familiar symbols of invading nations attacking Israel when she is secure in the last age. The source is Ezekiel 38, 39, where, however, Magog is the land of Gog and not another individual. Ezekiel is not clear at what point in the messianic age this attack is expected. Apocalyptic literature developed the two into mythlike symbols for anti-Messianic forces (Sibylline Oracles 3:512; 2 Esdras, 13:34; Enoch 56:5-8; 90:13-15; Test. Jos. 19:8 and numerous passages in the Jewish Talmud). In spite of the divergent Jewish opinions as to the time of the assault, Revelation is expressing a conviction or revelation that following the millennial period of triumph there is to be expected a resurgence of the attack (perhaps a renewed persecution). It is often suggested that John may not have intended the sequence to be chronological and that he means that once the thousand years of the martyrs' reign have begun (that is, when the victory is complete), though Satan has lost his power at large (in Rome's defeat), he will continue the battle as local conditions and situations permit. The lesson is that even in times of the church's greatest triumph, or perhaps even because of it, saints are in danger of Satan's deception.

REV. 20:7-9 *Last Battle*

⁸ **and will come out to deceive the nations which are at the four corners of the earth, that is, Gog and Magog, to gather them for battle; their number is like the sand of the sea.** ⁹ **And they marched up over the broad earth and surrounded the camp of the saints and the beloved city; but fire came down from heaven**ⁿ **and consumed them,**

ⁿ Other ancient authorities read *from God, out of heaven,* or *out of heaven from God*

Only in keeping God at the center of their lives are Christians safe. The Jewish apocalyptic writers seem to hit upon the truth that in the age of the messianic kingdom, evil—even apostasy—would multiply. Such was one of the signs of the last days (1 John 2:18; 1 Tim. 4:1ff.).

[8] The details are drawn largely from previous materials. Gog and Magog go out to **deceive the nations,** ever the work of Satan. They **gather them to battle,** inasmuch as throughout the Revelation Satan's opposition is seen in terms of conflict (note the use of Ps. 2). The breadth of the attack is shown in that the nations involved come from **the four corners of the world** (a frequent symbol of universality) and that their number is **like the sand of the sea** (a frequent simile for a great force).

[9] Continuing the figure of battle, John says that the armies of the nations **marched up over the broad earth and surrounded the camp of the saints.** The term "camp" recalls the resting stations in the wilderness wanderings. And then **the beloved city,** Jerusalem, is surrounded. John means the church, the Jerusalem from above which is the mother of us all (Gal. 4:26) or the New Jerusalem from above in anticipation. It has often been pointed out that here John has not reached the point of revealing the New Jerusalem. But the church already in her ideal situation is a continuing potential of that future anticipation. So Paul's statement shows, and so the letter to Philadelphia has implied (3:12).

John's use of apocalyptic symbol is shown by the manner in which the armies of Gog and Magog are defeated: **but fire came down from heaven and consumed them.** So Ezekiel saw the defeat: "I will send a fire on Magog" (39:6; cf. 38:22; and so also the Sibylline Oracles 3:673). The armies are

Great White Throne REV. 20:10, 11

¹⁰ and the devil who had deceived them was thrown into the lake of fire and sulphur where the beast and the false prophet were, and they will be tormented day and night for ever and ever.

¹¹ Then I saw a great white throne and him who sat upon it; from his presence earth and sky fled away, and no place was found for them.

---

consumed, but Satan does not come off so easily.

[10] Like the beast and false prophet before him (19:20), **the devil** is **thrown into the lake of fire and sulphur where ... they will be tormented day and night for ever and ever.** This is the biblical Gehenna. As seen from the moment of the cross, the Almighty is victorious over Satan. God is ultimately triumphant.

The Final Judgment, 20:11-15. The visions John has been spectator to have spanned the centuries. He is now shown the end of the great conflict and indeed the world's destiny, the final judgment.

[11] **Then I saw a great white throne.** At the beginning of the visions (4:1ff.) John saw a throne with one who sat upon it. Such a throne has been called the central image of the Apocalypse. Now the throne is described in its purity and magnitude as **great and white.** This contrasts with the thrones upon which those who reigned with Christ sat during the thousand years. In the final judgment there is only one judge. This judgment is stated in the New Testament as well as in apocalyptic writers (2 Esdras 7:33ff.; Enoch 90:20ff.). Though elsewhere in Christian writings Christ is said to be the judge (and even in Revelation this is recognized, e.g., 2:7, 10), the visions follow the apocalyptic model, and God is the judge. Christ is the agent through whom God judges (Rom. 2:16; cf. 2 Cor. 5:10; Rom. 14:10).

With the end of history comes the end of the world order: **from his presence earth and sky fled away.** This is in accord with earlier descriptions (6:14; 10:20; 16:20) of the removal of everything before the presence of God, but it especially emphasizes the expected removal of all things of creation: Isaiah 40:8; 51:6; 2 Peter 3:6-13; Matthew 5:17; Hebrews

REV. 20:12, 13 *Books Opened*

¹² And I saw the dead, great and small, standing before the throne, and books were opened. Also another book was opened, which is the book of life. And the dead were judged by what was written in the books, by what they had done. ¹³ And the sea gave up the dead in it, Death and Hades gave up the dead in them, and all were judged by what they had done.

12:27; compare Daniel 2:35.

[12] The picture of the great judgment is in simple detail. The general resurrection is assumed. John **saw the dead**, from all stations of life: **great and small, standing before the throne**. The righteousness of God's judgment is emphasized by the reference to **the books** being **opened** (see comment on 3:5). God has a book of remembrance of all that has happened, except what he has chosen to forget through his forgiveness. Therein are recorded the deeds of both good and bad (18:5; cf. Jer. 31:34; Dan. 7:10; 2 Baruch 24:1-4; 1 Enoch 90:20; 2 Esdras 6:20).

There exists another book, **the book of life**, with the names of those written therein from the foundation of the world (17:8; cf. 13:8). For those redeemed by the Lamb, the record of human deeds is nullified, except for the contingency that one's name may be removed from the Lamb's book (3:5). All will be judged by what is written in the books. It will be terrible for those who cannot plead Christ's mercy through his blood; their judgment will be **by what they have done.**

[13] The universality of the judgment is emphasized by the total general resurrection. The ancients, who put great importance in proper death rites, feared death at sea. But even **the sea gave up the dead in it**, as did **Death and Hades**, that **all** might be **judged by what they had done**. Here Death and Hades are not merely the abodes of the dead (these in 6:8 were personified as riders on one of the horses). Though they are elements of the retributive consequence of sin in the natural world. God is able to use them to accomplish his divine purpose. Paul sees death as an enemy of man to be destroyed (1 Cor. 15:26, 54).

New Heaven and Earth REV. 20:14–21:1

¹⁴ **Then Death and Hades were thrown into the lake of fire. This is the second death, the lake of fire;** ¹⁵ **and if any one's name was not found written in the book of life, he was thrown into the lake of fire.**

¹ **Then I saw a new heaven and a new earth; for the first heaven and the first earth had passed away, and the sea was no more.**

[14, 15] Now that their evil has been fully exposed, they are revealed for what they are—the enemies of God and man, whose end is that **they were thrown into the lake of fire** (14:10) to join the beast and the false prophet (19:20). This is the second death (2:11; 21:8). Only those whose names were **written in the book of life** escaped the same fate.

The New Heaven and New Earth, 21:1-8. The final scene of the vision (which began with an invitation to John to view the judgment of the great harlot) is a revelation of the eternal bliss of the saints. Here is offered a picture of the final state of God's children, so often foreshadowed or promised in the Scriptures (John 14:1ff.).

[1] John **saw a new heaven and a new earth**. It may seem surprising that the final spiritual abode is described in terms of creation—a new heaven and earth. Heaven and earth stand together for the total creation of God (Ps. 101:25; Acts 4:24; 17:24). The spiritual counterpart already promised and anticipated by Isaiah as the work of the messianic age (65:17; 66:22) includes both areas. Some apocalyptic writers had thought that the present earth would merely be transformed (Jubilees 1:29; Enoch 45:1), though others predicted that "the first heaven will pass away, a new heaven will appear" (Enoch 91:16). This accords with the New Testament expectation (Matt. 5:18; 2 Peter 3:12; Heb. 12:27), though John does not describe the process of destruction. He has said, ". . . earth and sky fled away, and no place was found for them" (20:11).

The destruction of the old order is complete; even **the sea is no more.** In John's typology the sea represents the abyss, the reservoir out of which the beast arises (4:6; 11:17; 13:1; 17:1) and which supports the harlot. John is probably saying that all the evil aspects of the old

REV. 21:2, 3 *New Jerusalem*

² And I saw the holy city, new Jerusalem, coming down out of heaven from God, prepared as a bride adorned for her husband; ³ and I heard a loud voice from the throne saying, "Behold, the dwelling of God is with men. He will dwell with them, and they shall be his people ° and God himself will be with them; ᵖ

° Other ancient authorities read *peoples*

ᵖ Other ancient authorities add *and be their God*

creation are gone with its physical destruction.

[2] As there is a new earth, so there is a new capital. John sees **the holy city, a new Jerusalem, coming down out of heaven from God**. Jerusalem often signifies the whole Hebrew people organized under the covenant of Moses (Isa. 40:1f.; Matt. 23:37; cf. Gal. 4:25). In the Old Testament the way a person or people treated Jerusalem was determinative of their attitude and standing before God (just as was their attitude toward Abraham, Gen. 12:3). The new spiritual order, the church, even in its earthly existence knows itself as "the heavenly Jerusalem" (Heb. 12:22), "the city of the living God." The church has as its mother "the Jerusalem which is from above" (Gal. 4:26f.), and its members are citizens of heaven (Phil. 3:20). So, too, the Christians of Philadelphia had the promise of having the name of **the new Jerusalem coming down** from God written upon them (3:12). The earthly description, that which has been seen by faith, now becomes a heavenly reality. The city comes down from heaven and the anticipatory experience of the church becomes a fact. The city is **as a bride adorned for her husband**, which recalls the previous invitation to the marriage feast of the Lamb (19:7f.).

[3] **A loud voice from the throne** interprets the holy city: **Behold the dwelling of God is with men**. "Dwelling" is the Greek *skene*, used regularly in the Septuagint for the tent of meeting (tabernacle). This itself was a symbol of the presence of God among his people. Out of this *skene* in heaven the seven angels of the bowls had come (15:5). God is seen as having his dwelling in heaven, a dwelling which has also been identified with the inhabitants of heaven themselves. The actualization of this association and habitation with God which has been anticipated in the earthly fellowship of the

No Tears REV. 21:3-5

⁴**he will wipe away every tear from their eyes, and death shall be no more, neither shall there be mourning nor crying nor pain any more, for the former things have passed away."**

⁵**And he who sat upon the throne said, "Behold, I make all things new." Also he said, "Write this, for these words are trustworthy and true."**

---

church is described. **He will dwell with them, and they shall be his people, and God himself shall be with them**. Behind this lay a long list of promises to ancient Israel of the new hope (Exek. 37:27; Zech. 8:8, Greek; cf. Lev. 26:11). One significant change in the wording of these promises is made in the present revelation. The Greek word for "people" is actually plural (literally "the peoples themselves shall be his"), probably recalling the fact that those who will dwell with him in the celestial city are the great multitude of the faithful from "every tribe and tongue and people and nation" (5:9).

[4] Part of the effect of God's dwelling among his saints has been anticipated in the scene of the triumphant church, which was interpreted proleptically: **He will wipe away every tear from their eyes**. The setting here, as in 7:17, is from Isaiah's "Little Apocalypse," the original prediction of the messianic banquet (cf. Isa. 25:8). Thus in heaven, not only will tears be taken away, but **death shall be no more, neither shall there be mourning, nor crying, nor pain**. Death, crying, and pain belong to **the former** (more correctly, "the first") **things**, those of the old heaven and earth; they **have passed away** with the creation to which they belonged.

[5] Assurance of such happiness comes as the voice of God himself is heard for the first time since the opening of the Revelation. God the father, **the one sitting upon the throne** (4:21.; cf. Isa. 6:1; Ps. 47:8) says, **Behold I make all things new**: the new heaven and earth are new creations, with absolutely new conditions. The nearest anticipation of this (cf. Isa. 43:19) is in 2 Corinthians 5:17, which is spoken of the individual Christian and not of his future surroundings. The promise also fulfills John 14:1. The voice gives further confirmation. But **also** he says, "**Write this, for these words are trustworthy and true.**" The words which are guaranteed as

> [6] **And he said to me, "It is done! I am the Alpha and the Omega, the beginning and the end. To the thirsty I will give from the fountain of the water of life without payment.** [7] **He who conquers shall have this heritage, and I will be his God and he shall be my son.**

true evidently are the previously spoken description of the absence of death and sorrow in the new heaven.

[6] God declares the complete and permanent character of the new creation: **It is done!** The voice which had spoken at the beginning of the Revelation (1:8) to give double emphasis to the characteristics of God speaks again: **I am the Alpha and the Omega, the beginning and the end**. These words of his eternal nature do not merely mean that God is at the beginning and end of history. Rather, God is the ground and goal of all existence because he is its author and sustainer. At the beginning of the Revelation this was evidently intended to assure the suffering church that God had not absconded from his world but knew and had a purpose in their suffering; He was ever in control. So the God who will dwell in the midst of his people in the holy city is the same God who is met in the processes of history and who has ever revealed himself as the beginning and end, the first and last, the A to Z. Compare Exodus 3:14; Isaiah 44:6; 48:12.

Now **to those who thirst** the Lord promises, **I will give water without payment**. The promises of Isaiah (55:1) and Zechariah (14:8) were seen as fulfilled in the church as "fountains of living waters shall flow out of his heart" (John 7:37). But in a deeper sense those who have had the deep yearnings for God (Pss. 42:1; 63:1; Matt. 5:6) and who have known the source of their strength will have their thirst slaked from the fountain of life itself (cf. 22:17).

[7] But the consolation belongs most to the **one who conquers** (see comment on 2:7). All that has been said of the heavenly bliss will be the **heritage** (inheritance) of the martyrs, who by their faithfulness unto death have aided in the triumph of the faith. The martyr's death was not for a lost cause; it will turn out to his own glory when as God dwells among his people he **will be his God and he shall be my son**.

The Unfaithful

⁸ **But as for the cowardly, the faithless, the polluted, as for murderers, fornicators, sorcerers, idolaters, and all liars, their lot shall be in the lake that burns with fire and sulphur, which is the second death."**

This promise of God has been one of the prominent features of God's covenant promises from the first promises to Israel (2 Sam. 7:14; Jer. 31:9; Isa. 43:6; 2 Cor. 6:18). It has often been noted that both in the teachings of Jesus and Paul the family is one of the favorite metaphors for the church and its relationship with God and his Son. So John is assured in the heavenly sequel that that relationship is for the faithful.

[8] As these words just spoken have the martyr in view, so the words to follow are to be seen in the context of those who have failed in the conflict (cf. 14:9-11).

Those whose lot shall be **in the lake that burns with fire and sulphur** include **the cowardly and the faithless**. The word "coward" (Greek *deilos*) is related to the verb in Jesus' warning his disciples, "Let not your hearts be troubled, neither be fearful" (John 14:27). Here it undoubtedly refers to those who lack courage to stand before the threats of the monster. The same is true of the adjective with which it is coupled: "faithless." The victory over the beast was won by those "called and chosen and faithful" (17:14), but those who compromise with the beast are faithless. These are not the usual sins of immoral conduct; John thinks only of the great conflict and its consequences.

Others consigned to the fiery lake—**the polluted, murderers, fornicators, sorcerers, idolaters, and all liars**—have participated in the worship and loyalty to the dragon and the harlot. **The polluted** are those who have had fellowship with the abominations of Babylon (17:4f.); **murderers** are the allies and agents of the beast who have shed the blood of the martyrs (13:15; 17:6; 18:24). **Fornicators, sorcerers and idolaters** imply those who participate in idolatrous worship (2:14, 20f.; 9:21; 14:8). The greatest **liars** are those who have denied the testimony of God and his faithful witness and have upheld the lie of the false prophet who made the whole world worship the beast and his image.

REV. 21:9 *Fourth Vision*

⁹ **Then came one of the seven angels who had the seven bowls full of the seven last plagues, and spoke to me, saying, "Come, I will show you the Bride, the wife of the Lamb."**

VISION OF THE NEW JERUSALEM, 21:9—22:5

The fourth and last major division of the Apocalypse, like the others (cf. 1:10; 4:2; 17:3), is identified by John's being taken "in the Spirit" to a high mountain, where he is shown the Lord's bride, the holy city Jerusalem.

This section repeats some of the features of the last section. There (21:1-8) the picture of the city served as the conclusion to the sequel to the fall of the city of Rome, coming at the end of the last judgment. Now John is given another and more detailed picture of that celestial city where God will dwell with his people. This is not the first time in the Revelation that a subject is introduced in its proper sequence only to become the subject of a more detailed and elaborate account later (cf. the fall of the city in 16:17-21 and 17:1ff. and the great battle, 16:12-16 and 19:11ff.) The preceding section proclaimed the coming of God to dwell with his people, and the mention of the holy city was an incidental part of that theme. It identified the place where the dwelling is to be. Now in a separate vision, that city in all its perfection and splendor is described. Such a vision and the assurance it gives that the Lord has prepared the place which he promised to go to prepare before he comes again to receive his disciples (John 14:1ff.) are a fitting climax to the apocalyptic vision.

John Invited to View the City, 21:9, 10

[9] It is **one of the angels of the seven bowls** (15:6ff.) that comes now to speak to John and invites him. It may seem strange that the guide to the holy city is one of the angels who had poured out the bowls of wrath on the harlot city (17:1-3). But there is a close connection between the introduction of this vision and that of the destruction of Rome. Both guides are associated with the bowls, both disclose a woman clothed with jewels, and both take John away in the Spirit. A contrast

Lamb's Bride

¹⁰ And in the Spirit he carried me away to a great, high mountain, and showed me the holy city Jerusalem coming down out of heaven from God,

---

in the two cities is probably being suggested. The city which is the Bride of the Lamb is the heavenly state of the church; the city of Babylon, a travesty of the church in its earthly state.

The city is first called the **Bride** (or the betrothed, Greek, *numphe*) and then (by prolepsis or anticipation) the **wife** (*gunaika*) of the Lamb. The church in its earthly state has been betrothed to Christ (Mark 2:19; 2 Cor. 11:2; Eph. 5:32). Now the invitation to the wedding feast (19:6-9) and the statement that the city is the Bride indicate the heavenly realization of that betrothal.

[10] Once again (cf. 1:10; 4:2; 17:3) it is **in the Spirit**, that is, in an ecstatic trance, that the vision is given to John, indicating that this is the fourth, and last, of the major visions of the book. Much of the following description is dependent upon the vision of Ezekiel of the new city of Jerusalem, which he idealized for the Jews of the return from Exile. It may be for this reason that like Ezekiel (Ezek. 40:2) John is **carried** by the angel **to a great, high mountain** where the city was located. The earthly counterpart of the city, the site where the Lamb stands with his army, is Mt. Zion. In the first glimpse of the holy city (21:2) it was called the new Jerusalem, as it is here (vs. 10). It is thus probable that the mountain is intended to be that of the city itself. There is a rich association in prophetic literature in which not only Mt. Zion but also a "holy mountain of God" (usually located in the North) plays a part. There are good reasons for thinking that this has influenced the vision here. In Ezekiel 28:11-16 the King of Tyre was reminded that he had been set "on the holy mountain of God"; he was "in Eden, the garden of God"; and he was adorned with "every precious stone" (a list of twelve stones is given), but he had fallen from that mountain. That John's vision is connected with this is indicated by (1) the combination of the mountain city and the garden or paradise concept (Rev. 22:1ff.) and (2) the fact that

[11] having the glory of God, its radiance like a most rare jewel, like a jasper, clear as crystal.

John borrows Ezekiel's list of precious stones. That mountain of the North, too, had been the place aspired to by the king of Babylon (Isa. 14:12-14), a figure John had already used (Rev. 8:8). As a figure for the original location of innocent but later wicked kings, it becomes a foil for Jerusalem, which as the city of God's delight is the true "city of the far north" (Ps. 48:2, "Mount Zion, in the far north, the city of the great King"; cf. Isa. 2:2; Micah 4:1; Zech. 8:25; 14:16). From this background Jerusalem was exalted to become the attraction for the nations of all the earth. So there was precedent for combining the mountain, **the holy city** of the new **Jerusalem**, and the garden or paradise of Eden as John's vision now does.

The city has twice before been described as **coming down out of heaven**: once to the church at Philadelphia (3:12) and in the first account of the new Jerusalem (21:3). This may describe the heavenly origin of the city or the abiding nature (even in John's day) of the city (so that the heavenly city is anticipated in the life and experiences of the earthly church—see comment on 3:12).

The City's Outward Appearance, 21:11-23

[11] The first section of John's description concentrates on the outward appearance of the holy city. The word **glory** which in ordinary Greek means "reputation" or "fame," took on a distinctive meaning in the Old Testament as the translation for the Hebrew *kabod* (first the "weightiness," then the "honor" or "glory" of God). The **glory** here refers to the majesty, power, or the manifestation **of God**. In particular it was used of the brightness or fiery splendor with which God revealed himself on Sinai (Ex. 24:16), in the tabernacle (Ex. 40:34), or temple (1 Kings 8:11). In Isaiah the glory of the Lord will fill the rebuilt city of Jerusalem so that "the sun shall be no more your light by day, nor for brightness shall the moon give light by night" (Isa. 60:1f., 19f.). It is

Twelve Gates REV. 21:11-14

¹² **It had a great, high wall, with twelve gates, and at the gates twelve angels, and on the gates the names of the twelve tribes of the sons of Israel were inscribed;** ¹³ **on the east three gates, on the north three gates, on the south three gates, and on the west three gates.** ¹⁴ **And the wall of the city had twelve foundations, and on them the twelve names of the twelve apostles of the Lamb.**

---

obvious here, as in verse 23, the prophetic hope is being spiritualized as a description of heaven. But the radiance of that glory is also like the **jasper** which John had already seen shining from God's throne (4:3).

[12] In describing the **twelve gates** of the city John once again utilizes the symbolism of Ezekiel's new city (Ezek. 48:31-35). There, however, the gates are mentioned in connection with the allotted territory of the twelve tribes and are considered exits through which presumably the tribes go to possess their inheritances. In John's revelation the gates are entrances, ever ajar for the nations of the world to come in. **At the gates** stand **twelve angels** or messengers, perhaps suggested by Isaiah's city which had guards or watchmen placed by day (Isa. 62:6), **and**, again, as in Ezekiel, **on the gates the names of the twelve tribes of the sons of Israel were inscribed.**

[13] The enumeration of the **gates** on each of the **three** sides is similar to Ezekiel (Ezek. 48:31ff.). John seemingly chooses the order of the directions in Ezekiel's measuring of the city (42:15ff.), i.e., **east, north, south, west** rather than the more normal north, east, south, and west. Both John and Ezekiel seem deliberately to have avoided using the gates in the order observed in the astrology of the day.

[14] The stones which he will soon name form **the foundation stones,** inscribed with **the names of the twelve apostles of the Lamb**. This picks up the idea that the church is built upon the foundation of the apostolic tradition and witness to the teachings of Jesus (Eph. 2:20). Also mention of the apostles as foundations certainly recalls the fact that—by the twelve tribes (see 7:1ff.)—John means the church as the new Israel rather than the ancient Israel.

REV. 21:15-17　　　　　　　　　　　　　　*City Foursquare*

¹⁵ **And he who talked to me had a measuring rod of gold to measure the city and its gates and walls.** ¹⁶ **The city lies foursquare, its length the same as its breadth; and he measured the city with his rod, twelve thousand stadia;**ᵠ **its length and breadth and height are equal.** ¹⁷ **He also measured its wall, a hundred and forty-four cubits by a man's measure, that is, an angel's.**

ᵠAbout fifteen hundred miles

---

[15] Still closely paralleling the vision of the prophet Ezekiel, the angelic guide now is revealed to have **a measuring rod of gold to measure the city and its gates and walls.** The purpose of the measuring is not clear. In 11:1 it seems to be for the purpose of protection, for which there is little need here. From the context the intent would seem to be to heighten the enormity, the symmetry, and the beauty of the holy city.

[16] **The city lies foursquare, its length the same as its breadth.** This was true of Ezekiel's city (Ezek. 48:20), though the dimensions are much larger: twenty-five thousand cubits for his; **twelve thousand stadia,** or roughly fifteen hundred miles, for the new Jerusalem. Parallels in rabbinic writers exist for heightening the dimensions of the new city, though with them the city merely stretches to Damascus, some one hundred and fifty miles away. The most astounding thing, however, is that John's city is a cube, for its height is equal to its sides! It staggers the mind to contemplate a city this large, with buildings towering into the sky as far as the walls extend in each direction. But this undoubtedly is hyperbole, its size exaggerated to indicate spaciousness. There is room in the city for the innumerable hosts from every tribe, nation, and tongue.

[17] Equally astounding, the **wall** of the city is only a **hundred and forty-four cubits** (about two hundred and sixteen feet). It is not clear whether this is the height or the breadth of the walls. If the height, there is a disproportion between the height of the city and that of its walls (this is usually interpreted to mean that the walls are there because the ancient city was always enclosed but that in John's city there is no

Precious Stones REV. 21:17-20

[18] The wall was built of jasper, while the city was pure gold, clear as glass. [19] The foundations of the wall of the city were adorned with every jewel; the first was jasper, the second sapphire, the third agate, the fourth emerald, [20] the fifth onyx, the sixth carnelian, the seventh chrysolite, the eighth beryl, the ninth topaz, the tenth chrysoprase, the eleventh jacinth, the twelfth amethyst.

---

need of the protection usually afforded by walls). While all this is quite beyond human thought, John makes the point that the measurements are not different from those ordinarily used by human beings: they represent **a man's measure,** which is the same as **an angel's.** The measurements are neither heightened nor lessened by using a different heavenly measuring rod.

[18] A touch of splendor is added in that the **wall** was **built of jasper; the city** itself was of **pure gold,** so pure, in fact, that it is **clear as glass.** Since throughout the Revelation heaven is thought of as conforming to the pattern of the temple or tabernacle, it is possible that the burnished gold of Herod's temple is responsible for the symbol here. In this aspect the heavenly city is the idealized temple.

[19, 20] **The foundations of the wall were adorned** with precious stones. There is much difficulty here. First, it is difficult to equate ancient names of jewels with the modern terminology for them. Secondly, precious stones in the cosmology of the ancient world were linked to astral and astrological lore. There exists evidence that the stones in the breastplate of the High Priest of Israel (Ex. 28:17ff.; 36:17ff.) and in Ezekiel's list of the foundation stones of the city of Tyre (Exek. 28:13) are generally the same as those associated with the signs of the zodiac (Philo, *Life of Moses* 2:24; Josephus, *Antiquities* III. vii. 7). But Ezekiel's order of listing, in exact reverse of the zodiac, is the one adopted by John here. The conclusion sometimes drawn (as with the order of directions in vs. 13) is that the reversal is deliberate so as to indicate both awareness and rejection of these astrological and mythical elements.

REV. 21:21, 22 *Gates of Pearl*

²¹ **And the twelve gates were twelve pearls, each of the gates made of a single pearl, and the streets of the city was pure gold, transparent as glass.**

²² **And I saw no temple in the city, for its temple is the Lord God the Almighty and the Lamb.**

---

[21] In describing the gates of the city John reverts to Isaiah's description of the renewed Jerusalem (cf. 54:11f.). He takes the Hebrew word for the stone of which the gates are made (*'eqdah*) to mean "pearl." **The twelve gates were twelve pearls,** with each pearl so large that a gate was cut in it. It is interesting that there is a rabbinic parallel. A third-century rabbi said that God would make the gates of the new Jerusalem out of pearls thirty cubits both ways, out of which he would cut passageways twenty cubits by ten. Though not known to the Old Testament, the pearl has New Testament connections (Matt. 13:46; 7:6; 1 Tim. 2:9) to indicate something of very great value.

Just as the city as a whole, so also **the street of the city was pure gold.** The use of the singular does not mean that the city had only one street. Just as one says "in the street," the word is used here in a collective or generic sense. John goes on to explain "pure" gold as meaning **transparent as glass**. These symbols, probably having no special significance in themselves, are used to convey the richness and splendor of the heavenly home.

[22] The most singular thing about the entire vision is that John saw **no temple in the city.** The temple is the central attraction in the prophetic visions of the new Jerusalem which have so greatly influenced John's descriptions (Isa. 44:28). This is a good illustration of how John has reworked the images he drew from these sources to make them serve the Christian theology. The temple is spiritualized to refer to the Christians as the living sanctuary of God (John 4:21, 23: 1 Cor. 3:16; 1 Peter 2:5). This is known in Revelation too (3:12). No temple is needed in the holy city because, as it has already been emphasized, the Lord God dwells with his people; **the Lord God Almighty and the Lamb** are the **temple.** The temple in Jewish worship is an imperfect representation of the presence and workings of God. It is replaced here by

Universality of the Church REV. 21:22-24

²³ **And the city has no need of sun or moon to shine upon it, for the glory of God is its light, and its lamp is the Lamb.** ²⁴ **By its light shall the nations walk; and the kings of the earth shall bring their glory into it,**

God himself, signifying direct and personal interchange and dealings between God and man.

[23] In like manner, there is **no need of sun or moon or lamp** for **light,** for the city is lighted by **the glory of God and the Lamb.**

The Inhabitants of the City, 21:24-27

[24] One is somewhat surprised to read that **by** the city's **light shall the nations walk; and the kings of the earth shall bring their glory into** the city. These things are more characteristic of the earthly city of Jerusalem than of the heavenly city. This may be John's anticipation of the universality of the church. Such a worldwide acceptance of the gospel is implied earlier in the Revelation (5:9f.; 7:9), and John expected it to be the result of the great martyrdom (15:4). If such was to be true of the earthly church, then the heavenly city also would be composed of all nations. Though the nations, by which John means the heathen people, along with their kings, had once opposed and made war against the Lord and his people (11:2; 18:3; 19:15), John had been shown that they would be won over to the side of the Christ by the sacrifice of the faithful martyrs (1:5; 6:15; 15:4; 17:2, 18; 18:3, 9). Their service and tribute to the Father and to the Redeemer will continue in the divine presence.

The **glory** of the **kings** which they will bring into the city is naturally interpreted as earthly or kingly splendor (as in 1 Peter 1:21; Matt. 4:8). In verse 26 it is combined with "honor," and the two together in other writers (Dio Chrysostom 4:116; 27:10; Josephus *Antiquities* XII:118) usually mean earthly possessions or things of value. If this is the sense here, it hardly means that John expected a material city in which commerce like that described in connection with the earthly city of Rome (18:15ff.) would go on. Here

REV. 21:24-27 *Open Gates*

²⁵ and its gates shall never be shut by day—and there shall be no night there; ²⁶ they shall bring into it the glory and the honor of the nations. ²⁷ But nothing unclean shall enter it, nor any one who practices abomination or falsehood, but only those who are written in the Lamb's book of life.

---

again John is transferring to heaven his expectation for the church in its age of triumph. He expects that after the church becomes the universal rule of God the whole secular world and its culture will be brought under the allegiance of Christ and made to serve his cause. That condition is then idealized for the heavenly state of the church.

[25] Isaiah had foreseen that **the gates** of the city would be always open—**never shut by day** or night (Isa. 60:11), and John sees this fulfilled in the holy city. Likewise, "The sun shall not set for you, for the Lord will be an eternal light" (Isa. 60:20). The reference to the gates implies openness and accessibility (as previously, also that the city has gates on each side, vss. 12, 13). There will be freedom from all of the hostility and warfare which called for the protective walls and the great gates guarding the passageways of ancient cities. It has already been noted that the glory of God so fills the city that there is no need of lights, even of sun or moon. In fact, **there is no night there** (cf. John 9:4; 1 Thess. 5:5-7 for a metaphorical use of **night**).

[26, 27] The open gates has implied that none is excluded of any nation or king who owns the right to the city. Only the unclean cannot enter. **No one** shall come in **who practices abomination or falsehood** (cf. vs. 8). Even the assurance that **the nations** will walk in the city and the kings of the earth will **bring their glory and honor into it** does not defile the city, for it has been already implied that through the redemptive work of Christ these have been brought into the service of God. But **only those** shall enter the city **who are written in the Lamb's book of life.** On this see comments on 3:5 and 20:15.

The Provisions of the City, 22:1-5

In this final section of the vision of heaven the emphasis is on the delights and pleasures of the garden of Eden. In his description John is dependent on Ezekiel 47:1-12.

River of Life REV. 22:1-3

¹Then he showed me the river of the water of life, bright as crystal, flowing from the throne of God and of the Lamb ²through the middle of the street of the city; also, on either side of the river, the tree of life' with its twelve kinds of fruit, yielding its fruit each month; and the leaves of the tree were for the healing of the nations. ³There shall no more be anything accursed, but the throne of God and of the Lamb shall be in it, and his servants shall worship him;

> ʳ Or *the Lamb. In the midst of the street of the city, and on either side of the river, was the tree of life, etc.*

[1, 2] In this vision the river which flowed from the temple has become **the river of the water of life** (already mentioned in 7:17 in a passage anticipating this one). It flows **crystal** clear, not from the temple and altar, but **from the throne of God**, who is the city's temple (21:22). Instead of watering the desert countryside, it runs **through the middle of the street of the city** itself. Again, whether the singular "street" is used generically or whether John saw one street winding throughout the city is not clear. One thinks immediately of the Psalmist's vision of "the river, whose streams make glad the city of God" (Ps. 46:4). The fruit trees along the banks of the stream become **the tree of life** which had grown in Eden, from which man had been banished, with the loss of eternal life, when he sinned (Gen. 2:9; 3:22ff.). It bears **fruit each month and** its **leaves** are **for the healing of the nations.** Here again John is emphasizing that the nations who once made war on the Lamb have now been conquered through his love and the love of the martyrs and that they now live within the city.

[3] The first Eden had been closed to man by sin, and the earth was cursed for man's sake (Gen. 3:17-19). But in the Eden restored, where **the throne of God and of the Lamb** will be, **there shall no more be anything accursed** (cf. Zech. 14:11, where the prophet looks forward to the day that Jerusalem would no more be cursed).

Jeremiah had foreseen the day when Jerusalem would be the throne of God (Jer. 3:17). By emphasizing again (cf. 21:3, 7, 22) the presence of **God and of the Lamb**, expression is

REV. 22:3-5

⁴ they shall see his face, and his name shall be on their foreheads. ⁵ And night shall be no more; they need no light of lamp or sun, for the Lord God will be their light, and they shall reign for ever and ever.

---

given to what, after all, is the ultimate reality of eternal life: the essence of heaven is to be with God and with his son, the Lord Jesus Christ. There **his servants shall worship him.** This is the fulfillment of what had been seen as the role of the triumphant church in 7:15, where one of the elders had described the condition of perpetual ("night and day") service or worship which would exist when the redeemed who had washed their robes in the blood of the Lamb stood before the throne. The scene is actualized here. But the worship is no more with the eye of faith; the worshipers will bow in his presence.

[4] **They shall see his face**, a privilege denied even the great lawgiver Moses, who so earnestly desired that sight (Ex. 33:17ff.). "We shall be like him, for we shall see him as he is" (1 John 3:2). The worshipers of the beast had the mark of the beast upon their **foreheads** bearing the moral and spiritual image of their master (13:17 and contrast 14:1). Undoubtedly John means to imply that the heavenly worship of the Father and the Son comes naturally out of the transformation of the redeemed, who have now been changed into the likeness of his glorious body (Phil. 3:21).

[5] Because the **Lord God will be the light** of the city, the inhabitants **need no lamp or sun,** and there is also no night. It has been noted that the service of the temple and the tabernacle was interrupted by night. Perhaps this is the reason for mention of perpetual light in the city. Also night had metaphorical significance of sin and ignorance. In such surroundings the saints **shall reign for ever and ever**. Israel was promised that she would become a royal or kingly priesthood. Peter interpreted this as being fulfilled in the church as the new Israel (1 Peter 2:9). But the doctrine finds its best expression in the Revelation. In 1:6 Christians have already become "kings and priests" through the redemptive action of Jesus. In 5:10 they are again called kings and priests, and it is said that they reign (or shall reign?) on earth. In the

Epilogue

⁶And he said to me, "These words are trustworthy and true. And the Lord, the God of the spirits of the prophets, has sent his angel to show his servants what must soon take place.

---

thousand-year reign (the triumphant age of the victorious church after the fall of Rome) the martyred saints "reign with Christ." But all those reigns are temporal and limited. They are foretastes of the perpetual reign of God's children in his presence: **they shall reign for ever and ever.**

THE EPILOGUE, 22:6-21

The Apocalypse closes with an epilogue, which in many respects resembles the opening section of the book. The epilogue is a sort of appendix after the visions have ended. This is accounted for, partly, by the fact that the book, though an apocalypse, is also written in the form of an epistle. Its introduction and address, as well as the epilogue, are in the literary tradition of the Hellenistic letter.

In content the epilogue consists of parting utterances from the principal characters of the drama. Since the construction is somewhat loose, it is often difficult to know just who is speaking. As in the earlier portions of the Revelation, there are affinities to the closing of Daniel's apocalypse, particularly in that the chief speaker is the angel who has guided John in the ecstatic visions. The angel tells him (in direct reverse to Daniel) not to seal the book.

The section is intended to give assurance to the churches of the genuineness of the material revealed in the visions, through the testimony of God as well as of others involved in revealing them. The authority of the Revelation as scripture is emphasized; its promises and warnings are enforced. There are further hints that the book is liturgical in nature, closing with the prayer for the coming of the Lord.

[6] The speaker must be the angel who had been sent to be John's guide (1:1). This angel (and not the one of 21:9) is indicated by the repetition of the words spoken at the beginning: **God has sent his angel to show his servants what must soon take place.** But John understands the words as the words

> [7] **And behold, I am coming soon.**
> **Blessed is he who keeps the words of the prophecy of this book.**

of the Christ, who had sent the angel. Thus in verse 12 the words take the first person and become the very words of the risen Christ, who had spoken to John at the beginning of the vision (1:10ff.). The voice assures John, **"these words are trustworthy and true."** By "these words" probably the entire content of the Revelation is meant. The same endorsement had been given (by the voice of the "one sitting upon the throne") the vision about the new heaven and the new earth (21:5).

This divine assurance affirms that what John had seen and heard had come from **the God of the spirits of the prophets.** Again this recalls 1:1-3, where the book was described as both an apocalypse and a book of prophecy. It can hardly be determined whether the reference is to the prophets of the Old or New Covenant, for the same Spirit of God (the Holy Spirit) inspired the hearts of prophets in both covenants. The emphasis is that the message of the book of Revelation is in line with the plans and purposes that God had revealed in ages past to "his servants the prophets" (10:7). Much of the material in the Revelation has been a reflection of words, images, and the general contents of prophetic books like Isaiah, Ezekiel, Zechariah, and Daniel. The Apocalypse has taken up and revealed the great plan of God which had begun in the Old Testament prophets. The purpose has been to show that what was to happen to the churches in the great crisis of impending persecution was a part of God's great purpose.

[7] The timing of that crisis is important to the Revelation and to an understanding of it: **And behold, I am coming soon.** How this promise has been treated in the book has been repeatedly commented on. John believed (along with the rest of the New Testament writers) that he lived in the realized Kingdom of Heaven (1:9), which was the unseen but great reality of his world (cf. Luke 17:21). John and his fellow Christians were a part of the city of the living God, which here and now comes down from heaven (3:12, 21:2). Within

Revelation Authenticated REV. 22:7-9

⁸ **I John am he who heard and saw these things. And when I heard and saw them, I fell down to worship at the feet of the angel who showed them to me;** ⁹ **but he said to me, "You must not do that! I am a fellow servant with you and your brethren the prophets, and with those who keep the words of this book. Worship God."**

---

that sphere the living Lord of creation worked; he was constantly "coming" in the events of history in fulfillment of his promise to be with his disciples always, to the end of the world. Part of the message of this book has been to warn the church (as in 2:5) that they must not fail to see the coming of the Lord in the events facing the church (cf. 16:15).

The beatitude pronounced by Christ himself (as in 16:15) says, **Blessed is the one who keeps the words of the prophecy of this book.** Revelation ends, then, as it began (1:3), with a blessing on the students who take the message of the book to heart. Through study the disciples would be prepared to face the great ordeal.

[8] To the divine assurances given, the writer adds his own: **I John am he who heard and saw these things.** The simple identification, without title or description, implies that the John to whom the revelation of Jesus had been made known was one well known to the readers. Since they had confidence in him as a teacher and leader, they could accept his affirmation that he really heard and saw the things he had described in the book. This is the authentication from the human side.

Probably only such an experience as John is avowing could have accounted for the next incident he records. At this point he says, **I fell down to worship at the feet of the angel who showed them to me.** From a human point of view it was natural that an experience so profound (as the vision of the victory of the church and its heavenly destiny) should have evoked the worship of the heavenly visitor who had shown John the visions. But **the angel** forbids the worship:

[9] **You must not do that!** Angels are God's servants (Heb. 1), but so was John and so are all those who have ministered in the prophetic office. The angel was no more worthy to be worshiped than was John himself. In a more

REV. 22:9-12 · *The Time Is Near*

> [10] And he said to me, "Do not seal up the words of the prophecy of this book, for the time is near. [11] Let the evildoer still do evil, and the filthy still be filthy, and the righteous still do right, and the holy still be holy."
> [12] "Behold, I am coming soon, bringing my recompense, to repay every one for what he has done.

---

general sense, all Christians—all **those who keep the words of this book**—are said to be on a level with the angel as God's servants. This is not said to degrade the angel but to elevate John as God's messenger. The terse command emphasizes the prohibition to worship the angel: **"Worship God."** It is possible that this is also recorded against the tendency of some in Asia Minor to worship angels (Col. 2:18).

[10] The command to John **Do not seal up the words of the prophecy** is explained by **the time is near.** This is another way of saying (see comments on verse 7) that the impending "coming" is not the parousia but the beginning of the persecutions. At the end of his apocalyptic visions Daniel saw an angel lift his hand to swear that Daniel's vision did not belong to his own day but was for a future time. He was told to seal up the vision "for it pertains to many days hence" (Dan. 8:26) or to seal it up "until the time of the end" (Dan. 12:9).

John had seen this vision repeated. In the vision of the little book (ch. 10), too, he had seen an angel stand and swear by God that in the days of the sounding of the seventh angel the "mystery of God" would be finished; there would be "no delay." This deliberate reversing of Daniel's vision was a way of saying that John's and Daniel's books differed. The sealing up until a future time became a standard literary device in the Jewish apocalypses. John's book, now complete, pertains to the immediate and not the distant future. The events foreseen are about to begin.

[11] As the time of fulfillment of the book is at hand, so is the time of repentance. The hardening of the heart is deceitful, and the day which is beyond repentance (even for some within the church, Heb. 6:1ff.) will come. Hence the warning to hear God "while it is still called today" (Heb. 3:13).

[12] For the second time in the epilogue the voice, seemingly this time the voice of Jesus himself (cf. 1:12ff.), says,

Coming with Recompense REV. 22:12-14

¹³ **I am the Alpha and the Omega, the first and the last, the beginning and the end."**

¹⁴ **Blessed are those who wash their robes ˢ that they may have the right to the tree of life and that they may enter the city by the gates.**

ˢ Other ancient authorities read *do his commandments*

Behold I am coming soon, bringing my recompense, to repay everyone for what he has done. At the sounding of the seventh trumpet (11:15, 18) John had described the end of that series of visions as "the time for the dead to be judged" (11:18). Since the visions have shown that the beginning of the great ordeal lay in the near future for John and his era, the "coming" he speaks of here could hardly be the immediate coming of the parousia. Several things in the context show that this conclusion is correct. First, **I am coming, bringing my recompense** is a direct quotation of Isaiah 40:10, which speaks of God's coming to lead his people from the exile of Babylon. It is thus probable that the promise here is intended to encourage and give hope in the persecutions facing the new Israel. Such temporal events can be described in terms of the final coming because they anticipate that event.

The Lord who is coming in the impending crisis brings his reward with him. In the Isaiah passage the reward is usually interpreted as the little flock or faithful remnant of the exiles who constituted the Lord's own reward. The phrase **to repay everyone for what he has done** suggests the idea of recompense for service. Every servant of God lives under responsibility, if not under an obligation of law or works, at least under one of loving service. The coming will not be a threat to those faithful servants whose justification (vs. 14) depends upon being washed in the blood of the Lamb and who thereby have a right to the city and the tree of life.

[13] This message again comes from the one who is **the Alpha and the Omega, the first and the last, the beginning and the end.** He who is the beginning of creation (Rev. 3:14), by whose word it became (John 1:3), is also its end.

[14] In verses 14 and 15 the voice speaking may still be the Christ, as in verses 10 to 13, the one who will resume

REV. 22:14-16 — *Outside Are Dogs*

15 Outside are the dogs and sorcerers and fornicators and murderers and idolaters, and everyone who loves and practices falsehood.

16 "I Jesus have sent my angel to you with this testimony for the churches. I am the root and the offspring of David, the bright morning star."

---

speaking in verse 16. But the words may come from the writer John, who is usually the one who applies the truth revealed to the readers. Here the words form a doublet. There is a blessing to **those who wash their robes that they may have the right to the tree of life** (growing in the midst of the new Jerusalem, vs. 2) **and that they may enter the city by the gates**, and a warning to those for whom these privileges do not exist. There seems to be a double significance in John's words. Christ upon the cross provided the means by which one washes away his sins and is made eligible to wear the white robe. But the victory won there must be ratified in the great conflict by the willingness of the martyrs to sacrifice their own lives (7:14).

[15] The solemn warning continues with the declaration that **outside** (the holy city) **are the dogs and sorcerers and fornicators and murderers and idolaters, and every one who loves and practices falsehood.** The list is very much like that of 21:8 and is to be taken also in light of the practice of idolatry, which is the crux of the great struggle. **Dogs** is the metaphor for the outcast and the unclean, especially in the heathen and idolatrous sense (Deut. 23:18; Ps. 22:16, 20; Phil. 3:3) or in the New Testament perhaps simply of heathen or Gentiles (Matt. 7:6; Mark 7:27). John has in view those polluted by its abominations, as in 9:20; 21:8. In one sense the language signifies the final reward of those on both sides of the great struggle. But John's tenses are present. By their choices in this struggle men qualify themselves for their eternal destiny. But they also indicate which of the two great cities owns their allegiance and in which they have their abode: either the new Jerusalem coming down from heaven or the harlot city which is full of the abominations of the earth.

[16] Again there is a divine attestation to the Revelation. It is the voice of Jesus certainly now being heard. Here is the

Morning Star REV. 22:16, 17

¹⁷ **The Spirit and the Bride say "Come." And let him who hears say "Come." And let him who is thirsty come, let him who desires to take the water of life without price.**

---

authorization for the writing of the book. This makes it "the revelation of Jesus Christ" (1:1). The sanction given the finished product is made on the basis of the exalted position held by the risen Lord. He is **the root and the offspring of David**, that is, he is the messianic king sprung from the royal line of King David (2 Sam. 7:14; Isa. 11:1; Ezek. 34:23; Hos. 3:5; Amos 9:11). Further, he is **the bright** and **morning star**. This designation is taken from the prophecy of Balaam (Num. 23:17) and was quite frequently applied to the Messiah in apocalyptic writers (Test. Levi 18:3; Test. Judas 24:1ff.). The conqueror has already been promised the morning star (2:28). This is a metaphor of the well-known morning star, which, outshining all other stars, promises the dawning of the new day. Compare the use made of the figure in 2 Peter 1:19. The Messiah who warns and promises, who comes with his reward, and who attests to the truth of these visions is the one who comes to all readers of the Revelation with the possibility of enlightenment in their lives.

[17] The church has a response to the repeated declarations that the Lord comes quickly. It is the response of those who "love" (2 Tim. 4:8) and who "look for" (Titus 2:13) and even "hasten the coming of the day of the Lord" (2 Peter 3:15). It was the answer given around the Lord's table in the assemblies of Christians as they uttered the early prayer *"Maranatha,"* or "Our Lord, come" (1 Cor. 16:22). There is evidence from early sources (*Didache* 10:6-7) that this was a liturgical prayer used in the ritual of the Lord's supper. Jesus had promised to break bread anew with his disciples, at his table, in the Kingdom of God (Luke 22:16). At that table they saw his presence with the eye of faith and took it as a pledge of his ultimate manifestation at the parousia. In the spirit of humble submission the seer knows that the church will join the Holy Spirit in saying as **the bride** of Christ **"Come."** In whatever manner of visitation the Lord

¹⁸I warn every one who hears the words of the prophecy of this book: if any one adds to them, God will add to him the plagues described in this book, ¹⁹and if any one takes away from the words of the book of this prophecy, God will take away his share in the tree of life and in the holy city, which are described in this book.

---

chooses—in the tribulations of earthly turmoil, in the affliction of the great ordeal, or in the final manifestation of his glory, John knows that the church will say, "Come, Lord Jesus" (vs. 20).

Indeed, everyone who hears the promise and the responding answer is invited to say **"Come."** But there is more; here is an invitation to all to join with the saints in order to anticipate the reward promised to the Christians. Obviously the church restricted the participation in the worship around the Lord's table to those of their own number (*Didache, ibid.*). Those who could not join in the prayer "Come, O Lord" are invited to come themselves —that is, to cast their lot with the churches—to quench their **thirst** with **the water of life without price** (cf. 21:6; John 4:14). This invitation to the saving message of the gospel echoes beyond the pages of the Revelation through the centuries.

[18, 19] In measured language which carries forward the solemnity of the other parts of this section, John now adds a warning against any alteration of the Revelation. **If one** who hears **adds** to the words of the prophecy **God will add to him** its **plagues, and if any one takes away from** them **God will take away his share** from the privileges **of the tree of life and in the holy city.** The language recalls warnings in the Law of Moses (Deut. 4:2; cf. Deut. 12:32; Jer. 26:2; Prov. 30:6). The warning became a literary convention also with the apocalyptists (Enoch 104:10; 2 Enoch 48:7, 8) and other writers, even the later Christian writers like Irenaeus. But with John it is more than a convention. From the beginning he has the commission of Jesus to write; he knows whose message it is; Revelation is designed to be read as scripture in the churches. He intends his message to be treated as scripture.

I Am Coming REV. 22:20, 21

²⁰ He who testifies to these things says, "Surely I am coming soon." Amen. Come, Lord Jesus!
²¹ The grace of the Lord Jesus be with all the saints.'
Amen.

' Other ancient authorities omit *all;* others omit *the saints*

---

[20] Finally, and for the third time, the voice of the Lord Jesus, as the one who has testified to the visions, is heard saying, **"Surely I am coming soon."** Again, and this time with a solemn acknowledgment of consent, the answer is that of the communion prayer of the church: **Amen. Come, Lord Jesus!** This is to be prayed, not merely as a ritual because it has become the weekly prayer of the Lord's supper, but as the answer of the "one who hears and keeps the words of this book." It is to be the prayer of one who has learned that in the coming of the Lord he may well soon face the trials vividly portrayed in the book, which threaten that the "beast will make war on the saints and conquer them" (13:7). Once the Lord's coming meant Calvary for him; it will mean Armageddon for the saints. But through accepting that role victory will come.

[21] The salutation, reminiscent of Paul's epistles, is part of the style of a letter. Though the book is an apocalypse, it is intended to be read in the churches as a message of Christ through John. The letter style pertains, as well, in the formal benediction: **The grace of the Lord Jesus be with all the saints. Amen.**